SILENT ACCOMPLICE

For my Mother and my Father

SILENT ACCOMPLICE

*The Untold Story of France's Role
in the Rwandan Genocide*

Andrew Wallis

I.B. TAURIS

LONDON · NEW YORK

Published in 2006 by I.B.Tauris & Co Ltd
6 Salem Road, London W2 4BU
175 Fifth Avenue, New York NY 10010
www.ibtauris.com

In the United States of America and Canada distributed by Palgrave Macmillan
a division of St. Martin's Press, 175 Fifth Avenue, New York NY 10010

ISBN 10: 1 84511 247 4
ISBN 13: 978 1 84511 247 9

A full CIP record for this book is available from the British Library
A full CIP record for this book is available from the Library of Congress

Library of Congress Catalog Card Number: available

Printed and bound in Great Britain by CPI, Bath
From camera-ready copy edited and supplied by the author

Contents

Abbreviations and glossary   vii
Preface   x
Map of Rwanda   xiv

1. *A Policy of Bad Habits*   1

2. *Invasion and Intervention*   14

3. *Civil War and Peace Talks*   37

4. *Militia, Massacres and Arusha*   51

5. *Retreat*   79

6. *Arming the Genocide*   102

7. *Operation Turquoise*   122

8. *Bisesero and Withdrawal*   146

9. *Burying Genocide*   180

Conclusion   206
Notes   217
References   228
Index   233

Roho z'Intungane Ziri Mu Biganza by 'Imana,
Kandi nta n'igitotezo kizongera kubageraho.
Mu Maso y'ibipfamutima bameze nk'abapfuye burundu,
barigendeye basa nk'aho bagushije ishyano,
bagiye kure byitwa ko barimbutse nyamara bu bibereye mu mahoro.

But the souls of the virtuous are in the hands of God.
No torment shall ever touch them.
In the eyes of the unwise, they did appear to die,
Their going looked like a disaster
Their leaving us, like annihilation,
But they are in peace.

Wisdom 3, verses 1–3.
(Notice above the door of the Kaduha genocide memorial)

Abbreviations and Glossary

AEMG	Autorisations d'exportation de Matériels de Guerre. An export licence the French Ministry of Defence gave for arms shipments
AFP	Agence France-Presse
Akazu	Literally 'little house' or inner circle around Madame Habyarimana, which became a meeting point for Hutu power extremists and the planning group behind the genocide
APC	armoured personnel carrier
bourgmestre	local government leader in charge of a 'commune' or district. There were 229 communes
CDR	Coalition pour la Défense de la République. A fervently anti-Tutsi Hutu extremist party
CEA	Central and Eastern Africa
CEPGL	Communauté économique des Pays des Grands Lacs
CIEEMG	Commission interministérielle pour l'étude des exportations des matériels de guerre. French commission that gave official sales notice to arms exports
CNN	Cable News Network. American news channel
CRAP	Commandos de Recherche et d'Action en Profondeur. Elite reconnaissance/special forces unit based within French regiments
DAMI	Détachement d'assistance militaire et d'instruction. French military training and assistance troops based in Rwanda from late 1980s to instruct Habyarimana's army
DGSE	Direction générale de la Sécurité extérieure. French external secret service comparable to British MI6

DPKO	Department of Peacekeeping Operations (United Nations)
DST	Direction de la surveillance du territoire. French interior secret services
EICA	Escadron d'Intervention des Commandos de l'Air
ETO	École technique officielle. Technical school run by priests near Kigali and massacre site after UN and French troops pulled out in April 1994
EU	European Union
EUC	end user certificate needed for arms shipments
FAL	fusil automatique léger – light automatic rifle
FAR	Forces armées rwandaises. Rwandan government army
FIDH	Fédération internationale des ligues des droits de l'homme (international human rights federation)
FMLN	Farabundo Martí para la Liberación Nacional
GIGN	Groupe d'Intervention de la Gendarmerie nationale. French police anti-terrorist branch
IBUKA	Rwandan association of genocide survivors
ICTR	International Criminal Tribunal Rwanda. Based in Arusha, Tanzania, set up under UN auspices to judge the main organizers of the genocide
IFRI	Institut Français des Relations Internationales
Impuzamugambi	'Those who have the same goal'. CDR youth militia involved in the genocide
inkotanyi	'those who fight bravely'. Term often used for RPF, but with older monarchical connotations
Interahamwe	'Those who work together'. MRND youth militia and leading participant in the genocide policy
inyenzi	'cockroaches'. Nickname given to Tutsis in 1959 with a view to dehumanizing them
IRIN	Integrated Regional Information Networks
MAM	Military Assistance Mission. French military campaign in Rwanda
MilOb	military observer
MRND(D)	Mouvement républicain national pour la démocratie (et le développement). Habyarimana's political party implicated in the genocide
MSF	Médicins Sans Frontières. French medical aid agency

NATO	North Atlantic Treaty Organization
NGO	non-governmental organization
NRA	New Resistance Army. Ugandan army Museveni recruited and from which RPF was formed
OAU	Organization of African Unity. Umbrella body of African nations
ORINFOR	Office rwandais d'information
PSD	Parti socialiste démocratique (Democratic Socialist Party) Rwandan opposition party
RDP	Régiment des dragons parachutistes
RGF	Rwandan Government Forces (also known as FAR)
RPA	Rwandese Patriotic Army. National army formed from RPF after its victory in 1994 – military wing of RPF
RPF	Rwandese Patriotic Front. Mainly Tutsi guerrilla army that fought against the Habyarimana regime
RPIMA	Régiment parachutiste de l'infanterie de marine (d'Assaut). Regular army parachute regiments that served in Rwanda from late 1980s
RPR	Rassemblement Pour la République. French right-wing political party
RTLM	Radio Télévision Libre des Mille Collines. Radio station set up in 1993 as mouthpiece for genocidaires and Hutu extremists, with links to the Habyarimana government
SHZ	safe humanitarian zone
Sofremas	Société française d'exploitation de matériels et systèmes d'armement contrôlé par l'Etat.
UNAMIR	United Nations Assistance Mission to Rwanda, deployed in October 1993 in line with the Arusha accords
UNAMIR II	United Nations Assistance Mission to Rwanda II, voted into being on 17 May 1994, it was eventually deployed to relieve Operation Turquoise in August 1994
UNDP	United Nations Development Programme
UNICEF	UN children's fund
UNICOI	United Nations International Commission of Inquiry

Preface

In 1991 I set out for the tiny central African country of Rwanda, lured like so many Western tourists with the prospect of trekking into the dense jungle of the Volcano Park region in search of the legendary mountain gorilla. Unfortunately, the tour operator had forgotten to mention that the country was in the middle of a civil war, with the result that my travel companion, a journalist with a local newspaper in Devon, was barred from leaving Kigali after intimating his line of work on his landing card. It was the first sign we received of a regime with more than a little to hide from the outside world, as it set about massacring its own people. My interest was heightened when I discovered that behind this Rwandan government, with its increasing catalogue of human rights abuses, lay the unconditional support of a permanent member of the Security Council and a nation that prided itself on democracy and the 'rights of man.'

While in France individuals and pressure groups such as Survie have have worked tirelessly to bring the truth to light, the English-speaking world has largely ignored the collusion of 'one of its own' in this shameful matter. It is hoped that this book will go some way towards encouraging further debate on the subject, not least because, as the recent tragedy in Darfur has shown, genocide is still occurring. Public debates about how to respond to genocide are framed around whether the international community can be made to do more. The point gets overlooked that genocide often occurs because of too much, not too little, Western interference.

It is no longer excusable for Western nations to write off African conflicts as 'ethnic wars', and to rekindle the usual racist arguments that such violence is to be expected from 'uncivilized' and 'black' peoples. What, after all, does that make the civilized 'West' that continually arms and trains the participants in the African wars?

In 2004 the Canadian, and former UN mission commander, General Romeo Dallaire returned to Rwanda a decade after the genocide. It was his misfortune to be in charge of the tiny United Nations force based in Rwanda during the genocide, and to end up an unwilling bystander to the slaughter. He spoke to a crowd in the Amahoro stadium in Kigali, a place where thousands had sought refuge during the genocide, and where hundreds had been killed by disease, shell-fire and marauding militiamen. In a highly-charged speech the former UN commander admitted his own failure to save those who were killed – but went further, attacking the very mindset of the West and its politicians in allowing the slaughter to take place without question or concern.

> The world is ruled by a belief that will permit other genocides. The superpowers had no interest in you, they were only interested in Yugoslavia. Thousands upon thousands of soldiers were sent there, and here I barely had 450. The guiding principle was that in Rwanda it's tribalism, it's history repeating itself. In Yugoslavia, it's different...It's ethnic cleansing. It's European security. It's white. Rwanda is black. It's in the middle of Africa. It has no strategic value. And all that's there, they told me, are people, and there are too many anyway.

France, under Mitterrand, was the only Western nation to take an interest in Rwanda in the years leading up to, and including the period of the genocide. Unfortunately for its people, this interest was borne out in supporting a government that was intent on solving its political problems by mass murder. Paris had few qualms about its political and military backing for Habyarimana and the later interim government that organized and so effectively carried out the genocide. Each day, each cabinet meeting, each debriefing session of returning officials from Rwanda gave Mitterrand and his selected officials, who included his own son Jean-Christophe, the chance to admit a massive policy failure and to change tack. Instead, then, as now, the French government is in denial about the effects of its actions, and its responsibility second only to the murderers themselves, in the final genocide of the twentieth century. 'Never again' to Mitterrand spelled out only 'never without gain'; while there was perceived cultural and strategic value for France in keeping a genocidal government in place in Rwanda that took precedence over any amount of killing.

This work has been made possible by the immense kindness and support of a number of individuals. Many of the unique testimonies are from interviews carried out in early 2004 by Georges Kapler, and I am very grateful for being allowed to use them here for the first time. Georges produced a documentary 'Rwanda, Un Cri d'un Silence Inoui', and is a member of Support Rwanda – an association that helps survivors of the genocide. The testimonies here are from former militiamen and genocide survivors, each of whom witnessed, first-hand, French action in Rwanda. I am very grateful for the assistance of Dr Andrew Brown in Cambridge for his help in translating these testimonies, and Betty Vainqueur in Bradford. The Department of Peace Studies at the University of Bradford has given me space and support for this project, and in particular I am indebted to the enthusiasm of Professor Shaun Gregory to undertake the work, and Professor Paul Rogers and Dr Jim Whitman for their encouragement and publishing assistance. This project could never have happened without the tremendous help of James Bell and John and Beth Maynard, Sean Terrell for the thankless task of proofreading the work, Dr Fraser Watts, Cecile Carlsson in Stockholm for her biting assessments and humorous critique and the calm atmosphere of the Community of the Resurrection, Mirfield as a retreat from the research frontline when needed. And to Tony MacDougal, who shared that initial trip to Rwanda and whom I hope one day will finally get to see those gorillas.

In Rwanda the hospitality of many made my visits both enjoyable and constructive. To protect identities I have changed the names of all those whom I interviewed for this research and, indeed, this is also true of those Georges Kapler interviewed. However, I am particularly grateful to the following for their help. Aloys, Veneranda, Speciose, Apollinaire, Moses Rugema, John Rusibuka, Tom Ndahiro, Marie Immaculée, African Rights in Kigali, François, Benoit at Ibuka, Jean-Damescene, Martin Ngoga, Frank Rusagara and editors of the Rwandan press; also to members of the ex-FAR, local government, businessmen and villagers who consented to testify to what they had seen. Finally, I wish to thank the survivors at Bisesero for reliving the horror one more time. I am equally grateful for the hospitality and help of those Rwandans working in Arusha at the War Crimes Tribunal, and for news agency staff there who gave me important assistance.

In France, this research has benefited immeasurably from the knowledge and professionalism of Sharon Courtoux at Survie, and the dedication of all who work at this organization, notably the late and much-missed Francois-Xavier Verschave, who died in summer 2005 after many years of exposing the complicity and corruption of *La Françafrique*. I have benefited enormously from the advice and support of Patrick de Saint-Exupéry and Mehdi Ba, and the calm analysis of Frédérick Charillon. The very helpful staff at the Institut des Hautes Etudes de Défence Nationale and the Bibliotèque IFRI in Paris found me important material and made visits very welcoming.

Finally my love and thanks to my mother for her incredibly positive outlook that has kept this project afloat.

Note from the translator
The interviews by Georges Kapler, conducted in Kinyarwanda, which I have translated here, have posed a number of difficulties. The French version is rather rough and ready, and at times grammatically approximate; furthermore, the respondents – as would be expected from people who have experienced horrendous events first hand – often find it difficult to express what they witnessed. Occasionally, they repeatedly use pronouns (in particular 'they') in a way that leaves it unclear to what the pronouns are referring, so that a certain amount of interpretative re-creation is necessary if the original situation is to be understood by an English-language reader. Given these constraints, I have tried to preserve some of the colloquial and informal nature of the respondents' speech, while at times clarifying their statements in the interests of greater intelligibility.

Dr Andrew Brown, Cambridge

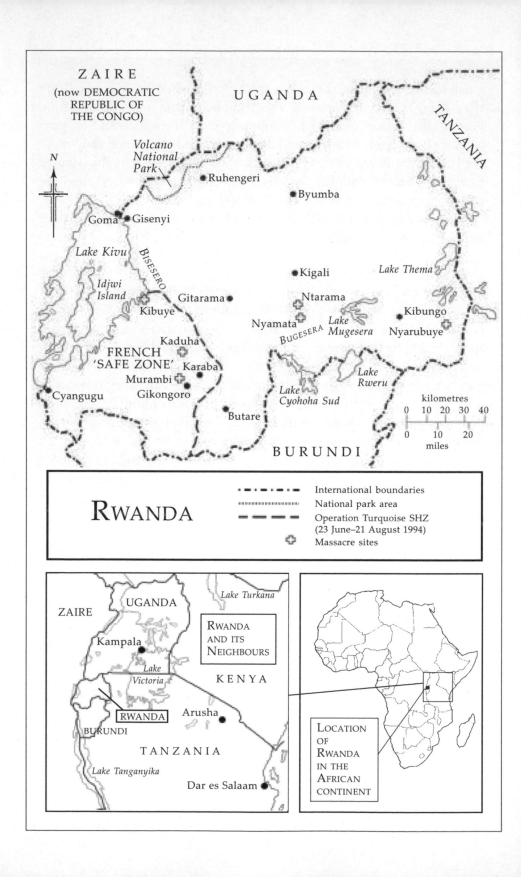

Chapter 1

A Policy of Bad Habits

T
he convent was a cool respite from the heat and humidity outside. We had crossed a large, flat and well cared for lawn to reach the ex-colonial residence, home to members of this religious order of sisters. Just a few years before, dismembered bodies, some still in the pitiful throes of life, had surrounded this same red brick building, rather than the pleasing green expanse of well cut grass that now reassured in its tidiness and vibrancy. A place of inferno and murder had again become tranquil with the song of red grosbeaks and the gentle Rwandan breeze.

Sister Ignatia was the last European left here in this religious order. She sat, upright and dignified in what passed for a German living room circa 1930, with tapestries, books and bowls full of fresh fruit providing colour and domestic incidence. Lending an air of humour was her grey parrot, Edu, which peered down on proceedings from its window perch, looking faintly puzzled by these unexpected guests. The Sister herself was a striking looking woman in her late fifties, her vocation to the people of Rwanda reflected in her eyes. She calmly told us her story.

For the past 30 years she had lived in this rural area near Gikongoro in southwest Rwanda helping to run a health centre for a community without access to electricity or running water amid the all-embracing poverty that characterized the villagers' subsistence lives. The local Tutsis, the minority ethnic group making up around 12 per cent of the population, had become more and more the target for a violent backlash from the extremists in the majority Hutu population. The Rwandan president, the Hutu Juvénal Habyarimana, who had seized power back in 1973, had continued an 'apartheid' system that all but banned Tutsis from working in the army, civil service and professional jobs. But, however terrible life under his despotic reign had been for

1

his Tutsi subjects, his death on 6 April 1994 in a plane crash was the trigger for a 100-day genocide that left up to a million dead.

One day after Habyarimana's death a Hutu priest turned up at the convent carrying a terribly injured young Tutsi, with deep machete wounds to his head and body. The Hutu extremist *Interahamwe* militia had beaten the priest for being a traitor for trying to help the child but the cleric was less badly hurt. Despite the Sisters' medical help the boy died of his injuries soon afterwards. It was then that four local Hutu leaders arrived at the convent.

I was told I must be quiet about events which were happening because there were people who were disobedient. They [the officials] asked for money and fuel and one soldier for a room in the convent. I learnt afterwards that this team of four were the organizers of massacres in the area. The Tutsi were very frightened – there had been massacres before and rumours abounded that the extremists were planning similar 'exter- inations' of these people they referred to as 'cockroaches.' Many Tutsi had trekked several kilometres with their families, avoiding roadblocks and constant attack to seek sanctuary at our church.

People streamed into here seeking refuge in the church, health centre and on the grass and outbuilding outside, and by 21 April there were more than 21,000 – mostly women and children. The church was packed and so was the school building. Many people were badly wounded, after being attacked by the militias as they fled. I hid our Tutsi staff here [in the convent itself] and closed all the doors and windows.

The soldier who we had allowed to stay knew that Tutsi staff were here but didn't do anything – he said he guaranteed us [the sisters] there would be no problem. I later learned this was a lie – he was here to keep watch, and find out if any Tutsis were being hidden. A few local Hutus helped the refugees. Others robbed and beat them as they came to seek shelter here. Those inside the church were mostly old and very weak, many with terrified infants. They were camped on the grass outside too. During the nights we tried to help in the church by feeding the refugees and giving them medicines.

Already by 20 April this place was surrounded. The killers

approached quietly and in the night – though we could hear them singing war songs. Some were wearing banana leaves as they approached. That night, 20 April, soldiers told us to go into the house [convent] and lock the doors and windows, and not to come out. If we did they could not guarantee our safety. At midnight we heard the Magnificat being sung in the church and the bells being rung and we asked each other what was going to happen. At 2.00 a.m. on the morning of the 21st I heard the sound of grenades exploding, guns being fired and the terrible cries of more than 22,000 men, women and children being killed.

The militia even went to the medical centre where there were around 100 patients. But they left after we told them they must kill my assistant and me before they could kill those in the beds. In the other health centres they killed everyone, small babies in cradles, mothers and the elderly too sick or injured to escape.

When there was no one left to kill, the head of the military came and asked for a caterpillar truck to move the bodies into a mass grave but I refused. In the end we paid 300 local Hutus to help bury the bodies properly.'

We left the convent on 15 June, and went south to Cyangugu and then to Bukavu where we saw the French soldiers. They refused to let us return to the convent as they said it was unsafe and our names were on a list of those the militia wanted to kill.

Eventually, Sister Ignatia did return, although all the other European sisters decided to return to safer Western countries in an attempt to get over the trauma of the nightmare they had witnessed.[1]

Imagine the horror of having to listen to the sounds of mass killing – the shrieks of the injured, of mothers pleading for the lives of small children whose skulls were often smashed against the walls of the church to save the killers wasting a bullet. To walk out at dawn to a church, only metres away, congregated by butchered corpses and literally mounds of bodies, some still in the agony of death. The trauma of what must be a daily reliving of such barbarities is etched on the sister's face, in her nervous hand gestures and in her calm but breaking voice as she recounted the horror. Every night, the same screams and cries haunt her efforts at sleep. It is an unending nightmare.

Opposite the church today there is a memorial to the crime that happened here. Rows of wooden, glass-topped cabinets inside an anonymous red brick building display the contorted bodies of small children and adults, often curled up in a fetal position as a last comforting gesture before death. Bookcases inside the doorway contain row upon row of skulls, the empty eye sockets staring out searchingly at the inquisitor. Around the walls the pictures are of the church and convent during and after the genocide – a true vision of hell.

Travelling around Rwanda today such memorials shatter the notion that this was an event best forgotten, as it was by all but France at the time. At Nyamata church, a few kilometres from Kigali, where up to 10,000 died, the altar is still covered by its bloodstained cloth, from the Tutsi 'sacrifices' made here one day in April 1994. The tabernacle and font are riddled with bullet and shrapnel holes. Inside the twisted iron doorway, which was blown apart by grenades, is a small room, ten foot across. Here the stench of death is pungent. Blue body bags lie half open. The contents sprawl out onto the floor – various barely recognizable body parts, some skulls, some decomposing limbs with rotten clothing clinging to them. They had been recently recovered from the latrines and ditches by the very killers who had put them there – part of their punishment after they were caught. Not content with blowing the terrified civilians apart by grenades or battering and bludgeoning them with their farming tools, the *Interahamwe* delighted in dousing some small children with petrol before setting them ablaze near the front door. One 12-year-old survivor spoke of seeing small children 'writhing from the burns completely alive, truly. There was a strong smell of meat, and petrol.'[2]

Behind the church is another crypt. Descending down its darkened staircase 'to the dead' is a visit to hell under the earth. In the first dark, airless and stale-smelling room rows of seemingly endless skulls and bones are stacked high. A corridor leads along to a further 48 such rooms, each housing unknown numbers of smashed discoloured bones. Outside, the figure of the young taxi driver who has brought me here sits hunched by the white crypt stone entrance, his head in his hands, sobbing. Epimaque Rwema, my guide, tells me softly, 'It is his first time here.' Does it get better after 1000 times I wonder?

At Ntarama, a few kilometres away, the genocide site is hidden up a dirt track, beyond the ironically named 'Nelson Mandela Peace Village'. A sign outside the church compound announces matter of factly,

'Eglise Ntarama genocide plus/minus 5000 persons'. The guide is a middle-aged woman. Her parents, husband and four young children were slaughtered here. Now, as in some appalling Greek myth, she is forced to stave off starvation by daily revisiting the horror for visitors.

Inside the church, shafts of the midday sun break in through massive holes in the red brick walls. Most of the stained glass windows have also gone, blown out by the grenades the militia used on the terrified refugees inside. The wooden pews are still covered with the debris of those who once sought refuge here for several days before the killers came. Small yellow eating bowls, woollen hats, red plastic children's shoes and school exercise books; a child's comb balances on a tiny plastic blue necklace. Walking is almost impossible without standing on the clothing, bones or 'relics' of the dead. When the killers entered the church, shooting and hacking with their machetes as if cutting down sorghum plants, some Tutsis fled to other outbuildings, but these were set on fire with the families inside; today there are just blackened bricks, bones, discarded shoes and clothing – and sacks of skulls.

The killing sites cover Rwanda. Between April and mid-July 1994, while the world sat glued to the trial of O. J Simpson, mourned the death of depressed rock idol Kurt Cobain and gloried in the inauguration of Nelson Mandela as South Africa's first president, an estimated 937,000 innocent Africans died solely because of their ethnic group. Like all genocides, this one had been meticulously planned and organized up to two years in advance. It was not the work of 'savages' or 'typical African intertribal warfare', as most of the West consoled itself as it sat on its hands and justified doing nothing. It was a genocide that intelligent, professional, university educated people had masterminded.

The killing became a daily ritual throughout the country. Hundreds of thousands either took part or quietly looked on as their neighbours were murdered. For the 'workers' it became as typical as getting in the harvest, using the same equipment – machetes, hoes and axes, but this time cutting down limbs and lives instead of sorghum, banana and mango. *Interahamwe* militiamen, bedecked in their uniforms of banana foliage with manioc leaves entwined in their hair, were happy in their 'work,' often drunk on *ikigage* (sorghum wine) or the ubiquitous *urwagwa* (local banana wine), as well as the taste of blood. For some, forced into killing on pain of death, alcoholic oblivion was needed to machete their elderly, bed-bound neighbours, or the children and infants who had played happily in the dirt alleyways only days before. For other *Interahamwe*, there was great joy to be had in literally cutting proud Tutsis down to size; tall Tutsi women sometimes had their legs hacked off before being left to die as a way of 'teaching them a lesson' for their alleged superior size and manner.

Yet, despite the numbers involved, the killing in each commune was systematic, precise and structured. Transport was laid on for the murderers to travel swiftly to their place of 'work', and they were rewarded with food and endless drink. Husbands killed their Tutsi wives and in-laws. Hutu hate radio RTLM warned listeners that Rwanda's troubles had begun by letting children and pregnant women survive the anti-Tutsi pogroms of the early 1960s. This time the laughing DJs demanded that no Tutsi should be allowed to live.

Where was the rest of the world? Much, rightly, has been made of the United Nations' failure to give adequate resources to preclude the genocide. The United States, in the guise of President Clinton and his official adviser to the UN Madeleine Albright, stand accused of monumental arrogance and indifference as they prepared to watch Rwanda and its people burn for political and electoral reasons. John Major's government in the United Kingdom also chose to turn its back on the unfolding tragedy, resulting in the killers effectively gaining a 'green light' from the international community to continue the slaughter.

However, one permanent member of the UN Security Council was heavily involved in Rwanda – before, during and after the genocide. France, the 'protector' of its former African colonies and the power behind some of the worst dictatorships on the 'black continent', is implicated to its core in the deaths at Nyanza, Ntarama and throughout the tiny central African nation. While apologies have been forthcoming in the past decade from nations that now 'regret' their inaction in the light of the immense suffering of which they were all too aware, the French government has remained silent.

In this book I uncover the untold story, a tale the Élysée would prefer to conceal, of how the politicians and military of a nation with a history of creative genius, invention and civilizing zeal chose to form an alliance with a genocidal regime and to arm, finance and train this regime and its soldiers.

Would the genocide have taken place without the support of Mitterrand and of the government he backed in Kigali? A Human Rights Watch report on the arms trade concluded:

> The people wielding the machetes in Rwanda operated in an environment in which a heavily armed movement (a combination of government and militias) provided the necessary protection and encouragement for the killers. If this environment had been different, if the government and allied militias had not been so well armed … there might have been a nasty conflict perhaps but not a genocide.

As the Canadian general, Romeo Dallaire, who commanded the United Nations Assistance Mission to Rwanda (UNAMIR) during the genocide, pointed out, Rwanda just did not matter. While the Bosnian crisis provoked full-scale diplomacy by the West and the deployment of hundreds of thousands of NATO and UN troops, the same countries treated Rwanda with indifference. This left the way open for Mitterrand to use it as a pawn in his francophone game, a pawn that could easily be damaged or smashed without consequences because it was in Africa and the rest of the world was not interested. The charge France faces of being implicated in the deaths of a million civilians is serious, and explains why politicians have fought shy of bringing the matter to light.

The reaction in France to its Rwandan policy has been muted, though not avoided. Several key pressure groups, including the Paris-based Survie, academics and African analysts such as Gérard Prunier, David Ambrosetti, François-Xavier Verschave and Antoine Jouan have all investigated this subject in great depth. The French media have also become increasingly involved in exposing areas of its national policy that are both painful and distressing to a nation steeped in a tradition of freedom and justice. Journalists and publishers such as Patrick de Saint-Exupéry, Mehdi Ba, Belgian writer Colette Braeckman and Jean-François Dupaquier have all contributed substantially to the debate by use of their eyewitness accounts, in the case of Saint-Exupéry, or by uncovering new and important sources. Yet, while this subject has been exposed to the French public for the past 12 years, it has rarely made any impact or impression on the English-speaking world, which perhaps is all too anxious with its own current foreign policy headaches and skeletons to want to look too closely at those of François Mitterrand.

There are important lessons to be drawn from the Rwandan genocide for both France and the West. The present situations in parts of Africa and the Middle East show how easy it is for Western governments, with their own private geostrategic and monetary agendas to inflame rather than solve the difficulties of states they earmark for political or military 'solutions'. The question is who is such a solution really for? In Rwanda, the French intervention in 1990 was very much aimed at ensuring the continuity of French influence in the country, and the continuation of a brutal, corrupt and 'apartheid-based' regime. At the base level of every such intervention, every such 'solution', though rarely at the forefront of the political minds that carry them out, are the civilian men, women and children who inevitably carry the brunt of any conflict. In the dehumanizing eyes of some Western political and military chiefs, such people become mere 'collateral damage': in Rwanda, such 'collateral damage' from the resulting genocide stands as a lesson of a cynicism gone mad.

***

Le pays des mille collines, the land of a thousand hills, is one of Africa's treasures. Unlike its neighbours Zaire (now the Democratic Republic of Congo), Tanzania and Uganda, Rwanda is a tiny country, the size of Wales, insignificant at first sight on the African and, indeed, world stage. Bordered by Lake Kivu and the Volcano National Park to the north and west, most of its eight million people survive their daily battle with poverty by relying on agricultural subsistence. Its only claim to fame before the 1994 genocide was through the highly dedicated and eccentric naturalist Dian Fossey and her attempts to save mountain gorillas in the beautiful northern rain forest.

Life in Rwandan villages is often short and always hard for the average 48 years each man can hope to live, or for the 'more fortunate' women who can expect to survive an extra two years of toil. The small huts that dot the lush green valleys and hills, with scarcely a flat plateau in sight, are a picture of the world of yesterday. No televisions, no cars, no computer games for the children who instead run around playing happily with discarded tyres. Water is more often than not carried up from the valleys to homes on the slopes by a mixture of the old and young. There is no retirement here and no social services to bail out the sick or elderly. Banana groves provide each family with its staple food, eked out perhaps with a chicken or rabbit on special occasions. These are cooked in charcoal fires as electricity is still a wonderment of the future. While the population has grown in the urban areas – the capital Kigali in the centre of the country, Ruhengeri and Gisenyi in the north and the university town of Butare in the south – Rwanda is primarily a rural economy. It relies on its tea and coffee plantations for commerce and on the occasional tourist coming to see the gorillas. It has no mineral or diamond riches with which its neighbour the Democratic Republic of Congo has been blessed, or some may say cursed.

To add to the mix of poverty and deprivation, Rwanda has become synonymous with the myth of ethnic division. Most Europeans who know anything about the genocide will venture the statement 'that was something between Tutsi and Hutu wasn't it?' as a catch-all summary of the disaster. While Rwanda is made up of three ethnic groups, the Hutu majority of around 85 per cent, the Tutsi minority of roughly 12 per cent and the Twas, about 3 per cent, the reality is that there is no intrinsic difference between them. It took the introduction of identity cards bearing a person's ethnic grouping by Belgian colonizers in the 1930s to distinguish accurately between Hutus and Tutsis. And this was for political reasons – part of the classic 'divide and rule' tactic so beloved of colonizers everywhere. While the European stereotype places the majority Hutu people as short and stocky and the Tutsis as tall and lean, outside ancient anthropological and racial theory textbooks such distinctions are meaningless. A trip to any Kigali or Butare market will quickly prove that years of intermarriage have blurred any easy distinctions. Instead, the Rwandan people – Hutu, Tutsi and Twa – have been bound together for centuries, speaking their own language, Kinyarwanda, tilling the same soil or breeding cattle and worshipping the same ancestral deities – or more recently the Christian God.

Colonization by Germany in the 1890s, then by Belgium after the First World War until independence in 1962, had a devastating effect on dividing Rwandans. A country that until 1880 was ruled by a king (Mwami), with the help of a village hierarchy and ancestral tradition, was split apart 100 years later by a 'modern' world in pursuit of geo-strategic, economic and political ambitions.

9

The Belgian rulers favoured the Tutsi, who took advantage of the imbalance to gain increased land and local prestige. Shortly before Belgium pulled out of the country and independence was declared on 1 July 1962, the legacy of its policy of ethnic partiality became apparent. Belgium and the Catholic Church switched their hand to supporting the majority Hutu 'underclass', thereby creating a counter elite. Recognizing the political expediency of allowing the majority to be in control once the state became independent, Belgium stood idly by as its former colony was bathed in a frenzy of killing from 1959 to 1962. Hutus 'settled scores' with their Tutsi masters who had been given control under the colonial system. Hundreds of thousands were killed or fled to neighbouring Uganda, Tanzania and Burundi, a problem that was to return to haunt Rwanda in 1990. An estimated 700,000 Tutsis ended up in or around refugee camps.[3]

After Belgium's withdrawal in 1962, there was a slow but steady incorporation of Rwanda into *la Francophonie*, the loose collection of former French colonies now part of a 'French-African commonwealth'. With its former colonizers now more interested in a pure economic aid relationship than in political and military links, France moved in to take advantage of the cultural and linguistic roots already in place.

The French Cultural Centre and embassy in Kigali encouraged continued reliance on Paris for all areas of life – language, arts, finance and military. Basic areas of society became saturated with the trappings of the richer Western country. Like other such African countries, Rwanda became 'a little island of France, where French papers are available on the day they are printed, and everything else, from telephone systems and tanks to paté, are French'.[4] The pre-1990 Rwandan army took part in training exercises with French legionnaires and relied on its Western counterpart for support should a war break out.[5] In almost every aspect of Rwandan life, France made sure it was present. It was classic neocolonialism – the tiny African state becoming a 'victim of an indirect and subtle form of domination by political, economic, social, military or technical means'.[6]

On 20 October 1962 President de Gaulle and Rwandan head of state Grégoire Kayibanda signed an agreement of 'friendship and cooperation', which was broadened to include civil cooperation clauses (economic, cultural and technical) by the end of that year. The Rwandan president, a former teacher turned journalist whose anti-

Tutsi pogroms had already caused some horrific massacres that continued until he was overthrown in 1973, made an official visit to
France in 1962, where he was effusive in his praise of de Gaulle. A
French ambassador to Rwanda was appointed in 1964 and, within ten
years of independence, Rwanda had become a fully-fledged Parisian
suburb.

French intervention in Rwanda in the late 1980s and early 1990s was
first and foremost an attempt by Paris to keep its beloved *francophonie*
intact. It was symptomatic of 30 years of military intervention by Paris
on the continent. Despite appalling human rights abuses by its 'client'
African governments, France has continued to support dictators and
regimes whose murderous policies towards their own people have been
well documented. The continuity of this policy is as striking as its
longevity through Presidents de Gaulle, Pompidou, Giscard d'Estaing
and Mitterrand, and has survived changing times, values and world
politics. Indeed, the term François-Xavier Verschave coined to
highlight the connection between France and its 'client' African states –
la Françafrique – is not without irony, with 'fric' being French slang for
money. Speaking in 1996, a diplomat in the Ivory Coast summed up
the equation, 'You could talk about the French presence for hours and
hours but it comes down to two things – prestige and business.'[7]

A number of different government departments in Paris, not all advo-
cating the same strategy, worked out French policy towards Rwanda
and other client francophone countries. Institutional competition was
endemic in the politics of African affairs. The ministries of defence,
foreign affairs, cooperation and the General Directorate for External
Security (DGSE) – the secret service – all vied for their own budgetary
and bureaucratic well-being and influence in policy making. The
Ministry of Cooperation had been set up precisely to decide on and to
implement policy towards the newly independent states. Known
somewhat sarcastically as the 'Ministry of the African Neo-Colonies',[8]
its decisions seemed to reflect the interests of French politicians rather
than the good of the states in which it operated. In fact, the real power
behind African policy lay with the president at the Élysée. Decisions
were based on his judgement or that of his personally appointed
adviser at his special consultative body, the secret Africa Cell, also
embedded at the Élysée Palace. This 'individualistic' diplomacy was
given a public display of openness at the francophone political sum-

mits, when the French president invited friendly African heads of state to a show of unity and hospitality.

French policy in Africa has always been based on personal ties between respective presidents, their ministers and business leaders. In Rwanda it was these personal ties that were to lead Paris into the heart of genocide. The red carpet welcome that greeted the Rwandan president Juvénal Habyarimana on his many visits to the French capital, with banquets, shopping trips and business deals to cement relations, was symptomatic of how policy was made. Mitterrand's son, Jean-Christophe, made personal links with African elites when his father appointed him head of the Africa Cell. Such high level 'cronyism' gave the president a secure, uncritical voice in African affairs. Jean-Christophe, now with the rather appropriate nickname *papa m'a dit* (daddy told me to), claimed that the difference between the French and Anglo-Saxon way of dealing with Africa was down to the hot-blooded Gallic nature. 'The French culture corresponds better with the Africans' than the English culture does – it's our Mediterranean side. Our ties are so much more personal.' His successor in the Africa Cell office, Bruno Delaye, romantically reflected, 'France and Africa are like an old couple. We argue, we disagree, but in the end we cannot separate. We have too much, too many friends, in common.'[9] For both men, and indeed the whole edifice of francophone Africa, personal ties, deals done over bottles of wine and contacts made in Paris clubs and Brazzaville mansions were the way to unlock the many benefits that such close relationships had to offer.

The personal, political, military and economic justification for intervening in this far-off region was to be found in a cultural and linguistic heritage. In the Rwandan tragedy Paris was fearful not just of losing a client government with which it could do business, but of having it replaced by that most vilified of projected rivals '*les anglais*'. The anxiety that French Africa is under constant threat from the Anglo-Saxons pushing a zone of influence from Ethiopia to South Africa has become almost pathological. It is an area of policy that continues to unite socialist and Gaullist political groups and seems to override all other political, military and strategic viewpoints and, in the case of Rwanda, human rights and morality as well.

This latter-day fear of Anglo-Saxon encroachment had its origins in the fiasco at Fashoda a century earlier. In 1898, rather than risk war with Britain over its African dependencies, the French government had faced a humiliating climb-down by withdrawing its garrison under Commander Marchand from the Sudanese town of Fashoda in the face of Kitchener's British expedition. Since then a sense of 'never again' has motivated the policy of the Élysée, the French foreign office at Quai d'Orsay and the military. It is a mindset, not official policy, but it cannot be ignored. Central Africa was a francophone zone and Rwanda, the perceived border of this French-speaking area, became in French official thinking a 'Rubicon' that might allow an entry into *la Françafrique* for perfidious Albion, and more importantly the United States.

This rivalry, born in the colonial era, has been exacerbated by French military defeats in Indo-China and North Africa and the systematic march of American culture and the English language around the world. François Mitterrand, as minister of justice in 1957, declared, 'All problems that we French have had in West Africa are not to do with a desire for independence, but with a rivalry between French and British areas. It is British agents who have made all our difficulties.'[10] Rwanda became a 'linguistic Maginot line'.[11] One French commentator compared France with:

> a large hen followed by a docile brood of little black chicks. ...
> The casual observer imagining that money is the cement of the whole relationship would have the wrong impression. The cement is language and culture. Paris's African backyard remains its backyard because all the chicks cackle in French. There is a high symbiosis between French and francophone African political elites. It is a mixture of many things: old memories, shared material interests, delusions of grandeur, gossip, sexual peccadilloes, in short a common culture.[12]

A French journalist commented wryly, 'In Africa, France does not have a policy, only bad habits.'[13] In Rwanda's case, this 'bad habit', which politicians and the public in Paris shrugged off, resulted in corpses decomposing outside Nyambuye and throughout the tiny insignificant country. Ten years after the killing Sister Ignatia still sits in her convent, reliving daily the screams of the murdered. 'I don't understand how people can hate each other so much,' she sighs. 'God created all men equal.'

Chapter 2

Invasion and Intervention

The invasion, when it came, was hardly a surprise. Rwandan Patriotic Front (RPF) troops moved over the Ugandan border into northern Rwanda in their trademark Wellington boots catching President Habyarimana's ill-prepared government off guard. It was October 1990 and to outside eyes it seemed the start of just another low-level African civil war, blamed conveniently on 'intertribal' tensions and political deadlock between the two sides. But, as the exiled RPF leaders led their well-armed and trained recruits back into their homeland for the first time in many years, few could have envisaged that the end result of this war would be genocide, with Habyarimana's Rwandan government planning the most desperate of all measures to hold onto power – the complete annihilation of its Tutsi opponents – or indeed that the French government would send in troops and munitions to keep the killers in power.

The mists that blanketed Rwanda's valleys, rivers and hillsides in the years before the 1990 invasion were indicative of a political system hidden from all but those closest to Rwandan President Juvénal Habyarimana. He had built his dictatorship into a fearsome, all-controlling dominance. Only his most trusted henchmen were allowed to dip their fattened fingers into the spoils of state wealth and prestige. His 17 years in power had consolidated a stranglehold on every area of Rwandan life – political, military and economic.

Born on 8 March 1937 at Gasiza in the commune of Giciyi in north Rwanda, Habyarimana was, like many African dictators, a product of the army rather than of a distinguished family. As a student he studied in neighbouring Zaire, first reading humanities and mathematics at St

Paul's College, then medicine at Lovanium University, also in Mobutu's poverty-wracked country. Deciding that a medical career was not for him, the young ambitious Juvénal scented change in the air on his return to Rwanda; he joined the officers' school in Kigali in 1960 and, within a year of Rwandan independence in 1962, was appointed army chief of staff. His first military action followed soon after – the savage repression of a Tutsi uprising. In the same year he married Agathe Kanzinga, a highly ambitious aristocrat. By 1965 he was minister of defence and chief of police in President Kayibanda's government. He built his power base among officers in the northern Gisenyi region, a traditionally strong Hutu area given to extremist elements. On 5 July 1973, two years after Idi Amin had seized power in neighbouring Uganda and two months after Kayibanda had promoted him to major general, Habyarimana took control of Rwanda after launching what he later claimed to be a 'popular' coup. Kayibanda was shuffled off to prison to be starved to death – the new president was superstitious and afraid of 'spilling the blood' of his predecessor in case it came back to haunt him.[1]

Like his wife Agathe, Habyarimana was an impressive disciple of the Roman Catholic Church, which represented the majority of Christian believers in Rwanda, and liked to give the impression of being close to God. The pulpit was still a vital tool to any government in radiating friendly propaganda in a country where literacy levels were low and the church was still a trusted and vital part of society. The gospel of the White Fathers – a Catholic missionary society founded in 1868 – was of obedience to authority. This religious foundation, more than any other, threw its weight behind ethnic division and authoritarian rule. By the 1960s the church and state had bonded into one entity, preaching the same gospel of Hutu supremacy and total loyalty to the leadership in the capital Kigali.

Habyarimana spent much of his time in his ornate Kigali palace, sprawled along a hillside overlooking the capital city and conveniently near the airport. Guests would be left in no doubt that this dictator was a spiritual man of refinement, learning and intellect. A tour would include the glitteringly decorated chapel and a study stuffed full of hunting trophies, with antlers lining the walls like those of a Habsburg's palace and portraits of the brave dictator standing beside his bloodied kills. Bookshelves crammed with literary volumes assured guests of the African leader's learning and intellect. The weightiest

15

tome, an embossed two-volume *Dictionnaire de Littérature de Langue Française*, was a gift from President Mitterrand, given in 1986 to symbolize the close ties between the two French speakers.[2] Like his predecessor Kayibanda, Habyarimana was obsessed with Hitler and the Third Reich. Some of his most prized possessions included Super-8 films, books and cassettes about the German dictator, including a copy of *Mein Kampf* – except for Jews, Habyarimana now read 'Tutsis'.

The French ambassador Georges Martres was one of Habyarimana's biggest fans, telling one interviewer:

> I knew President Habyarimana personally. He was a man who expressed himself very well in French, who had an interesting political vision, who gave the impression of a great morality. President Habyarimana prayed regularly, assisted regularly at mass. I'm not saying these were the elements that brought about the support of President Mitterrand but I believe that in general the face that President Habyarimana and his family presented to President Mitterrand was received in a favourable manner. I do not think I am mistaken in arriving at this judgement.[3]

Habyarimana's regime reinforced ethnic stereotypes to consolidate its hold on power. All Rwandans, from the newborn to the elderly, were pressed to join the sole political party, the MRND (*Mouvement républicain national pour la démocratie et le développement*), founded by the Rwandan dictator in 1975. Western donor nations, including Germany, the USA and Canada, felt their funding was safer in this tiny central African state than in neighbouring Uganda, where Obote's massacres had replaced Amin's horror; Zaire, where the aid budget lined only Mobutu's hidden bank accounts; or Burundi, with its ongoing ethnic killings on a massive scale. Though a rise from seventh from bottom of the World Bank's GNP per capita in 1976 to nineteenth from the bottom in 1990 was a success of sorts, the Rwandan economy had come to rely not on exports but on foreign aid.

Habyarimana's smiling face beamed down on his people from posters in shops and homes, on badges and T-shirts and massive roadside advertising sites. His quintessential bouffant haircut and tall, upright figure cut a dash in the streets of Brussels and Paris where his regime increasingly looked to make representations. Rwanda was small and lacking in raw materials, but by playing the francophone card the president made the most of his powerful European ally. Kigali cemented its position in 'la Françafrique' by hosting the Franco-African conference in 1979. Three years earlier, in 1976, Rwanda became a co-founder of the Communauté économique des Pays des Grands Lacs (CEPGL), a French-run organization promising possible new trade routes and business deals.

The 'land of a thousand hills' had by 1991 become 'the land of a thousand foreign aid workers' as external aid provided nearly a quarter of its GNP. Such aid came from Belgium, its main donor, France, Switzerland, Germany, Canada and the USA. Under Habyarimana the country seemed to offer a stable and economically forward-looking strategy, a dictatorship that was acceptable to outsiders with well-intentioned donations.

But things were less rosy in Rwanda than the donor nations believed. Habyarimana had two battles to fight in the 1970s and 1980s, and both would explode in the early 1990s. The first was an internal struggle for power and wealth within the Hutu elite. The president, from Gisenyi in the north, favoured this area over Kayibanda's previous regime's prefer-ence for elites from the central town of Gitarama and areas to its south. By the 1980s northern favouritism had become highly restrictive and many Rwandans, suffering from over-population and increasingly reliant on food aid, bitterly resented the greed for land and power of a small clique around the president. Although Habyarimana won the 1988 election with 99.9 per cent of the vote, a splendid result even if no opposition parties were allowed to stand against him, resistance to one-party rule was on the increase. Intellectuals, the business class and middle-ranking bureaucrats objected to the way a close-knit group around the president controlled the government, money and army. With coffee and tea prices nose-diving in the late 1980s, drought deci-mating harvests in the east and tin mining shut down because it was unproductive, starvation was becoming increasingly prevalent among much of the population. Meanwhile, Habyarimana's family and friends had grown rich in power and had become addicted to the corruption now prevalent in every area of the country's political life.

The MRND had built its impressive power base on knowing every individual in the country. In Rwanda each person was part of a ten-house group, the sous-secteur, which in turn was part of a larger *secteur, colline* or hill. Further up the administrative scale were communes, administered by *bourgmestres* (mayors), and prefectures, each represented with government loyalists. The Hutu majority had an almost total monopoly on jobs. An 'apartheid' system was savagely enforced, even keeping Hutu and Tutsi children apart at school and making sure only the former could later gain government or professional employment. It was another irony of the Rwandan genocide that while the Western world got so excited about the demise of apartheid in South Africa, a similar system was in place 1500 miles north. But the Tutsi did not have a Nelson Mandela to champion them. In fact, the only Tutsi who managed to become a prefect during the 20 years of Habyarimana's rule was Jean-Baptiste Habyarimana (no relation to the president), who administered the Butare prefecture in the south. He was killed at the start of the genocide.

The presidential hold on the army was even tighter and made use of former colonial practices to ensure recruits were loyal Hutus. In the early 1960s the Belgian colonel Guy Logiest had introduced the 'Pignet' system to keep Tutsi recruits out of the army; after independence the newly formed *Guard Nationale de Rwanda* continued this military 'apartheid'. In local administration and the civil service Tutsis were also shunned. Only in business were they allowed some degree of tolerance – due to the money they could bring the regime and its supporters.

The Rwandan dictator had survived both endeavours to dethrone him. Two coup attempts, by Colonel Théoneste Lizinde in 1980 and Colonel Stanislas Mayuya in 1988, failed. Habyarimana became adept at playing a balancing act between Hutu extremists – many of them his own relatives – desperate to hold onto power and growing calls by moderate Hutus for multi-party government and press freedom.

A far more dangerous threat was building up across the border in Uganda. The Rwandan Patriotic Front (RPF) was born out of the pogroms and bloodshed in Rwanda during and after independence, which cost hundreds of thousands of Tutsis their lives. Up to 700,000 Tutsis had fled their homeland in the 1960s, many of them to Uganda where life under Amin and Obote was only slightly less horrific. A small group of refugees joined rebel leader Yoweri Museveni and his National Resistance Army to attack the Obote regime, forcing him into exile in January 1986; despite their role in liberating Uganda, the local population far from accepted the Rwandan Tutsi refugees, for they resented the influence they now had over President Museveni and his new government in Kampala. While the international community dithered over how to get the refugees back to Rwanda, and Habyarimana blocked any solution, the RPF was formed in December 1987 with a view to returning them, by force if necessary, to their homeland.

The 1990 invasion of northern Rwanda was anything but a surprise. Habyarimana had been trying for two years to infiltrate the RPF in Kampala and assassinate its leading players. In turn, RPF leaders General Fred Rwigyema and Colonel Paul Kagame had a firm eye on the international situation, using information from both Britain and America on the state of Habyarimana's government and the possibility of an international response to their invasion. From July 1990 the RPF began a military build up of its forces near the Ugandan–Rwanda border. While the RPF plotted, with apparent help from the Ugandan regime in Kampala, Habyarimana was looking to France for his security and to the father/son combination that currently held sway in the Élysée – François Mitterrand and his appointed head of the presidential Africa Cell, Jean-Christophe Mitterrand. The fate of Rwanda in the early 1990s was inextricably linked to the policies and political careers of this *père/fils* combination. Their decisions, taken at the Élysée presidential palace in Paris, a building whose grandeur reflected their own sense of personal worth and respect, were to have terrible repercussions among the people living in simple huts and brick houses that make up Rwanda.

François Maurice Mitterrand arrived at the Élysée in 1981 after a presidential campaign lasting more than 20 years and a political career reaching back to the dark days of the Second World War. He had made great capital in his election campaign *à la* Blair of a 'new way' in France's view of the world and an ethical foreign policy that would sever the link between aid given and favours expected. Mitterrand 'pledged to defend the rights of oppressed people everywhere, champion a fairer system of international development and work for world disarmament'.[4] He championed a reduction in France's sale of armaments by stressing that his country should aim to export goods that did not further destabilize the third world with the threat of civil or international war in the way that arms do. Given that by the time Mitterrand won the 1981 election France was the leading arms exporter per capita in the world, such a pledge was quite a commitment.[5]

The start was auspicious. By appointing Jean-Pierre Cot as his first minister of cooperation and development Mitterrand signalled his intention to remain true to his word. The president intervened in South America to support the Sandinista National Liberation Army's struggle against the USA in Nicaragua in the early 1980s, as well as the FMLN (*Farabundo Martí para la Liberación Nacional*) guerrillas fighting the US-backed government in El Salvador.

But the honeymoon policy of supporting the 'poor and oppressed' was short-lived. Cot resigned in 1982 and with him left Mitterrand's only attempt to live up to his promised ethical foreign policy. Arms sales flourished again, the idea of increasing budget aid to developing countries to 0.7 per cent GNP was dropped, while political and military assistance to dictators with appalling human rights records continued apace. Realpolitik came before real aid. In effect, 'a policy of subsidized export of arms and equipment was pursued, and a small group of private advisers to the president saw to it that the bulk of French development aid would continue to flow into the pockets of those African heads of state who had always proved faithful friends, though not necessarily effective developers of their countries.'[6]

Mitterrand's policy in Africa was consistent with his Machiavellian outlook on politics and his cynical regard for life in general. His rise from a humble background – his father was a stationmaster and vinegar factory owner – was due to a chameleon-like ability to match his face to the current public need. His decision-making on Rwanda was symptomatic of his political career and was in no way exceptional. This was a man who had fought for both sides in the Second World War, beginning as a member of the right-wing nationalist group the *Légion française des combattants*, a militia used later to track down and deport or kill resistance fighters and Jews. A friend of Marshal Pétain and René Bousquet, leader of the Vichy government and its chief of police respectively, Mitterrand's service to the pro-Nazi hierarchy included publication of articles in journals given to fervid anti-Semitic writing, while he had no moral difficulty accepting the '*Francisque*' from Pétain – the highest award the Vichy regime could give. Correctly perceiving the political and military wind of change as Germany's prospects waned, Mitterrand joined the resistance and later made great capital from helping to liberate Paris from its German occupiers.

In office under the Fourth Republic from 1954 to 1957, Mitterrand took a hard line on the Algerian independence movement; a French general later accused him of sanctioning torture in the French colony. The ensuing conflict cost more than half a million lives and both French forces and their opponents committed appalling atrocities. Mitterrand reinvented himself as a socialist in the 1960s and 1970s as a way of getting back into power, and was elected in 1981. Political and personal scandals marked his two terms in office, but with typical gusto the president ensured his survival through one presidential re-election campaign in 1988 and two periods of 'cooperation' with right-wing prime ministers in 1986–88 and 1993–95.

Mitterrand's genius was in keeping under wraps a storm of immense political proportions. When finally the lid came off the president was too ill and the public inclined, as ever, to forgive and forget amid the 'nostalgia' of Mitterrand's reign.

For his son Jean-Christophe, his father's election to the Élysée in 1981 was like winning the lottery. Within five years this little-known journalist was parachuted into one of the top jobs in France. Six years later, he ignominiously left the post as head of the presidential Africa Cell after constant insinuations of corruption and malpractice. By the end of the decade he was under investigation for illegal arms trafficking and money laundering; he spent Christmas 2000 in a prison cell.

After a childhood neglected by his parents, Jean-Christophe dropped out of university and at 23 was working on a kibbutz in Israel before turning to a career in journalism in Africa with Agence France-Presse. Out of this scarcely impressive background he was thrust into the secret world of the Élysée and African politics in 1986 as head of the Africa Cell – part of the presidential office tasked with advising Mitterrand on the so-called 'black continent'. His alleged close relationship with Jean-Pierre Habyarimana, the Rwandan dictator's son, made Jean-Christophe prey to rumours about his own behaviour. Being seen, according to *New York Times* journalist Frank Smyth, 'carousing together in discos on the Left Bank [in Paris] and in Rwanda at the Kigali Nightclub', hardly helped Mitterrand junior's image.[7] Life heading the Africa Cell was a mixed bag and was never dull. It involved wining and dining visiting heads of states from francophone countries, providing them with suitably expensive gifts, or even 'arranging the supply of French prostitutes to the Gabon president'.[8]

In his autobiography *Mémoire meurtrie* ('Battered memory') Jean-

Christophe vehemently denied all allegations of corruption.[9] All the sins of the father had, he alleged, been thrown on him. The result, according to Jean-Christophe, was that he was left to carry the can of worms. This father–son combination was certainly one out of which nightmares are made when it came to establishing an ethical and beneficial foreign policy towards the people of Africa. The corruption, greed and ambition so prevalent in the Élysée were in many ways matched by the client francophone governments with which they were so intimately connected. It was small wonder that the plight of 'ordinary' Rwandan citizens was of little concern.

Habyarimana was one of many French-backed dictators to fly to the Franco-African summit held at the pretty resort town of La Baule in June 1990. It was the usual back-slapping occasion and time for the home nation to parade its power on the continent to the 40 leaders of client African states who turned up. Mitterrand, as ever keeping up with the times, announced in his keynote speech on 20 June that aid to African states would be tied to human rights and democratic reforms. Foreign Minister Roland Dumas summarized the president's thoughts; the wind of change had blown in the east (Europe) and should now blow in the south, namely Africa. Allied to this was the fact that there could be 'no development without democracy and no democracy without development', with Mitterrand making clear his support for human rights and democracy in francophone states. 'France is putting all its effort into efforts that will produce greater liberty', he declared to some open-mouthed African dictators. Indeed, the French president had begun to sniff the 'wind of change blowing through Africa's coconut trees', as he delicately put it.[10] However, the effect on dictators like Mobutu, Eyadéma, Bongo and Habyarimana, who had delighted in a previous decade of French-funded human rights abuses, with help from the International Monetary Fund, World Bank and other Western nations, can only be imagined. Was this the same French president who supported Hassan II of Morocco in his authoritarian regime with a 38-year history of human rights abuse or whose secret services had been implicated in the 1987 murder of President Sankara in Burkina Faso – an African leader who stood against 'la Françafrique'?

Sitting in his new government office in a smart suburb of Paris, the youthful and engaging defence analyst Frédéric Charillon gave me his take on the La Baule phenomenon.

After the end of the Cold War, France, like other European powers, had to search for an updated foreign policy. But here [in Paris] there were no policy think-tanks or discussion groups, especially on Africa which was a closed, family affair. Mitterrand's France pretended to still be a global power, not just a regional one – and the answer to that lay in Africa.[11]

Habyarimana recognized that any 'democratic' reforms he implemented in Rwanda could conveniently be tailored to fit his authoritarian needs. With continued control of the military, the heralded multi-party reforms and democracy were always more of a concept than an actual policy. There were ways to split the opposition, to buy off political rivals or have them murdered if necessary. He gambled correctly that support for Mitterrand's new stance was more a matter of words than deeds. It was in neither president's interest to have a powerful Rwandan opposition that could in the future unseat both Habyarimana and his cosy client relationship with France.

Throughout the 1980s Habyarimana had ingratiated himself with Mitterrand. Like other African francophone leaders, he enjoyed the ego boost of walking along the red carpet to the Élysée, and the pomp and ceremony of standing alongside Mitterrand for the gathered press photographs, pictures that could be seen on the front pages of Kigali papers the next day. All the while his family could use their French funding for expensive shopping trips along the Champs-Élysée, or allegedly to do some hard bargaining on arms deals.[12]

The personal ties extended from the husbands and sons to the wives of the two presidents. Agathe Habyarimana was of 'noble' blood and, unlike her husband Juvénal, was from an 'aristocratic' Rwandan family from Gisenyi. As such she made sure her trips to Paris made her feel like the royalty she felt she was. Her wardrobe was an impressive array of fine snakeskin dresses, gold jewellery to match and shoes for the ballrooms of Europe and her husband's palaces, with horn-rimmed sunglasses as a final touch. Press pictures from an official visit to Paris in 1990 show Madame Habyarimana perched happily on an Élysée couch handing over presents to Mitterrand's wife Danielle, her gold necklace, watch and rings glittering impressively. But then, as British journalist Christian Jennings has written, 'when you are Agathe Habyarimana buying white leather cocktails dresses and red acrylic hot pants with dollars that you have stolen from your country's international budget, it feels doubly right. You are, after all, only returning the money to the country from which it came.'[13]

The RPF invasion on 1 October 1990 caught most players unawares. Habyarimana, ironically with Ugandan President Museveni, was at a UNICEF banquet in New York. Colonel Paul Kagame, a leading RPF commander, was also in the USA, while François Mitterrand, the defence minister Jean-Pierre Chevènement, the foreign minister Roland Dumas and the general-secretary to the presidency Hubert Védrine were all on a state visit to the Persian Gulf.

On the evening of 3 October 1990 the French president was dining aboard his frigate moored off Abu Dhabi when, between fine wines and food, he was disturbed. Jacques Lanxade, at that time Mitterrand's personal military adviser, related what happened. 'A telegram from Paris arrived in which Habyarimana said his country was being invaded and he needed urgent French military help. Immediately the president asked me to [go to] Rwanda. Jean-Pierre Chevènement tried in vain to present a few objections but his arguments on the neocolonial stance of France were brushed aside by the president.'[14] The following day the panic-stricken Rwandan leader sent another telegram alleging that his capital Kigali was now being threatened, which led to a decision to double the French force sent out to help him.

Back in Paris, as misfortune would have it, the only player in his office when the invasion started was Africa Cell chief Jean-Christophe Mitterrand. Also there on unrelated business was African expert Gérard Prunier, who recounted the remarkable events that triggered France's first step into a quagmire of Rwandan death and hatred.

Jean-Christophe picked up the phone to listen to a worried Habyarimana plead for urgent French military intervention. Prunier related what he heard. 'After ten minutes I knew who he was talking to [Habyarimana]. After 20 minutes' conversation on the phone he [Jean-Christophe] said to me "we'll send old man Habyarimana a few troops; we're going to bail him out, it'll be over in two or three months"';[15] Prunier added, 'he believed his own stupidity'. Jean-Christophe later denied that this conversation with Prunier had ever taken place.

Despite Mitterrand's and his son's assurances that troops were on their way, Habyarimana was far from reassured. He knew his own forces were weak and that, despite promises from Paris, it was better to be safe than sorry. Three days after the RPF invasion he staged a 'firefight' in Kigali on the night of 4–5 October, which received a glowing account from Ambassador Martres who reported to the French foreign office that there was 'heavy fighting in the capital'. As a result the French troops were upgraded and Operation Noroît (north wind) breezed into the troubled African country with 600 elite paratroopers. It was a double whammy for Habyarimana who used the staged assault to round up 10,000 opposition suspects for 'interrogation'. The RPF was nowhere near Kigali and had nothing to do with this event, but it suited the French to believe otherwise, and was all the justification needed to encourage further intervention. Admiral Lanxade recounted in his memoirs how 'On 5 October a raid by the RPF at the heart of the capital seemed to give us reason for our intervention. The defence attaché sent an account of the clashes which had happened in the town and noted they took place close to our embassy.'[16] The geography of the attack was hardly surprising; the Rwandan president had designed it to ensure that France had every reason and encouragement to get involved. He was not to be disappointed.

Whatever Mitterrand's motives for intervening in a country that France had not even colonized, he may well have acted on a simple gut feeling that the decision to send troops to Rwanda would be quick and painless. It is possible that Mitterrand believed, as his son clearly did, that French support would not be needed for long. Like the First World War, it would be 'over by Christmas'. Mitterrand's close personal and family ties with Habyarimana were another reason to intervene. They were good friends and had a relationship that was mutually beneficial. However, the French foreign office and Ministry of Cooperation also advised sending in troops, as did French military intelligence in Rwanda and the embassy in Kigali. They needed to stop this francophone country becoming the first domino to fall in the feared anglophone 'invasion'. Fashoda may have been 100 years ago, but its effects on French political and military circles were undiminished. Habyarimana certainly played up the fear of an anglophone Tutsi plot to carve out a large new central African kingdom.

Loyalty to its francophone allies was also vital. 'If we fail to fulfil our promises', explained a French diplomat, 'our credibility towards other African states with which we have similar accords (Central African Republic, Comoros, Djibouti, Gabon, Ivory Coast, Senegal and Togo) would be seriously damaged, and we would see those countries turning to other supporters.'[17] Several African heads of state privately sent their congratulations to the Élysée for its military action.

From the start, Paris was keen to portray the RPF as nothing but the Ugandan army, which it accused of arming and training it. There was no attempt to get beneath the surface of the refugee problem, the massacres and the 'apartheid' system that had forced many Rwandan Tutsis to flee to Uganda in the 1960s and 1970s, or to understand that Habyarimana had stopped them peacefully returning to their homeland in the 1980s. Instead, Paris portrayed Rwandan Tutsis as Ugandan anglophones. It was pointed out that most of the RPF spoke English instead of French and had been to military academies in the USA rather than Paris. Ugandan leader and RPF supporter Yoweri Museveni was the very embodiment of an Anglo-Saxon, for he spoke English and threatened the French.[18] To work alongside him, as many of the RPF leadership did, was to be guilty by default.

A French mercenary dismissed Paul Kagame, a later RPF leader, as a 'very clever soldier. But he's a product of America, he's CIA. For a start he doesn't speak a word of French. He only speaks English. And he did all his training … as an officer in American military schools.'[19]

Besides deliberately discriminating against the Tutsis by refusing to regard them as Rwandan, the French government described the RPF as 'Khmer Noir' (Black Khmers), which, with its reference to the genocide and killing fields of Cambodia where Pol Pot and his Khmer Rouge supporters murdered two million fellow countrymen in the late 1970s, was highly destructive terminology. It was particularly ironic for the French government to besmirch the RPF with such a loaded reference, given that Paris had at the time supported Pol Pot and his bloody henchmen in their 'year zero' revolution.

To finish off the heady brew of prejudice against the RPF, some French politicians and military commanders dismissed it as a group of terrorists invading purely to wreak havoc and with no meaningful political agenda. 'The action the RPF started from Uganda was not a classic army action. It was a terrorist action with villages razed and children disembowelled. The men led by that guy Kagame were terrorists and killers.'[20] This view was especially ironic given that it came from Paul Barril, one time French secret serviceman and now a mercenary acting for a number of African dictators.

However, Mitterrand's initial decision, taken in a few hours, to send in troops betrayed a complete misunderstanding of the complexities of the Rwandan situation. Once the decision was made, French pride made withdrawal more difficult than continuing involvement in the bitter civil war. Previous successful interventions, notably in Chad and Zaire, had lulled Paris into a sense of false security.

In President Mitterrand's analysis, what was important above all was a global reasoning, there was no point of strategic application making Rwanda more important than Chad. He considered, as had his three [presidential] predecessors, that France had subscribed to a security role and that if she were unable to bring help in a case as simple as that of being a friend of the country suffering an armed invasion, then his guarantee of security was not worth anything anymore.[21]

Typically, there was no debate in the French parliament about troops being sent to intervene in Rwanda, or indeed at the UN from which France did not wait for a mandate for its action. Only two papers, *Libération* and *L'Humanité*, covered the intervention in any meaningful manner. French television barely got involved until autumn 1994 when images of post-genocide refugee camps and cholera victims were deemed newsworthy. One journalist had bemoaned his fellow Frenchmen's silence during the first Gulf War, asking 'where are the collective appeals, the petitions, the committees, the meetings, the marches?'[22] The same was true of the intervention in Rwanda, which both public and politicians met with deafening indifference and silence.[23]

Once the decision was taken to send a military force to Rwanda, the next step was to cloak its duties and aims in a public relations smokescreen of 'humanitarianism'. Thus, Operation Noroît was sold to what little of the French public was aware of it at all as purely a device to protect and evacuate French citizens. The French prime minister, Michel Rocard, told his apathetic nation on 6 October 1990 that 'we have sent troops in to protect French citizens, and nothing more. This is a high security mission and a republican duty.'[24] This position was reiterated for the next two years, with Daniel Bernard at the foreign office telling the French press 'the presence of French forces has no other objective than to assure the security of our residents.'[25]

In the first two weeks of Operation Noroît in October 1994 313 French nationals were flown out of the country, leaving a force of more than 300 heavily armed elite troops to protect the remaining 290 French civilians. Though their mission was allegedly based in the capital Kigali, reconnaissance to Butare in the south and Gisenyi in the north reported an enthusiastic welcome for French soldiers by the local population and government troops, the FAR (Forces armées rwandaises).

The RPF invasion started inauspiciously enough. Within a week it had lost its commander General Fred Rwigyema, killed in unknown circumstances, and the attack petered out into a guerrilla war in the north of the country. Crucially, it failed to anticipate the military help that France was to send to keep the Rwandan dictator in power.[26]

While the RPF struggled to make an impact, Habyarimana's forces struggled to know from which end of their rifles they should fire. The president's ramshackle troops numbered little more than 3000 at the start of the war and they were poorly trained, tactically naive and inexperienced in any form of battle. As in so many francophone countries, the government troops were a shambles of military incompetence and weakness, with leadership given as a reward for political service rather than tactical awareness. This was precisely because the president could always call in external French forces to do the fighting. French mercenary Paul Barril was appalled at what he found. 'When you take a peasant, you take a pupil. You can put him in a military uniform, but that doesn't make him a soldier. You understand what I am saying? These guys have got absolutely no training, no motivation. No special commandos, no special action guys, they're a balloon full of wind.'[27] Habyarimana saw within days of Noroît's arrival that the survival of his regime depended on the French staying put.

Use of French Gazelle helicopter 'gunships' was one method that helped stop any significant early advance by the RPF at the start of the war. Barril boasted that:

> France's official special services blocked in '90 the attack by the RPF terrorists and Uganda, [it was] a DGSE (French Secret Services) job. A remarkable job which was a source of great pride in the first phase of the war. There were heroes on the French side who will never be known, extraordinary stories of guys who took crazy initiatives, who went out and blasted all around them

with just a few helicopters and a few guns. There is material for a
book on the heroism of the Secret Services in Rwanda, against
Uganda and the RPF ... which explains their hatred for France.[28]

An RPF tactician, who backed this account, said that the helicopters
were one reason the RPF moved to a guerrilla-based attack rather than
a frontal assault near Byumba in the north.[29]

In December 1990 the Rwandan president begged French military
chiefs Admiral Lanxade and Colonel (later General) Jean-Pierre
Huchon to remain for at least another two months. This was despite
the RPF threat being confined to guerrilla skirmishes on a localized
level in the Ruhengeri area. Lanxade, who painted a flattering portrait
of the Rwandan dictator as a tall, amiable but reserved individual,
suddenly found he was pestered by phone calls from Habyarimana day
and night pleading for more French military help.

Mitterrand did not need much persuading to allow Noroît to continue into 1991. Intelligence reports made it clear the Rwandan army
was unlikely to be able to contain any new concerted RPF attack. At
the same time as 'protecting their citizens', French military know-how
was keeping Habyarimana safe. As Operation Noroît swung into action
in the second week of October 1990, so did the activities of the French
military's 'consultative' role for its Rwandan counterpart. Colonel
Gilbert Canovas, deputy defence attaché, was to 'provide appraisal and
advice' and to help equip Habyarimana's forces for the war. A number
of 'security' consultants were sent to the conflict zone in the north to
'instruct, organize and motivate troops ... who have forgotten the ele-
mentary rules of combat'.[30] Tactical advice on the protection of Kigali
and northern border towns like Gisenyi, Ruhengeri and Byumba was
vital for an army devoid of any real leadership or strategy. Equally
imperative was the swift recruitment and training of thousands of new
troops. In 1991 the Rwandan army had swelled to around 20,000, and
this was to further double in the next two years of French assistance.

On 23 and 24 January 1991, the RPF launched a sudden and impressive offensive against the town of Ruhengeri, freeing 350 prisoners
from its gaol. By 27 January the attackers had retreated again into the
surrounding national park. Habyarimana's response was immediate; the
indigenous Tutsi of Bagogwe were massacred as punishment.

In the 1990–94 period the French equipped the Rwandan government army with some of the most modern weaponry available. African civil wars are usually fought with old Russian or east European stocks and cheap Chinese weapons, but France ensured its allies had Gazelle helicopters, heavy mortars, radar equipment, Milan rockets, Panhard tanks and armoured vehicles, as well as a variety of small arms. The French, however, had to finance and ship the armaments to the FAR, and then train a highly demotivated and unskilled army to use the sophisticated weaponry.

The hawks at the Élysée, who wanted the RPF threat defeated in the field, made sure their Rwandan allies were not going to be outgunned. General Huchon, Mitterrand's confidant and assistant to commander-in-chief Lanxade at the Élysée, 'had at times to struggle at meetings of the Interministerial Committee for War Material Exports meetings to get approval for the impressive volume of lethal equipment which high government officials wanted to send to Kigali'.[31] One solution was to get the deals done through 'neutral' countries like Egypt.

In fact, arms were sent to Rwanda both officially and unofficially, with the latter either not registered or sent via a third party to avoid questions. Evidence showed '31 direct transfers of arms and munitions to Rwanda were carried out in disregard of correct procedure'.[32] There were also 19 'free' deliveries amounting to around $3.6 million, paid for by oblivious French taxpayers as a gift to their Rwandan allies.

France ignored a new 1992 EU directive aimed at 'ethical' deliveries of arms to regions currently in a state of war or internal unrest. The EU had just adopted eight criteria for selling weapons to its member states. The third criterion stated that EU members would take account, in selling weapons, of 'the internal situation of the country, according to the existence of conflicts or tensions inside its borders'.[33] Instead of abiding by these rules, the French pointed the finger at other countries that were also breaking the embargo. For example, South Africa had continued to sell arms to Rwanda in the early 1990s in contravention of an international ban (Convention 558 of December 1984) that embargoed the export of weapons from the apartheid regime.

Habyarimana's pleas for even greater destructive weaponry did not go unheeded by Paris. The Rwandan dictator begged for Jaguar attack planes to be used against the RPF, and was no doubt disconsolate when France, much to his surprise, deemed the demand 'over the top' and refused. Instead, it offered a meagre sop of nine Eurocopter Gazelle SA

342 attack helicopters worth $7.5 million, which were exported on 22 April, 1 July and 9 October 1992, each with the capability to use canons or rocket launchers.[34] Paris presumably regarded such helicopter firepower as non-excessive. The Gazelle helicopters were a utility craft able to strafe enemy positions, destroy tanks or be used for reconnaissance missions. In the mountainous terrain of northern Rwanda, they were vital for locating the movement of RPF infiltrators. At the start of October 1992, a Gazelle was responsible for destroying a column of ten RPF vehicles. It was alleged that a French instructor, who was suitably proud of his pupil's efforts, trained the Rwandan pilot. Whether the French instructor was in the helicopter at the time is suspected but as yet not proved.[35]

While Jaguar fighter planes may have been 'over the top', a whole arsenal of sophisticated weaponry was flown in to keep Habyarimana happy and Milan missiles, made by Euromissiles based in Fontenay-aux-Roses, were shipped in. Along with heavy 120mm mortars, they gave the Rwandan army an important advantage in the artillery war, for they could smash any armoured carriers and destroy RPF positions up to three miles away. Training was also given in the use of the Rasura radar system to detect RPF troop advances. Other French aid included day-to-day military equipment, tents, clothing, parachutes, spare parts for helicopters and artillery. CIEEMG records also show the sale of 20,000 anti-personnel mines and 600 detonators, though the defence ministry in Paris denied France had sold any such mines after 1986.[36]

For one of the poorest countries on earth, with most people earning less than a dollar a day, Rwanda was now involved in a hi-tech war with its forces using state-of-the-art attack weapons. 'Between 1992 and 1994, Rwanda was the region's [sub-Saharan Africa] third largest importer of weapons (behind Angola and Nigeria), with cumulative military imports totalling $100 million.'[37] While France provided some of the heavy military hardware to repel frontal attacks, its banks provided the legitimate means whereby Habyarimana could enter deals with other African countries to bring in light weapons.

Rwanda made secret contact with Egypt, liaising directly with Boutros Boutros-Ghali, then a foreign office official in Cairo before his elevation to UN secretary-general. The two governments concluded a deal in late October 1990 for nearly $6 million of weapons, including mortars and ammunition. The French government-controlled bank,

Credit Lyonnais acted as insurer for the money that was deposited, according to an unheaded document dated 30 March 1992, in the French bank's Regent Street branch in London.[38] Weapons shipped to the African country as a result of the deal included 70 mortars, 16,200 mortar shells, 2000 rocket propelled grenades, 450 Egyptian Kalashnikovs, 2000 landmines, 3000 artillery shells, six 122mm heavy artillery howitzers, plastic explosives and three million rounds of ammunition.

Noroît commander Colonel Philippe Tracqui noted that on 12 February 1993 a DC8 landed with 50 machine guns of 12.7mm capacity, together with 100,000 rounds of ammunition destined for the Rwandan army (FAR). Five days later another Boeing 747 arrived with 'discreet unloading by the FAR of 105 mm shells and 68 mm rockets'.

In total, France sold $24 million of arms to Rwanda during 1990–94, though this figure does not include non-authorized grants. It is clear that 'secret deliveries' outside the knowledge or authorization of the ministry of defence were taking place. Because of this secrecy there was 'a gap between the official commentary and the actual administrative reality'.[39] The imported weapons soon filtered down through black market traffickers and Rwandan military officials to towns and villages around the country. Much of the huge stocks received from France and Egypt were handed over to the civilian militia. In June 1993, a Western researcher noticed grenades being sold openly on a market stall in Kigali, alongside bananas and mangoes. He was stopped from photographing the scene by a policeman who told him such pictures were 'not nice'.[40] The grenades cost less than $2. Many would later be used to kill and maim the Tutsis gathered inside churches and community halls during the 1994 genocide.

According to Rwandan journalist André Sibomana, 'Kigali airport was allegedly used as a hub for French arms dealers who were secretly supplying Iran.'[41] The Habyarimana regime had become a key player in the drugs and arms trade, and the war from 1990 only increased the stakes. It now became less about selling for profit than buying for survival. When quizzed by a journalist on the French arming a regime known for its brutal violence against its own people, military attaché Colonel Bernard Cussac replied angrily, 'are you saying that the providing of military assistance is a human rights violation?' He added, when he learnt his questioner was from the USA, 'France and the United States have a common history, for example, Vietnam.'[42] It was

an unfortunate comparison, given the appalling human rights violations in that campaign, with napalm, Agent Orange and civilian
massacres hardly pointing to a common history to remember with pride.

From the start of the war, the Rwandan government had a number of
high-level backers in the French military. Leaving aside political
francophones like Jean-Christophe Mitterrand and Paul Dijoud,
director of African and Malagasy affairs at the foreign office, old-school
generals made it plain they felt the war in Rwanda was one that could,
and should, be won in the field. General Christian Quesnot, appointed
as personal chief military adviser to President Mitterrand from 1991 to
1995, 'shared and shaped Mitterrand's analysis of the Rwandan situation'.[43] In this he was joined by other leading military figures,
including Colonel Jean-Pierre Huchon, who was on the president's
military staff before becoming head of the military mission programme
in 1993. Quesnot had little time for the RPF and left little doubt about
where his sympathies lay in remarking, 'The RPF is the most fascist
party that I have met in Africa, and is akin to being Black Khmers.'[44]

Two parallel military missions were therefore taking place from
October 1990. While Operation Noroît was launched with hundreds of
well-armed marines and paratroopers, officially to protect French
citizens, the army training corps (DAMI or *Détachment d'assistance
militaire et d'instruction*) and the Military Assistance Mission (MAM)
were working behind the scenes in surveillance, training and tactical
support for Habyarimana. This resulted in the French effectively taking
over the command structure of the Rwandan government forces, with
the blessing of its grateful president.

Secretly, as with the arming of the Rwandan troops, Paris put in place
an officer who not only directed French forces, but also became head of
the Rwandan government army, with the role of direct military adviser
to Habyarimana and his chief of staff Colonel Laurent Serubuga.
'Lieutenant Colonel Chollet, head of the French Military Assistance
Mission, adviser to Habyarimana' would, in his new capacity be con-
sulted on 'organization of the defence and on the collaboration of the
military', duties that would require him to 'work in close collaboration'
with officers at all levels.

In effect, until the secret was exploded in the Belgium daily *La Libre
Belgique* on 21 February 1992, Chollet was head of the Rwandan armed
forces, 'advising the Rwandan chief of staff in such tasks as drawing up

daily battle plans, accompanying him around the country, and partici-
pating in daily meetings of the general staff.[45] A letter of 3 February
1992 from the Rwandan ministry of foreign affairs to French ambassador Martres noted 'he [Chollet] has just received unlimited power to
direct all military operations in this war ... our army is now run by a
Frenchman.' The letter described Chollet as an adviser since 1 January
1992. Once news was leaked to the media of his new position, the
French foreign office was forced to deny Chollet's role, and he was
smartly removed. After a suitable few weeks 'cooling down' period
Lieutenant Colonel Jean-Jacques Maurin was appointed to Chollet's
position as deputy to the defence attaché in Habyarimana's government
in April 1992. In effect, it was the same role as Chollet, but this time
without the 'official' notification.

More secret support was soon on its way. After the RPF attack on
Ruhengeri in January 1991, the constant calls from Habyarimana for
more French involvement did not fall on deaf ears. Georges Martres,
the French ambassador in Kigali, was sent a telegram from Paris on 15
March 1991 to tell 'old man Habyarimana' that a detachment of around
30 army trainers was to be sent to Rwanda for 'four months', though
given the way the civil war was heading it was clear this would be open
ended. These instructors upped the military stakes substantially. Their
aim was to train and run the war for the Rwandan government, using
surveillance to counteract RPF guerrilla incursions. Martres was told
that this new initiative should remain secret. Habyarimana expressed
himself well satisfied with this new turn of French support.[46] In fact
French military instructors had been in Rwanda since the late 1980s.
The 11th parachute division was made up of several regiments, which
in turn had smaller 'special forces' units attached. These *chuteurs
opérationnels* with the unfortunate acronym CRAP (*Commandos de
Recherche et d'Action dans la Profondeur*) had already set up a commando
school for the Rwandan Army with a view to basic military training.[47]

The trainers lived in camps outside the capital, where they worked
with their 'pupils', the new Rwandan army recruits. Many such bases
were located in the northern areas of Gisenyi and Ruhengeri, only a
few kilometres from the front line of the fighting. The French instructors were barracked at the commando training school at Bigogwe, and
in military camps at Gako and Gabiro. Training would consist of
tactical awareness, the use of heavy weapons such as 120mm mortars

and AML 60 and 90 armoured vehicles, mining and explosives. Night infiltration, encircling manoeuvres and building strategic roadblocks at the front were also included.

Janvier, a 22 year-old Hutu, was keen to put into practice the anti-Tutsi rhetoric he had learnt at an early age.

It started during our very first days at school; we were taught that it was impossible for a Hutu and a Tutsi to get on together. We'd realized that the enemy were the Tutsis, since they always act in bad faith. I grew up in this frame of mind.

When political parties were authorized and I was ready to play my part, the party leaders, the ministers and the prefects continued to drill this into us even more intensively.

In 1992, I was highly motivated, ready to volunteer not just once but twice and join a group of young Hutus selected from among the *Interahamwe* [youth militia]; we were to fight for our country, as we'd been taught to. Throughout the war we applied what we'd been taught.

I liked the French – they were people who'd given us a lot of help in Rwanda. First of all during the civil war [1990–93] between the Hutus and the Tutsis, between the ex-FAR and the RPF, the *Inyenzis*. The French gave us a lot of help. It was from them that we received the most help. Most of the military aides came from France. It was the French who trained our soldiers who, in turn, landed on the hills to train us. They brought us the equipment they'd received from the French, and they taught us how to use it in combat, when necessary.

The example I can give. ... Grenades, rifles of the FAL type it was the French who distributed all this equipment throughout the country.[48]

Diplomatic support went hand in hand with that of the military. The French ambassador to Rwanda, Georges Martres, was a personal friend of Habyarimana who visited his house and was free in his praise for the elderly diplomat. Martres, a tall bespectacled man in his sixties, was an old-style Africanist who had arrived in Kigali on 10 September 1989, having been head of the French mission of cooperation in other franco-phone client states – Mali, Niger, Senegal and Cameroon.

Martres's view was simple. There was unrest in Rwanda and a possibility of ethnic violence leading to disaster, so French troops were needed to help pacify the trouble. Interestingly, the troops Martres was keen to keep in Rwanda to defeat the RPF were, he later explained, not strong enough to stop massacres. When the killing of Tutsis began at the start of the war in 1990, Martres's reaction was to refuse to believe the evidence implicating his government friends.

Vénuste Kayimahe, who worked at the French Cultural Centre in Kigali, met Martres several times. He described him as 'more Hutu than the Hutus – more Habyarimana than the president himself. He certainly seemed less a representative of France and more of Habyarimana. In every meeting I heard him defend the president's views, explaining the Rwandan government's views as well as the government did itself. People wondered if he really worked for Habyarimana.'[49]

It was joked in Kigali diplomatic circles that Ambassador Martres 'was not the French Ambassador to Rwanda but rather the Rwandese [sic] ambassador to France.'[50] Martres was meant to be the eyes and ears of the Élysée, able to note, analyse and report back to Paris on the 'true' state of affairs. Instead, he was politically blind and deaf, refusing to countenance criticism of the regime whatever its faults. Given his personal friendship with Habyarimana and the closeness of the military leadership, it is unsurprising that unbiased coverage of the unfolding crisis in Rwanda failed to reach Paris.

When Martres was due to retire at the start of 1993 Habyarimana took the unusual step of intervening on his behalf, asking President Mitterrand to keep him in office. Mitterrand regretfully told the dictator that he could only keep Martres in Kigali for an extra few months, until April, due to retirement rules, at which point the French diplomat, as staunch a supporter of the regime as it could have hoped for, had to bid farewell to his friends at the presidential palace and return to a cosy retirement in Paris, congratulating himself on a job well done. As Martres flew out of Kigali, the killers who a year later would commit the genocide were already receiving arms and training from the French government he represented, and carrying out orders to murder hundreds of villagers.

Chapter 3

Civil War and Peace Talks

I t was a typically hot humid Rwandan day in April 1991, with temperatures hitting the mid thirties, that found Immaculée Cattier travelling in a minibus with a Canadian religious group, bumping its way along the potholed road outside the northern town of Ruhengeri. With the civil war going on all around her in this area of the country, Immaculée, like many Tutsis, was trying to escape the fighting and government reprisal killings of civilians. But the sweat on her brow inside the minibus was not just from the force of the sun; Immaculée was scared. Despite being in the van with her Canadian friends, she was well aware that if they were stopped, she could, with her identity card showing her ethnic group, be hauled off the vehicle and killed by Habyarimana's soldiers.

Suddenly, to her horror, she felt the vehicle slow to a halt as it reached a queue in front of an army checkpoint.

The tension was unbearable. From a distance I saw armoured vehicles ready to attack. Their drivers were white men. My Canadian friends whispered: 'the French'. ... We saw the soldiers who were in charge, and militiamen holding the gates while patting their machetes. My old [Canadian] guardian looked at me in the mirror with eyes that urged me to keep calm.

My prayers ceased inside me, I already believed myself to be dead. We went forward one or two metres as a car in front pulled away. I realized that among the soldiers there were also some French who were also asking to see identity cards where it was recorded 'Hutu, Tutsi, Twa'. The Tutsis were made to leave the

37

car and the French soldiers handed them to the angry militiamen who hit them with machetes and threw them into a gully (a water canal) very close to the main tar-macadamed Ruhengeri–Kigali road. After curfew, a truck came from the town to load the bodies and take them to another place I don't know.[1]

In spite of the orders of the Brothers to pretend to be calm, I glanced in the mirror of our Hiace minibus to see what happened in other cars and I saw a Tutsi who was made to leave a car not far from ours and after his identity card had been inspected, a French soldier and another Rwandan officer handed him to the militiamen who began, in front of the cars, to hit him with machetes and other weapons like clubs before throwing him into the gully. (It was done quickly so they could get ready for the next person).

When I saw this I looked about the gully where I saw a few bodies which lay without making any noise (they died without a sound). I closed my eyes, our motor ran without stopping for a long time and I understood that we had authorization to leave without injury. … No one in our car commented on what had happened, just the head Brother who asked for a small prayer in our hearts for the people who had been killed.[2]

Despite pronouncements that Noroît would not interfere in internal matters, witnesses like Immaculée and photographic evidence show French soldiers directly assisted Rwandan army units in civilian areas. A Human Rights Watch investigation in 1992/3 'observed French soldiers manning checkpoints [just north of the capital Kigali] on the roads to Ruhengeri and Byumba. They were armed with 5.56 mm FAMAS automatic rifles, as well as Wasp 58 assault rocket launchers and other infantry support weapons. Like Rwandan army troops, French troops demanded identification from passing civilians.'[3]

Such identity cards, which carried the holder's name, address and ethnic origin, were to become a vital component of the genocide. The cards were a legacy of colonial times. Belgium introduced them in 1933 and for the first time categorized the ethnic origin of the populace. Despite opposition, the cards were retained when Rwanda gained independence and by Habyarimana when he seized power in 1973.[4] Despite diplomatic pressure from several foreign donor countries to change the cards, Habyarimana's militia was already using them to identify Tutsi victims in massacres that took place in northwest Rwanda in 1993. French paratroopers from Operation Noroît working alongside their FAR and presidential guard colleagues at roadblocks also used the cards to 'spot' Tutsis. With all Tutsis seen as possible if not probable RPF members, the cards often spelt a death sentence to innocent civilians. It was as if they were walking down a street in 1930s Munich with a yellow star emblazoned on their coats.

Video footage taken during this early period of Operation Noroît shows smartly dressed French soldiers with automatic rifles by their sides and green berets atop their traditionally shaven heads surrounded by Rwandans at a roadblock. The Gallic soldiers have stopped a minibus and are taking their time to study identity cards. Other pictures show soldiers from Operation Noroît setting out from their barracks, each fully armed, including one carrying a missile launcher. One French soldier was quoted as saying: 'It is well known that the Tutsi are the enemy.'[5]

Not surprisingly, the French troops formed close bonds with their FAR counterparts with whom they trained, worked and socialized. A student studying history at Ruhengeri University from October 1991 to April 1994 related how French soldiers frequented local bars 'where we could sit with them. They would tell us they were here because of the cooperation between the two governments. We often saw them with FAR troops, and the RPF were always seen as "the enemy". But they were easy enough to chat and have a drink with.'[6]

According to this Rwandan witness, some of the French paratroopers expressed sympathy for the regime they were defending, the 'underclass' Hutus against the 'aristocratic émigré' Tutsi – the 'Ugandan enemy'. This was an entirely understandable reaction from troops with little knowledge of the complexities of Rwandan history or politics. Less explicable are the views of a French army general who, according to Prunier, declared to Bruno Delaye, head of the French presidential Africa Cell, that it would be 'an act of high treason' for Paris to order his troops out of Rwanda.[7] The intervention had already become, in the minds and imaginations of many top ranking French military a France plus Hutu government/people versus RPF/Uganda/Tutsi rationale. It made any withdrawal and objective decision-making at the Élysée and on the ground in Rwanda a far more difficult proposition.

A letter from the Rwandan foreign ministry to Ambassador Martres in Kigali dated 24 December 1991 confirmed that France was engaged in a 'secret war' by expressing 'deep regret' over an incident at the northern town of Gatuna. French observers in this area, on the Ugandan border, came under fire from their Rwandan army friends on 1 December after the Rwandan government forces mistook them for the RPF.[8] It is hard to answer why French military observers were in such a forward position when they were meant to be defending their nationals and protecting Kigali airport unless it was understood that the French role was to provide significant frontline help to Habyarimana's regime.

In fact, France was strengthening its military support for Habyarimana as well as its political resolve that, come what may, the dictator would come out on the winning side in the civil war. At the beginning of March 1992 Daniel Bernard, the director of the cabinet at the foreign office, wrote to his colleagues at the ministry of defence pointing out the weakness of the FAR. He concluded, 'In this context, France doesn't seem to have any other solution than to accentuate its support, in particular its military support, to the Rwandan government.' Two months later, on 21 May, Paul Dijoud, director of African affairs at the foreign office, commented in an internal memo that, 'for the balance of the region and in the perspective of the negotiations, it is imperative that Rwanda is not in a situation of military weakness.'[9]

The RPF's continued probing attacks culminated in another offensive by its forces on 6 June 1992 at Byumba, about two hours north of Kigali. To make matters worse for the government in the capital, ill-trained and despondent FAR troops in the area chose this moment to mutiny, leading to a spree of looting and killing, with the predictable result that 150 more French troops were rushed to the area on 10 June. Again, the all-encompassing explanation from Paris was that its response was 'to prevent any violence against the foreign community'. An uneasy ceasefire, brokered at Arusha in Tanzania on 12 July came 24 hours before an RPF radio broadcast alleged that French soldiers were in combat next to their FAR allies, and that they were helping the government, especially in giving heavy artillery support.

By 1992 Rwanda was staring down a barrel and not just because of the civil war. The economy, barely adequate for peacetime needs, could not afford the millions of dollars being spent on heavy armaments and an army grown to eight times its 1990 strength. Foreign debt had more than doubled from $452.2 in 1986 to nearly a billion dollars in 1993, while the value of the Rwandan franc plummeted to half its 1987 level.[10]

Habyarimana had been expecting a form of power-sharing government. After La Baule, he loyally told Mitterrand that the 'democracy for French help' campaign would have his support. The question was how much power would be shared and with whom. Habyarimana saw new political parties as mere decoration – 'the whole point of the exercise being to please the French'[11] – while his MRND party carried on its solitary role of running the country. To give the correct public relations feel to anxious Western aid backers, in July 1991 an extra 'D' was added to the MRND's name, making it the 'Revolutionary National Movement for Development (and Democracy)'. It may have meant nothing to his people, but that 'D' for democracy pleased his French backers and European aid donors.

In the same vein of spin and public relations in June 1991 the president had announced a new multiparty system to govern Rwanda. The opposition, faced with the possibility for the first time since independence of a share of power and influence, quickly dissolved into infighting. The formation of the Hutu extremist party, the CDR (*Coalition pour la Défense de la République*), in March 1992 only added to underlying strains as its sole policy was to exploit ethnic tension.

Early attempts to form a transitional government showed a gulf between expectation and reality. A new cabinet appointed on 30 December 1991 included no members from any party other than Habyarimana's MRND; the president did not quite grasp that 'multiparty' government meant that more than one group should be involved. The result was mass demonstrations in Kigali by the opposition parties followed by a government clampdown and the first wave of political beatings and attacks on the demonstrators by Habyarimana's thugs.

While these half-hearted efforts to establish a 'multiparty system' were underway in Rwanda, talks started in Paris to resolve the civil war. Paul Kagame, now effective head of the RPF, arrived in the French capital on 17 September 1991 to meet Jean-Christophe Mitterrand. Interpreters were in place because the anglophone Kagame spoke no French, a source of some irritation to his hosts. Two months later Habyarimana arrived for private discussions with the French president at a Franco-African summit held at Chaillot. The result was that a

French observation mission, composed of a diplomat and two soldiers, was sent to monitor RPF incursions into Rwanda from Uganda in violation of the current ceasefire. Predictably, the French chose not to send a mission to investigate their own gunrunning, which saw planes loaded with arms arriving in Kigali, also in breach of the truce.

Kagame flew back to Paris for a meeting with Paul Dijoud, director of African affairs at the foreign office, in mid-January 1992. It was clearly a stormy affair. The French politician told Kagame, 'If you do not stop the war, if you seize the country, you will not see your brothers and your family again, because they will all have been massacred.' Dijoud, an old-style Gaullist conservative, later denied in the press that he had any memory of this visit by Kagame, though in 2005 his memory 'returned' and he admitted the meeting took place even that he said such words, though he denied they were any kind of 'prophecy'.[12]

In 1991 and 1992 France had hosted a number of meetings in Paris with Kagame and Habyarimana aimed at resolving the conflict, while at the same time continuing to arm, train and supply the Rwandan army. This dual policy was symptomatic of a deep division in French strategy. Hardliners in the army, Élysée and Ministry of Cooperation made it clear they would stand by Habyarimana, and that talks with the RPF were a final resort, best avoided. Yet, some diplomats at the foreign office had a realistic 'soft' policy that accepted the need for a negotiated peace. However, by 1993 there had been three years of close wartime collaboration between the Rwandan and French armies and General Jean-Pierre Huchon firmly resisted any attempt to abandon their Rwandan allies now.

Huchon, who was now head of the military mission of cooperation in Paris, had been instrumental in pushing for greater French military involvement and undermining 'soft track' diplomacy. Accordingly, there was unsurprisingly little contact between Paris and its embassy in Kigali, which received 'little direction or instruction'.[13] Consequently, those favouring diplomacy were often isolated and unable to achieve their objectives. Only two French officials supported the Arusha peace process and were prepared to oppose Huchon's view, 'somebody in Tanzania and someone here in Paris at the Ministry of Cooperation'.[14]

However, according to analyst François-Xavier Verschave, Huchon's rigid pro-Habyarimana stance reflected Mitterrand's outlook. After all, when the president appointed the general he knew his views on Africa and fully backed his policies.[15] Mitterrand's personal pride was at stake, for other francophone nation heads were anxious to see if his help to the Rwandan government was unconditional. Habyarimana continued to flatter the French president and to reinforce the view that he was highly esteemed in Rwanda. The Hutu extremist journal *Kangura* carried a full-page photograph of Mitterrand in its December 1990 issue with the subtitle 'A true friend of Rwanda', along with the adage in Kinyarwanda, 'It is in hard times you know your real friends.'[16] In the same edition of this extremist paper were the appalling 'Hutu Ten Commandments' that urged racial purity by avoiding all contact with Tutsi and that effectively paved the way for their disappearance from Rwandan society. It was akin to having a full-page picture in a Nazi propaganda paper of the 1930s in which cartoons and stories vilified the Jews as vermin. Bizarrely, Mitterrand seems to have been flattered by the *Kangura* piece, which was just the reaction its editorial team of Hutu extremists wanted. The best way to the French president's heart, such as it was, seemed to be to appeal to his vanity. This was repeated later when Hutu extremists demonstrated in Kigali in October 1992 against the ongoing peace talks at Arusha during which the mob chanted, 'Thank you President Mitterrand, thank you French people.'[17] In fact, had the 'French people' known the truth about their president's policy in Rwanda and the ongoing massacres, they would have been horrified.

In this swamp of personal and military pride and the continuing fear of Anglo-Saxon intervention, it was US diplomacy that pushed the Élysée into action. When US deputy assistant secretary Irvin Hicks arranged for the RPF and Rwandan government to have talks in Harare in July 1992, alarm bells immediately rang in Paris over the audacity of the USA trying to hijack France's attempts to bring order to its own *pré-carré* (backyard). Nothing was more guaranteed to produce a swift reaction in Paris than the thought that the Americans may be about to tread on their own neocolonial toes.

In July 1992, after two years of inconclusive conflict, the two sides in the Rwandan civil war finally sat down in an effort to seek a diplomatic solution. The small dusty Tanzanian town of Arusha where the discussions took place became synonymous with Rwandan hopes and nightmares. Today it is the setting for the ICTR, the UN war crimes tribunal for Rwanda charged with finding justice after the genocide.

Back in the summer of 1992 it was the scene of hard diplomatic negotiations.

The talks were formally opened on 12 July 1992, with the Tanzanians acting as hosts and coordinators while the head of the Organization of African Unity (OAU), Secretary-General Salim Salim, played a prominent part in trying to mediate between the two sides. The difficulty was that the situation in Rwanda was becoming more politically pressured and dangerous, thus forcing the main actors into talks that were inappropriate. By summer 1992 President Habyarimana was under immense strain. With a new RPF strike expected at any moment, he knew he had to keep French troops in Rwanda, for without them he would face military defeat in weeks, if not days. He was also under sustained attack from the *Akazu*, the group of Hutu militants his wife Agathe led that would have no truck with Arusha. To make matters worse, Hutu moderates, now part of the multi-party government, were increasingly talking about gaining a greater share of power.

Habyarimana bowed to international pressure and, on 18 August 1992, Rwanda signed a first Arusha protocol on the rule of law, though the following day the president declared he refused to 'lead our country into an adventure it would not like'.[18] The next stage of the talks saw an agreement reached on creating a broad-based transitional government, though for part of the negotiations the Rwandan government was represented by its foreign minister Boniface Ngulinzira who, it turned out, was acting without Habyarimana's support. A second protocol was signed on 31 October agreeing to an eventual parliamentary system and downsizing the president's power to that of a ceremonial head. While the French were not officially represented at the protocol talks, Jean-Christophe Mitterrand's close friend Jeanny Lorgeoux took part in the negotiations as part of the delegation from the Habyarimana government.

The strategy at Arusha was highly complex, dealing as it had to with ending a civil war and reintegrating Tutsi refugees, soldiers and perceived political 'enemies of the regime' into Rwandan society. In particular, the two armies now intent on killing each other would have to be made into one 'national' army, and RPF leaders like Kagame accepted into a new transitional government, which would also give far more power to Hutu critics of Habyarimana and his MRND(D) party.

That Habyarimana was only taking part in the Arusha talks under duress presented a major difficulty. Without RPF forces effectively holding a trigger to his head he would not have been forced into the political corner he perceived Arusha to be. And, once cornered, he and the Hutu militants were at their most dangerous, for desperate times inevitably call for desperate measures. By mid-1992 extremist Hutu radio and newspapers were blurring in the public mind the precise identities of the regime's 'enemies'. The RPF and 'Tutsis' became interchangeable terms for those who threatened the state. The Hutu population was deliberately fed the lie that if the RPF won, the country would return to a pre-1960 period of Tutsi domination. The extremist CDR party led by Jean-Bosco Barayagwiza called for Arusha to be abandoned on the grounds that 'an enemy is an enemy. Anyone who cooperates with the enemy is a traitor to Rwanda.'[19] The French, having close ties with these militants and their leader, were in favour of the CDR being part of the democratic process, though in the event it was excluded after pressure from the RPF.

Two weeks after the first Arusha protocol, CDR leader Jean-Bosco Barayagwiza received a letter of thanks from the Élysée signed by Bruno Delaye, Jean-Christophe's replacement as head of the Africa Cell. The letter, dated 1 September 1992, came because Barayagwiza's extremists had produced a petition in favour of French intervention.[20] Delaye later said the letter and its compliments 'surprised' him, as if the CDR and its leader's poisonous agenda were not fully understood. If this was so, French observers in Rwanda must have been the only people to misunderstand the simple message that the extremists preached daily.

While politicians in Paris privately backed the regime, the French military made clear its abhorrence of any 'sell out' of its Rwandan army ally. A French general confided to Gérard Prunier on 10 October that to abandon Habyarimana would be an act of 'high treason'. Three days later General Quesnot arrived in Rwanda with a French delegation, visiting the northern front and meeting Habyarimana, the head of the Rwandan army and the Rwandan minister of defence.

At the end of 1992 and in 1993 Mitterrand and his government were focusing on events in a wider arena, on the Balkans, on the unfolding conflict in Somalia, on the effects of the Iran–Iraq war and on internal politics, which had seen the French president's popularity wane as political controversy and record low poll ratings led one of his prime ministers, Edith Cresson, to resign in April 1992 after a mere nine ineffectual months in office; her replacement, Pierre Bérégovoy, shot himself less than a year later. Such political flux in France allowed hardliners in the military and Élysée to push their own agendas. Martres, Huchon, Marcel Debarge, the minister of cooperation and Bruno Delaye, the shamed Jean-Christophe Mitterrand's replacement at the Africa Cell, all pressed for peace to be on Habyarimana's terms.

On 17 February 1993 *Le Monde* reported Debarge as saying, 'France has supported the Arusha negotiations which have led to an agreement between the government and the opposition to create a transition cabinet. ... In any case, the World Bank and the other donors keep their representatives in Kigali only because of our military presence which – need I remind you – is there only to protect our citizens.' Debarge did not say that behind the scenes the French military was keeping the RPF at bay and that his own president and military top brass were working towards keeping Habyarimana in power, whatever Arusha might bring. In an ideal world the Rwandan dictator would have no need for peace talks and political compromise at Arusha, and the French must have hoped, as Jean-Christophe Mitterrand originally predicted, that with Gallic military help, the RPF would have been crushed before now. The reality was that the French military presence had alone kept Habyarimana from defeat and exile, and that Arusha was now the best hope of keeping him and his Hutu hardliners in power – even if it meant some compromises.

On 9 January 1993 the two sides at Arusha agreed on the composition of a new national transitional assembly to run the country until new elections were held. In Kigali the news was greeted by CDR- and government-controlled Hutu extremist rioters taking to the streets to demonstrate against the 'sell-out' at Arusha. The violence lasted six days, with around 300 fatalities after murderous thugs had rampaged through the streets, torturing and killing as they went. The talks at Arusha collapsed and further negotiations were suspended.[21]

The ceasefire that had accompanied the Arusha talks was broken on 8 February 1993 as the RPF launched a well-coordinated and well-organized attack on the northern town of Ruhengeri. The effect was the usual débâcle for the government forces and the town fell within hours. As predictable as the defeat of Habyarimana's troops was the immediate arrival of French support as Paris swung into action two new military operations, Volcano and Chimera – the first to rescue trapped nationals, the second to shore up the FAR until politicians could reach a truce.

Operation Volcano began on 10 February with a remit to evacuate 67 foreigners now trapped inside the RPF-controlled town; 21 of these were French. A negotiated settlement was reached and the foreign workers were allowed to leave in three convoys. While this was happening, the French were stepping up their military strength because it had become obvious to their commanders that, without it, the FAR would be overwhelmed and the capital, Kigali, overrun. Colonel Bernard Cussac was informed that reinforcements were being rushed to the threatened area. On 20 February a second company of paratroopers arrived from Bangui, followed the next day by a heavy artillery section from Libreville.

On 28 February the French, under General Dominique Delort, set Operation Chimera in motion. It encompassed a detachment of special operatives (DAMI) as well as 20 paratroopers from the first RPIMA. Helicopters continued to be used for identifying RPF movements, while DAMI set up and managed artillery units, doing everything except firing the guns.

Such artillery was the difference between the two sides. With heavy mortar sited and aimed effectively by the French, the RPF attack was halted on 23 February. Human Rights Watch reported, 'according to one French "instructor", French trainers positioned the heavy artillery to bombard the RPF and then stood back to let Rwandan soldiers push the button to fire the weapon.'[22] Former Rwandan defence minister James Gasana admitted that the FAR were only allowed to employ artillery given by France after they had received permission from their foreign allies to use them.[23]

The fact that Paris had flown another 300 troops into Kigali meant that any RPF assault on the capital would inevitably be against the French and, as such, the advance stopped about 20 kilometres short of the seat of government. French intelligence operatives in Rwanda, the DGSE, and Tanzanian intelligence experts shared this view of the motive behind the RPF's sudden halt.[24] According to RPF Colonel Frank Rusegama, who helped lead the offensive, 'What was important was not occupying land; it was to establish a buffer zone, and to put pressure on Habyarimana.'[25] The RPF certainly managed this, as hastily arranged peace talks were convened at Bujumbura in neighbouring Burundi.

A legionnaire told the BBC in an interview just how involved Noroît had been in the battle in early 1993 and how near Habyarimana's government was to military defeat. 'The artillery is on the front. There would be an officer, in this case a French military officer, who would observe all lines of fire, who would regulate by radio to his under-officer, who would give the orders to the general soldiers on the ground their direction of fire.' The interviewer asked him: 'So when you say the French army officer was regulating by radio what was his actual role?'

'He was commanding the fire.'

'If the French hadn't been there what would have actually happened do you think?'

> The Rwandan army would have been totally incapable of defending the country, and since they scarcely knew how to use their weapons and they knew very little about military tactics, the war would have been lost. There would have been a very small battle and in a day it would have been all over if the French hadn't been there.[26]

His military and political superiors shared this legionnaire's assessment. Colonel Dominique Delort declared on 16 March that 'any reduction of our help would entail the quick defeat of the government army if the [RPF] offensive is renewed.'[27]

French information officer, William Bunel, told concerned Human Rights Watch investigators that 'French advisers are prohibited from entering combat areas, and may only advise Rwandan troops in fixed training centres.' The human rights group drew its own conclusions. 'Western observers, diplomats and Rwandan military officers said that French advisers had been observed in tactical combat situations with Rwandan troops during the 1993 offensive.' The new French ambassador in Kigali, Jean-Michel Marlaud, replied to this allegation in language that hardly suggested the opposite was true. 'When you are supposed to advise, you must advise however it is necessary.' He was also quoted as saying: 'I don't expect the Rwandan army to suppress the RPF by itself.'[28]

Military hardware accompanied this tactical advisory support. The French provided anti-tank guns and a complete battery of 105 mm mortars. A letter from Colonel Deogratias Nsabimana, commander in chief of the FAR, to the Rwandan minister of defence showed his delight with his Western allies but warned, 'the French work has been good, but they must be more discreet.'[29]

The number of French troops involved rose significantly with the RPF offensives in 1992 and early 1993, and by March 1993 had reached an official peak of 688. Other estimates put the number at nearer 850.[30] A French army colonel even boasted that, by cleverly rotating units and dates, it was possible to almost double, to 1000 men, the official figure of 600 soldiers.[31] On top of this was an unknown number of 'unofficial' secret service operatives from the DGSE involved in a shadowy game of protecting and shoring-up Habyarimana. After their 1991 action at Ruhengeri, 15 French soldiers were recommended for medals,[32] while another document thanked the French for assistance that was 'precious in combat'.[33]

Pierre, a 37 year-old lance corporal in the FAR, had first-hand experience of the French.

> In 1991–92, I was at Ruhengeri, in the Muhoza camps. The French (DAMI) were giving us military training in hand-to-hand combat. When they were training us, they told us that they were teaching us to defend ourselves in case we had to fight the enemy. We learnt from DAMI over a six-month period in 1992. Afterwards, I was sent to Ruhengeri at Butaro on the Muhabura volcano since there were attacks from the *Inkotanyi*s [RPF].
>
> There were French there, they had 'support rifles' that they fixed and then let us handle. It sometimes happened they took part themselves, like when we fought between Muhabura and Gahinga. They were firing on the *Inkotanyi*s, but the latter put up a good fight.
>
> It was only when the battle became difficult that the French came to support us with military training. They'd taught us and they could leave us on the field and watch us get on with it.[34]

Allegations were also rife that some French soldiers were helping to question RPF prisoners, a charge Paris dismissed. In November 1991 the International Federation for Human Rights declared that French officers had led 'strong-armed' interrogations of RPF prisoners.

Éric Gillet, former president of Amnesty International in Belgium, returned from Rwanda in August 1991. He reported that RPF 'major' Jean-Bosco Nyirigira had testified that French officers in Kigali prison had interrogated him for many days. Witness statements by 17 other RPF prisoners reported French soldiers questioned them.[35] Six years later Colonel Cussac said he was the only French soldier to have met military prisoners.

Vénuste Kayimahe, a middle-aged Tutsi living in Kigali, also had experience of the French 'interrogators'. His friend, Jean, who worked at the French Cultural Centre branch near Ruhengeri in 1990, had been arrested after an RPF attack and accused like many Tutsi of helping the enemy.

> A colonel in the Rwandan army tortured him, with a French captain also present. It took place at the gendarmerie school in Ruhengeri, where the French had established a place to train new police. Jean was tied up, and during questioning he was beaten with a large stick when his replies did not please his captors. He later fled to Belgium. I saw his professional file in Kigali; it was full of letters between the [French] Cultural Centre and the prosecutor's office. These French employers, instead of trying to protect this man who worked for them, instead seemed to take the side of those who considered him to be an 'enemy' because he was a Tutsi.[36]

Chapter 4

Militia, Massacres and Arusha

A gathe Habyarimana was no ordinary president's wife and mother. Those who had the dubious pleasure of meeting the terrifyingly ambitious wife of the Rwandan dictator were left under little pretence that she was intent on keeping her family in power – whatever the consequences. While her husband dealt with the imminent dual threat of a renewed RPF attack and a peace process that threatened to undermine his authority, Agathe began to plan her own solution to staying in control. From the late 1980s Agathe began to form around her a group of Hutu radicals and extremists. *Le clan de madame*, or *Akazu* (small house), was bent on one objective alone – a violent retention of power and influence. Here was a highly potent core of people, most of them her relatives, whose aim was to exploit the Habyarimana presidency for personal wealth and power. Even today, 12 years after the genocide, the dread this woman engenders makes it difficult to have any real conversation about her. A very real fear of Agathe and her *Akazu* network makes Rwandans from all walks of life, from villagers to army generals shy away from making any comment. Email and telephone conversations about her are courteously declined. It is the one subject that produces a degree of discomfort that is remarkable given that most individuals have lived through the genocide. It is a testimony to an incredible influence that lives on, even though she is now thousands of miles away in a comfortable European retirement. The fact that those who have intimated they were prepared to testify against her have ended up dead (see Chapter 9) is a powerful deterrent to any who underestimate her continued hold over a powerful network of militant Hutu extremists.

Born Agathe Kanzinga in the northern region of Bushiru, her marriage to ambitious military recruit Juvénal Habyarimana promised her and her family a return to power and greatness. Unlike her husband, she could trace her ancestry back to the royal line, when her Hutu forebears ran their own small independent principality.[1] Many Rwandans saw Agathe's unusual snake-skin outfits and horn-rimmed dark glasses as signs that she was a witch or sorceress.[2] To Rwandans, she became known as 'Kanjogera', an unflattering reference to the fabled murderous mother of former Rwandan King Musinga. Around Agathe milled a dozen or so *Akazu* members, including military figures Théoneste Bagosora, Elie Satagwa, Laurent Serubuga, and her three brothers Protais Zigiranyirazo, Colonel Pierre-Celestin Rwagafilita and Séraphin Rwabukumba. The group also included powerful administrators of the country such as the prefect and deputy prefect of Kigali, Tharcisse Renzaho and François Karera respectively, and the head of the communal gendarmerie in Kigali, Pascal Simbikangwa.

By the late 1980s, as the Rwandan economy dipped and internal opposition to Habyarimana mounted, the *Akazu* was already plotting to maintain and increase its slice of the profits of power. Those who stood in its way, like former presidential aide Colonel Stanislas Mayuya, were murdered. Others who threatened the clique were also eliminated, such as Colonel Alois Nsekalije and former commander of the Rwandan army, Colonel Innocent Rwaganyasor, who was poisoned after threatening to expose the *Akazu*.[3]

The *Akazu* had close working ties with the French, not to mention personal friendships. Chollet and Maurin met Colonel Serubuga almost daily through their military liaisons; Renzaho operated alongside French gendarmerie trainers and Théoneste Bagosora, a leading planner of the genocide, had been to a French military college and later commanded the military training camp at Kanombe, where French troops were also billeted. Agathe was a constant visitor to the Mitterrand household when she was in Paris where she was guaranteed a warm welcome and a few handsome trinkets.

The *Akazu* also lay behind the establishment of a death squad made up of soldiers, presidential guards and militia members. In 1992, Rwandan academic and former head of the Rwandan press and media office ORINFOR Christopher Mfizi went public, naming this group as Réseau Zero – Network Zero. He accused it of being behind the killings and disappearances taking place in the country during the previous two years. 'Réseau Zero was a hard core of men around President Habyarimana and of whom he was the centre. They expanded into the army, the civil service, the economy and even the churches with the intention of taking over the apparatus of the state and even putting it at their own service.'[4] When Mfizi, later Rwandan ambassador to Paris after the genocide, was asked if the French ambassador in Kigali, Georges Martres, had known of Network Zero he replied, 'Certainly ... I discussed this with the French ambassador at the time and he congratulated me on my analysis.'[5]

French intelligence had already worked out the dynamics of the political situation in Rwanda. In a report of July 1991 they pointed to three circles of power in the country, with the grouping around Habyarimana seen as the most militant. It makes it all the more remarkable then that 'Monsieur Afrique', Jean-Christophe Mitterrand, the man charged by his father to run the Africa Cell at the Élysée, denied that Network Zero existed.

> I know that's a phrase this person [Mfizi] came up with but I don't really believe there was such an organization. I mean give me some surnames and I'll agree with you there was corruption and maybe some gangsters. I mean there are affairs like this going on everywhere. There are gangsters everywhere. But in general you only know they are gangsters when they are arrested, not before. Someone says, you know, so and so's a gangster but you only find out for sure a couple of years later. You just don't know at the time. It's not marked on their foreheads, you know what I mean? At the time I knew Rwanda of course there were guys who said 'yes, there is corruption'. But try proving it! Well I'd have loved to. But I just didn't know anything.[6]

This was surprising given his close personal relationship with the Habyarimana family, visits to the country after 1990 and the quite considerable secret service, military and diplomatic information he was fed.

It suited Mitterrand's strategy to put the ever-increasing massacres of civilians and political opponents down to disorganized anonymous 'gangsters'. The truth was that the murders were a deliberate, ordered and centrally led terror by the very people in Rwanda with whom

French politicians, the military and the secret services were working on a daily basis. Even more frightening, new evidence points to the direct complicity of French troops in training the killers.

In a series of targeted and well-prepared massacres in the four years preceding the 1994 genocide, Hutu militants began to seek a 'final solution' to their 'Tutsi problem'. Thousands of Tutsi villagers were killed in attacks orchestrated by the *Akazu*, and carried out by Habyarimana's presidential guard, the regular army and, increasingly, the new illegal militia, the *Interahamwe* and the *Impuzamugambi*.

The militia were armed youth supporters of the MRND(D) and CDR parties, created by the government to use violence against its perceived enemies – the Tutsi and liberal Hutu opponents. The *Interahamwe*, literally 'those who stay together', was formed in 1992 and the *Impuzamugambi*, 'those who share the same aim', a short time later; both acted with the ruling elite's support but outside the law. Using unemployed, poor and easily politicized Hutu youth, these militia groups brought a new dimension of terror to Rwanda.

With direct instructions from their presidential backer, they could not effectively be stopped. Those who tried were the victims of assassination or torture. 'Like the army, [the militia] were divided into sections, each with a particular assignment to accomplish ... usually coordinated by the army.'[7] These killers were not just thugs roaming the streets and villages. They became a trained and disciplined outfit that killed to order, disrupted opposition political groups where and as required, and spread ethnic hate and fear in a coordinated manner, aided by government media support. Sibomana referred to the militia as the 'spearhead for the genocide'.[8]

The young militiamen were far from just clumsy wielders of machetes or axes. Most had special military training at the various army camps that had sprung up since 1990 where they learnt the tactics of war, and how to use small arms and grenades. Camps in the Nyungwe and Gashwati forests, and three in Kibungo prefecture and Bugarama in the south, became training grounds for the genocide. By March 1992 the militia were able to put their new skills in butchery into action at Bugesera.

Set up initially to discipline the Rwandan army (FAR) into a force that could repel the RPF, these training camps were not just for Rwandans. French specialist military trainers, the products of commando instructor courses at the Mont St Louis French army centre in the Pyrenees, were there too and their mission now was to train the FAR and presidential guard, both of whom took part in the genocide.

According to 35-year-old key witness ex-militiaman Aloys, who spoke of French involvement in his training, he

> was trained at the Bigogwe commando training centre at Gisenyi [in the north]. ... I'd received military training from French instructors at the Bigogwe camp. These were military exercises of exactly the same kind as the exercises performed by professional soldiers. Their intention was to do damage. In short, we were training them [the militia recruits] to run for long periods and to increase their powers of endurance, to climb up a rope, to kill with a knife; and they also practised shooting. They were taught how to use grenades.
>
> I can't remember the names of our instructors, but they were Frenchmen, they were the ones who first introduced the guns called 'machine guns', this was the first time they brought the guns to us at Bigogwe. As for me, I'd been entrusted with training the *Interahamwe*; I trained them for a long time. After that came the dreadful disaster affecting Rwanda. But before that, there'd been the war between the Tutsi cockroaches and us. Where I was, at Bigogwe, the French had trained us, saying it was so that we could go and fight the enemy, and the only enemy was the Tutsis. Eventually we killed the Bigogwe [villagers] who lived in the region. They were Tutsis, they were killed after the arrival of the French – who stood by and did absolutely nothing even though they were the ones who had taught us to inflict so much damage. ... We'd go there with the French, and then, one of the accompanying sergeants would tell us, 'go ahead, just slaughter those people, those Tutsis, they're the ones who are sending their children into the [RPF] army.' To begin with, we were scared because of the French presence, but this sergeant could go and discuss things with our French instructors, and to our astonishment they told us, 'of course, kill them – otherwise, don't be surprised when they come to attack you. I'm in training, true, but I wouldn't go into battle in your place! I'll give you all the equipment necessary, but if you let them carry on producing children they can send to the front, you'll never be done with them.'

Yes, the French knew that the Bigogwe were civilians but they were Tutsis, and the Tutsis had a great sense of solidarity and sent their children to the front. ... When the Bigogwe got massacred, they saw it all with their own eyes. What did they do? Well, they didn't do anything except support us in what we were doing there.[9]

In 1992, human rights investigator Jean Carbonare travelled to Rwanda to seek the truth behind rumours of widespread ethnic killing. He was part of an international mission of inquiry that consisted of four NGOs – including Human Rights Watch and FIDH (the International Federation of Human Rights). His key informer, Janvier Afrika, an ex-member of Network Zero who had turned against his former henchmen, testified to Network Zero's aim to eliminate not just political opponents but Tutsis in the villages. The investigators found bodies hidden in one mayor's garden, despite his denials that they were there.

Carbonare told the French newspaper *Le Nouvel Observateur*, 'I have seen what French military instructors did in the camp of Bigogwe between Gisenyi and Ruhengeri in northwestern Rwanda. In the presence of French soldiers, the Hutus were taking their Tutsi prisoners away in trucks to torture them and to kill them.' Carbonare said the bodies were then taken to a mass grave in Gisenyi, which human rights activists later uncovered.

Janvier Afrika, who went into hiding to avoid being killed by the very death squads of which he had once been a part, confessed he had been at a meeting of militia leaders in a Kigali building known as 'La Synagogue' on 1 September 1992, which Habyarimana and his wife Agathe had also attended. There the orders were given for opponents to be wiped out. He alleged the president told the meeting it was important to 'find all the politicians who were not with us. They were all considered to be RPF, because they opposed the killing of Tutsis, which Habyarimana wanted to have them do. And Madame Habyarimana, she addressed the meeting to advise how to neutralize opposition among women.' Afrika was later gaoled for opposing the killing, but escaped death when the RPF overran his prison. His revelations implicated the French military in the massacres now ripping through the country.

We had two French military who helped train the *Interahamwe*. A lot of other *Interahamwe* were sent for training in Egypt. The

French military taught us how to catch people and tie them. It was at the Affichier Central base in the centre of Kigali. It's where people were tortured. That's where the French military office was.

At the camp I saw the French show *Interahamwe* how to throw knives and how to assemble and disassemble guns. It was the French who showed us how to do that – a French major – during a total of four months training for weeks at a time between February 1991 and January 1992. The French also went with us *Interahamwe* to Mount Kigali, where they gave us training with guns. We didn't know how to use the arms which had been brought from France.

Afrika went on to testify to the effectiveness of the militia killers now they were armed and trained. 'In early 1992 we did our first killing. Around 70 of us went to Ruhengeri to kill Tutsis from the Bagogwe clan. We killed about 10,000 over one month, from our base at the Mukamira military camp at Ruhengeri. Two weeks later we went to Bugesera, where we killed about 5000 people.'[10]

The informer also produced photos of victims and said how he had been sent to see a local mayor to check that a massacre had been successfully carried out. His militia had 'massacred the Tutsi men one by one. They were ready to kill the widows and orphans too if I'd wanted.'

Carbonare told the BBC that he thought Afrika's testimony was 'perfectly credible. I don't say that everything he said was true, but there were a lot of interesting things he said that tied in with what we'd found out on the ground. And of course he didn't know where we'd been because he'd been in prison. So we knew some of what he was saying was true.'[11] There is also evidence of French instructors living with their 'pupils' in the training camp at Mukamira and commando centre at Bigogwe,[12] and of French instructors helping to train the presidential guard, the ultra-loyalist soldiers hand-picked by Habyarimana from his northern territory and responsible for many of the worst atrocities in the genocide in the preceding years.

Journalist Christian Jennings, on interviewing former MRND officials in Goma in 1994, reported them saying off-camera that 'the French made and kept the *Interahamwe*'. He commented, 'this is not strictly accurate. The French Special Forces instructors instructed Rwandan army soldiers … these men went on to massacre Tutsis or trained men who did. The French trained men who carried out a genocide, not to carry out a genocide.'[13]

It is difficult to know how much differentiation there was at the camps between the FAR, presidential guard and militia. It would have been easy for French instructors just to train all those in front of them, whatever their background. After all, they were all fighting the 'enemy' RPF and were loyal to the government. No instruction came from Kigali or Paris to ensure that the militia, which by 1993 had been named in a number of reports as complicit in killings, did not receive arms or training. Africa Watch reported that following the February 1993 offensive by the RPF 'Rwandan soldiers killed at least 147 civilians and beat, raped or arrested hundreds more in the four months following the offensive.' The use of rape and sexual crimes to 'dehumanize' the Tutsi population was to mirror its widespread use in the following year during the genocide. While it is easy to blame individual French military figures for failing to reassert the human aspect of any conflict, given the noises coming from politicians in Paris about the RPF being 'Khmer noir' and 'Maoist' Ugandan-backed anglophones, it is hardly surprising that DAMI military training specialists were content only to train those in front of them to kill – and leave their protégés to make the differentiation between civilian Tutsi and RPF soldier.

The first slaughter of innocent civilians had taken place only days after the initial RPF attack, between 11 and 13 October 1990. Ordinary villagers in the Kibilira commune near Gisenyi were targeted; more than 500 homes were set on fire and many families were forced to flee.[14] Following the massacre 10,000 mainly Tutsi 'suspects' were rounded-up, imprisoned, tortured and some even killed. André Sibomana, a priest who edited the church newspaper *Kinyamateka*, entered Kigali prison with an official human rights delegation that Habyarimana had organized to prove how well the prisoners were being treated. What he found when he managed to sneak away from the main delegation was horrifying. 'Under a blanket, I discovered a pile of bodies; some of them were motionless, others had been mutilated. Innocent people had been beaten, their backs slashed with bayonets. Some had deep cuts in their arms from being tied up.'[15] Sibomana published pictures of the scene in his newspaper, much to the government's disgust. Pressure on Habyarimana caused by this scandal helped to gain the release of many of those imprisoned, though the genocide of 1994 later 'finished' the job of murdering them. The death squads revisited Kibilira in March and November/December 1992, but it was not the only area to suffer.

Once the RPF invasion had begun, Hutu extremists also targeted the Bagogwe Tutsi who lived in the northwest. The initial massacres of October 1990 gave way to more systematic killing after the RPF attack on nearby Ruhengeri in January 1991, where 1000 civilians were murdered.[16] Between fighting the RPF and being trained by the French, Rwandan army soldiers helped round up the civilian victims. The region was targeted again in late 1992 and early 1993 with radio broadcasts announcing that the 'bush' (Tutsi) 'must be cleared', with dire consequences if it were not.

The Bugesera region in the south near the Burundian border was subjected to massacres in March 1992, though as elsewhere no one was convicted of organizing or taking part in them. With the initiators being government soldiers, local mayors and officials, MRND(D) members and, from 1992, the militia, this was not surprising. A Human Rights Watch investigation into the killings blamed 'authorities at the highest level, including the President of the Republic'.

> The Rwandan army slaughtered hundreds of civilians in the course of its military operations against the RPF. The army also killed civilians in support of the attacks by Hutu civilian crowds against Tutsi. In a number of cases the army assassinated or summarily executed civilians singled out for murder by local authorities. The army also killed RPF soldiers after they had surrendered and laid down arms.[17]

Nor did UN special rapporteur Bacre Waly Ndiaye mince his words after his mission to Rwanda of 8–17 April 1993. The French-trained FAR was, he said, playing an

> active and well-planned role at the highest level ... of killing of Tutsis by the population, notably with respect to massacres targeting the Bagogwe. For instance, soldiers of Bigogwe camp (Mutara Commune) are said to have organized fake attacks by rebels during the night of 4th February 1991, so that they could unleash indiscriminate and bloody reprisals against those alleged

to be responsible. The FAR are accused of incitement to murder and of giving logistic support to the killers.

The FAR's involvement in the killings has been confirmed by numerous reliable witnesses, and even by the findings of a commission set up by the [Rwandan] Government on 15 September 1992 to investigate allegations of massacres in the prefecture of Kibungo. It should be noted that these findings have not resulted in the imposition of any penalties on the accused military personnel.[18]

The report singled out officials (prefects, sub-prefects, mayors, councillors, sector and cell leaders) as 'encouraging, planning and directing' the massacres, as well as spreading rumours to 'exacerbate ethnic hatred'. It accused the militia of massacres and political assassinations and 'imposing a reign of terror with complete impunity', and being backed by the FAR, some in plain clothes, as well as the local authorities. Such militias, it found, had been 'trained by members of the Presidential Guard and members of the armed services'.

The report condemned the activities of the 'death squads', 'Network Zero' and the military 'Amasasu' – a militant group in the army that armed and worked alongside the militia – and called for them to be disbanded and all weaponry already distributed to civilians confiscated. Moreover, it reminded the Habyarimana regime that under its own 1991 law it was expressly forbidden to establish militias.

Ndiaye's investigation, issued a year before the 1994 apocalypse, described the massacres taking place up to 1993 as genocide because Tutsis were being targeted for no reason other than their ethnic identity. It reminded Habyarimana that he had acceded to the Genocide Convention in 1975. This UN report echoed one sent previously on 25 September 1992 to the Rwandan president, as well as reports by the international commission of inquiry of 7–21 January 1993. The evidence was damning about the 'genocidal' killings taking place.

Yet, the response of the French government, which had copies of all the reports and inside information from its own military and secret services, was to ignore them. It continued to sell arms to the FAR, despite evidence they were going to the militia. Extra DAMI personnel arrived to continue training the FAR and presidential guard, both explicitly cited for committing massacres. There is now evidence that the French were also actively training Hutu militiamen. While some areas of the French government, like the foreign office officials actively trying to reach a diplomatic settlement, may have been kept in the dark about the role of its special forces personnel and army units in Rwanda, it is clear that, from an early stage, Mitterrand and the hardliners in his government and military had chosen to ignore any moral or ethical questions arising from supporting Habyarimana and his extremists. Retaining the dictator was more important than villagers in Bugesera, and an RPF victory would have been intolerable.

Thierry Prungnaud, a sergeant with the elite GIGN (Gendarmerie Intervention Group) was one of a number of troops sent in to train the FAR and presidential guard during the Noroît campaign. He later went public with what he had witnessed, in direct contradiction of the denials of the Paris government. According to Prungnaud:

I saw French soldiers giving fire-arms training to civilian Rwandan militiamen in 1992. There were about 30 militiamen being trained. I am absolutely categoric about this. I saw them and that is all there is to it. They must have been militiamen because the soldiers used to go around in fatigues and these were civilians. It must have gone on till 1994. It didn't shock me – after all I didn't see how it all turned out. It just seemed normal.

Prungnaud alleged the troops were from the 1st RPIMa, a regiment noted for its hard line attitude, and one that would later be involved in controversy for its 'pro FAR' role in operation Turquoise in 1994.[19]

In March 1992, after learning of the Bugesera massacres, a group of Western diplomats confronted Habyarimana with their concerns. French ambassador Georges Martres refused to join them and dismissed the international commission of inquiry's findings on the killings in the northwest as 'just rumours', despite an avalanche of proof from witnesses, not to mention the uncovering of mass graves. It was a remarkably blasé approach even from an individual accustomed to tagging along in Habyarimana's slipstream.

The French ambassador's lack of objectivity was a crucial weak link in the communication chain back to his government in Paris. 'According to officials in the Ministry of Foreign Affairs and the Ministry of Cooperation, Ambassador Martres never reported on the rise of the extremists, Hutu power, and the continuous violence during his tour in

Rwanda from 1990 until 1993.[20] As a result, the foreign office was unprepared for and ill informed about what the Rwandan government it supported was doing. Members of Mitterrand's government and military mission shut out reality in favour of the usual 'RPF = Anglophone menace' mantra, with a member of the French foreign ministry asserting that Habyarimana's regime was 'rather respectful of human rights and on the whole concerned with good administration'. This same official declared that the massacres were the Tutsis' fault because their agents (*provocateurs*) had infiltrated and caused both the Bugesera massacre and the carnage at Bagogwe in 1991.[21] Philippe Decraene, a pro-Mitterrand journalist whose wife Pauline was long-time secretary to the French president, was still managing to write in April 1993 that Habyarimana was a 'moderate democrat ... whose image has been tarnished by the clumsiness and excesses of some Hutu extremists'.

Many other open sources were sending detailed information back to Paris about the atrocities, even if its ambassador was reluctant to confront the truth on the issue publicly. Secret service, military and media reports,[22] as well as evidence from human rights organizations and diplomats, all made the massacres and their perpetrators open knowledge. That elements in the French government, at the Ministry of Cooperation and the Africa Cell knew what was happening was not in question. Like Jean-Christophe Mitterrand, they blamed 'gangsters' and ethnic tensions created by the RPF invasion, but held to the view that the Rwandan president was a 'moderate democrat' whose good work Hutu extremists were puting at risk.[23]

It was becoming clear to human rights activists that they were wasting their time trying to help stop the killing by talking to the French. Regime critic and journalist André Sibomana approached the US representative in Kigali, Ambassador David Rawson, with a plea for help, but it fell on deaf ears and Sibomana did not even approach the French. 'I didn't have any contact with the French embassy,' he wrote, 'even if I had, what could I have learned or expected from the country which was the most open supporter of the Habyarimana regime?'[24] By 1993 Habyarimana and the Hutu militants were the only people left in Rwanda with any faith in the French strategy.

In France, as the political classes' intrigues reached boiling point in the build-up to the March 1993 elections, there were bigger fish to fry than the fate of a few thousand black Africans. The eventual right-wing victory ushered in a period of so-called 'cohabitation', with socialist president, Mitterrand, having to work with conservative prime minister, Édouard Balladur. The Élysée now had to deal with Michel Roussin, the new minister of cooperation, a former secret service officer and friend of General Quesnot. For the ailing 76-year-old Mitterrand, the election defeat reflected his personal unpopularity. He had finally replaced his tarnished son Jean-Christophe with Bruno Delaye as head of the Élysée's Africa Cell in a last ditch attempt to head off the criticism of corruption aimed at his presidency, but this had failed.

However, the new right-wing team in the French government was content to change little in terms of French policy towards Rwanda. Besides, the president made it crystal clear that Africa was still his personal policy item, dictated through Delaye at the Africa Cell, and Generals Huchon and Quesnot and the secret service networks.

On 8 February 1993 400 crack new French troops that had been rushed to Rwanda met the new RPF offensive that had come within 25 kilometres of the capital Kigali. Only two outcomes were now feasible, an RPF military victory or a negotiated peace. The third option, that the Rwandan army could on its own be strong enough to repel the rebels was no longer a possibility. French military intelligence had concluded that the RPF was on the verge of victory in the civil war.[25]

France's problem was how to keep Habyarimana in power given the current military position and increasing insecurity in the country. One option, never discussed, would have been to replace Habyarimana, who was already implicated in massacring his people, with a moderate candidate more acceptable to the RPF, at least in the short term while peace talks reconvened. Mitterrand's single-minded determination to keep Habyarimana in power was deeply flawed, for it gave the Hutu Power militants the time and resources with which to continue planning a 'final solution' to the 'Tutsi problem.'

As human rights reports detailing Habyarimana's French-trained forces' massacres of Tutsi civilians were published, Paris focused only on the RPF. Marcel Debarge promised not to ignore the reports of the government-instigated massacres, but then did so, never publicly denouncing the regime in Kigali and saving his venom instead for the RPF. The 64-year-old Debarge, the minister of cooperation, encapsulated the confused and highly ambiguous French position. In an interview with *Le Monde* on 17 February 1993 he announced that 'France has supported the Arusha negotiations which have led to an agreement between the government and the opposition to create a transition cabinet. ... In any case, the World Bank and the other donors keep their representatives in Kigali only because of our military presence which – need I remind you – is only there to protect our citizens.'[26]

It was in effect a 'have my cake and eat it' argument. According to Debarge, France was helping to mediate the Arusha agreement (to which it had assigned a solitary very junior diplomat). Meanwhile, its multi-million dollar military help protected French citizens and allowed aid projects to continue. In fact, according to Debarge, French efforts in Rwanda benefited everybody. He omitted to mention the massacres, now in full swing, that the government his soldiers were keeping in power were carrying out, or indeed the financial scams siphoning off millions of dollars of foreign aid money into the coffers of the *Akazu*.

Prejudice against the 'anglophone' RPF blinded any French policy reassessment. An African strategic expert confided, 'it is not possible to tolerate this attack from Uganda, 18 million people against Rwanda with only seven million. The Belgians have abandoned their old colony, and they are alone. But, thanks to us, the Rwandan army is able to hold off the coup.'[27] Remarkably, such views did not include the white Western French as 'invaders', only the RPF, who though mostly from Uganda were actual Rwandans forced into exile. It was the RPF that was seeking a return to its homeland, not the French who were merely asserting their neocolonial rights to intervene as and when it suited them in a foreign land – without even a UN mandate.

Ten days after his remarks to *Le Monde*, Debarge was in Kigali. On 28 February, the man tasked with finding a peaceful solution told the Rwandan opposition parties that they should make a 'common front' with Habyarimana against their 'enemies'. It was a simplification and underestimation of the whole Rwandan mess. According to Prunier, 'in such a tense ethnic climate, with massacres having taken place in recent weeks, this call for a "common front" that could only be based on race was nearly a call to racial war.' The result was a clear deline-ation in Paris of what the conflict was about. 'The equation thus suggested was "Uganda equals Anglo-Saxon equals RPF ... equals Tutsi. ..." This of course implied another equation: "Rwanda equals France equals common front equals Hutu".'[28]

There were dissenting voices in the French camp. On the release of a number of high-profile reports on human rights abuses in Rwanda in March 1993, Guy Penne, a former government minister and now vice-president of the senate commission on foreign affairs and defence, wrote to Prime Minister Balladur expressing his anxiety. He mentioned France being 'very implicated' in the situation, asked the prime minister to arbitrate between the ministries of foreign affairs, cooperation and defence, and stated the need to reduce the French military presence. Moreover, he expressed the view that any remaining troops should be used specifically for humanitarian work and to protect French citizens, and that cooperation with Habyarimana should be suspended until the international commission on human rights abuses in Rwanda was published.[29] Predictably, such views were swiftly consigned to the Élysée's ample wastepaper basket. France was not renowned for changing a stance merely for human rights abuses and Mitterrand, champion of Vichy and the Algerian campaign, was not about to let the fate of 'a few' Rwandan villagers upset his Rwandan policy.

An RPF press release, issued on 8 February 1993, the day it renewed its offensive, conclusively equated Habyarimana with France. As far as the RPF was concerned the new offensive it had launched was due solely to Habyarimana's intransigence and his French allies. The RPF press release was dominated by an attack on the continuing French role in Rwanda.

> Contrary to the terms of the ceasefire agreement [of July 1992], the French troops remain in Rwanda, six months after the ceasefire came into effect. Their presence has continued to sustain President Habyarimana's intransigence towards a peaceful negotiated settlement. Once again we remind the international community that these French troops not only participate in the president's efforts to make war but also train the security agents who are responsible for the genocide that has been taking place in Rwanda. It is against this background of genocide, rejection of a negotiated settlement to the current conflict in Rwanda and the persistent presence of the French troops in our country that hostilities have resumed.[30]

Habyarimana was not about to change tack, and his reply to the February RPF offensive was to plead with Paris for more troops and to announce a 'common front' to repel the offensive. In a presidential communiqué issued with the support of various representatives of the Rwandan political parties on 2 March, the RPF was condemned and the French military help welcomed. Government troops, which had been hastily shifted from massacre duties to fighting the RPF, were thanked for their 'bravery' and assured of full support.

The presence of the new French troops at the front was all too obvious. *Guardian* reporter Chris McGreal, one of the few to cover the war, found one RPF recruit in his position near Byumba disappointed not to have the opportunity to get to grips with this foreign foe.

> Shaban Ruta wears his French army uniform to make a point. He would like to have captured a French soldier inside it to prove that Paris has sent troops to fight in tiny Rwanda's civil war. Instead he has to confess that the uniform was still folded in its packet when it was abandoned by fleeing government troops last week.[31]

Spring 1993 saw the RPF still occupying positions threatening Kigali, despite a ceasefire signed at Dar es Salaam in March 1993 agreeing to retreat away from the *zone tampon* (buffer zone) to a previously held location. The CDR Hutu militant party's extreme reaction to this ceasefire had given all parties cause for immense concern. A CDR communiqué called the agreement 'high treason' and accused Habyarimana of letting down the Rwandan people. France complained to the international community about RPF aggression and called on the United Nations to act.

Inside Rwanda, law and order had broken down amid violence and corruption. By July 1993 'everybody was exhausted. The political rigmarole had reached a point of almost total absurdity. Hutu supremacists were sniping at President Habyarimana who was consorting with liberals who wanted to see him fall; in Arusha the RPF's appetite seemed to grow by the day; extremists were arming almost openly ... the only thing that seemed equally distributed between all the political actors was corruption money.'[32] And behind the scenes the *Akazu* was already formulating and carefully organizing the 'final solution' to the Tutsi problem.

The World Bank, along with the main donor nations, insisted that a treaty be signed by 9 August, otherwise funds to Rwanda would be halted. Given this was Habyarimana's main source of income the result was inevitable.[33] Habyarimana, with a heavy heart and no doubt a wife incandescent with rage, made his way to neighbouring Tanzania to sign the Arusha accords on 4 August 1993. He could hardly bring himself to smile for the waiting press, let alone make the correct noises about how pleased he was that the civil war was now over. For the international community there was much backslapping and relief that Rwanda could now be stabilized and, it was presumed, both the civil war and massacres stopped. The reality was far more complex and the accords were greeted with dismay in Kigali, with the hard-line Hutu CDR and *Akazu* activists decrying this 'sell-out.'

The accords were made up of a number of previous protocols on power-sharing and setting up a broad-based government, but included an agreement on the return of refugees and on the thorniest of all questions, the RPF's integration into a new Rwandan army. They were, however, deeply flawed. With neither the RPF nor Habyarimana prepared to accept an imposed peace and the political solution they offered, they were set to collapse before the ink on the treaty paper was dry. Underlying tensions festered and were not addressed. Habyarimana had signed an agreement neither he nor Agathe and her *Akazu* coterie could ever accept, while looking down the barrel of an ultimatum from Western bankers and Kagame's RPF. Reforms such as power-sharing, army-sharing and finance-sharing, undermined the whole corrupt ethos of Habyarimana's government. Plans for the genocide were already being carefully worked out before the Arusha accords were signed. The treaty was another piece of Munich writing paper, promising peace in our time when extremists were already in advanced preparation for the carnage to come.

Although several African leaders were represented at the Arusha talks, including Uganda's Yoweri Museveni, President Ali Hassan Mwinyi of Tanzania and Faustin Birindwa representing Mobutu's Zaire, France was the only country in regular touch with the Hutu extremists. Having been roundly praised in the radical paper *Kangura*, Mitterrand was definitely the flavour of the year as far as the CDR and *Akazu* were concerned. France had saved Kigali in February 1993, but there was no sign before or after the signing of the accords that Paris had a real strategy for dealing with the extremists. Was the idea of keeping them onside by ignoring their human rights abuses and violent statements a policy to keep them from even worse actions? Or was it a purely cynical exercise in politics – of wanting to keep a popular stance with what it perceived as the 'rank and file' Hutu majority and the many powerful military and government figures with whom it had been working for the previous two-and-a-half decades? Equally, were there extremist elements in French political and military circles that encouraged their Hutu counterparts to reject any peace that could curtail them? According to French analyst Jean-François Bayart:

> Some French military officers seem to have suggested, both to the Habyarimana regime and to his entourage, that the Arusha accord was neither good nor ineluctable. Even if they did not want this atrocious genocide, one may ask whether they had not put the seed of this idea among the extremists of the regime that this accord had to be sabotaged at all costs.[34]

For the peace deal to work a neutral military power was needed to assist in the new broad-based elections and to provide stability and security in the current knife-edge political situation. France agreed to withdraw Operation Noroît to allow UNAMIR (United Nations Assistance Mission for Rwanda) to take its place. However, operating under a Chapter VI peacekeeping mandate of the UN Charter that banned proactive disarming measures and with a chronic lack of well-trained and armed troops, the UN force was spineless. With the Bosnian crisis in full cry and the US embroiled in a Somalian nightmare, Rwanda got the fag end of UN help. Sub-Saharan nations without oil, international terrorists or political clout could count on little support from the UN despite every nation's theoretical entitlement to equal help.

General Romeo Dallaire, UNAMIR's charismatic Canadian commander, had no experience of Africa or UN missions in the field; his immediate reaction on being told that the UN was considering him for a mission to Rwanda was, 'Rwanda, that's somewhere in Africa, isn't it?'[35] When he flew to Rwanda for a pre-mission reconnaissance tour on 17 August he found both the politicians and military in a state of extreme nervousness, as well as thousands of refugees created by the recent civil war who were now living in camps that smelt a long way off of 'faeces, urine, vomit and death'. The UN commander made contact with the French para-battalion in Kigali 'but the visit yielded little except some map references of RGF (Rwandan army) sites around the city. The battalion too was close-mouthed about its strength and true mission in Rwanda. We rarely saw French soldiers, except at the airport or at night when they operated patrols and roadblocks in and around the capital.[36]

Dallaire soon became aware of rifts within the French political and military establishment. The UN commander met new French ambassador Marlaud before he left after his short two-week fact-finding mission.

> I took the opportunity to run some of my findings past him [Marlaud]. The ambassador thought my report reasonable, but as soon as I started to talk actual figures, the French military attaché leapt into the fray. He said he couldn't understand why I needed so many troops. France had a battalion of only 325 personnel stationed in the country and the situation seemed to be well in hand. There was an awkward moment as the ambassador reiterated his support for my plan and the attaché sat back in his chair silently fuming. The attaché's position made no sense to me, and I concluded that he was being deliberately obstructive. The incident alerted me to an outright split between the policy being followed by France's foreign affairs department and its ministry of defence.[37]

The division between the French military, which had worked closely with its Rwandan army and government counterparts for the past three years, and the foreign office, which was far less subjective about Rwanda, was clear. The French military saw UNAMIR as 'impinging' on its territory, even if that was presently filled with daily murder, violence and political hatred.

UNAMIR finally rolled into Kigali in late November nearly three months after Dallaire's initial mission and three-and-a-half months after the accords had been signed. It did so without key equipment, including APCs and helicopters. One less than enthusiastic UN official told the BBC that UNAMIR was just 'taking in France's dirty linen'.[38]

Operation Noroît pulled out of Rwanda on 10 December 1993, honouring a clause in the Arusha agreement on which the RPF had insisted. Habyarimana organized a hero's sendoff at Kigali airport to these troops that had literally kept his regime in power. French television treated the occasion as a cause for great celebration, with the commentator praising the 'humanitarian' help the paratroopers had given the Kigali government over the previous three years. After a smart march past on the airstrip by singing legionnaires, Rwandan government ministers gave the commander of the French force neatly wrapped gifts. But, as the planes carrying Operation Noroît took off, an unspecified number of French military intelligence and 'security' experts who remained began their secret role of continuing to support Habyarimana. Minister of cooperation Michel Roussin admitted that 40–70 French soldiers were still in Rwanda in early April 1994.[39] The shadowy world of the secret services, the DGSE, as well as maverick security 'experts' and 'parallel network' mercenaries like Captain Paul Barril, were to be another vital lifeline for Habyarimana and the Hutu extremists.

By late 1993 the undercover war in Rwanda had been going on for several years. French agents were already in the country in the late 1980s, at Habyarimana's request, looking at how to strengthen his security network. *La Françafrique* was interwoven with networks of ex-police, secret service agents, ex-marines and paratroopers.[40] Such men included Paul Barril, Jeannou Lacaze, Paul Fontbonne, Jean-Claude Mantion, Pierre-Yves Gilleron and Robert Montoya. With these 'operatives' doing the French political and military establishment's work but being paid by their African employers, the operation was cleverly disguised. If there were to be an operational failure, no blame would fall on the French government. Instead, the mercenaries, 'parallel networks' or their African employers would take the rap.

The French secret service (DGSE) had suffered a few high profile embarrassments in the recent past and badly needed to boost its credibility. In October 1981 an alleged coup took place in Chad and President Goukouni Oueddei disappeared. When Mitterrand demanded to know what was happening he was told that his two secret service men in the country were unable to help. One was on holiday and the other away from the capital.[41] Debacles like the *Rainbow Warrior* affair, when secret service operatives Alain Mafart and Dominique Prieur sank a Greenpeace ship in Auckland harbour on 10 July 1985, killing a photographer on board, did little to enhance the service's reputation. According to former DGSE head Admiral Pierre Lacoste, Mitterrand had personally approved the sinking of the ship.[42] True to form though, the French president issued a briefing six weeks after the murder denying that either he or his secret service was involved – though recent evidence has proved this to be yet more Mitterrand fabrication. Paris had put pressure on the New Zealand government at the time to release the two convicted DGSE operatives after serving little more than a year of their ten-year sentences. In 1987 they were flown back to Paris on 'humanitarian and medical' grounds. New Zealand protests were muted when it was pointed out that its butter and mutton market in France might suffer.[43]

In Rwanda, as in many francophone countries, there was fierce competition for the lucrative role of presidential 'minder'. Two mercenaries, Captain Paul Barril and former secret service agent Pierre-Yves Gilleron, who had served in the French counter-intelligence branch, the DST (Direction de la surveillance du territoire) saw a chance of making a profit on the back of Habyarimana's fears. Gilleron had also worked in the anti-terrorist cell of the Élysée (cellule antiterroriste de l'Élysée) under Major Christian Prouteau and alongside Barril in the elite state security police, GIGN. Both men had now left official Élysée service, Barril in disgrace after being found to have tampered with evidence in a court case, and had proceeded to undertake various semi-official contracts for African Presidents. Barril started his own security company, 'Secrets Inc', in 1992 and even opened a branch on the Avenue de la Grande Armée in the 17th *arrondissement* of Paris. With support from influential figures at the Élysée like François de Grossouvre, Barril was able to secure lucrative contracts guarding francophone leaders. Central African Republic president Ange-Félix Patassé paid him with diamonds and funds from the Libyan secret service. He also worked for Cameroon's dictator Paul Biya, training the president's security guards,[44] for Burundian president Melchior Ndadaye and by the late 1980s was on Habyarimana's payroll. But all these African adventures did not stop the Élysée in Paris employing him to run an unofficial 'dirty tricks' operation against Mitterrand's opponents.[45]

In Rwanda, Barril and friend, now rival, Gilleron, who had founded his own company, 'Iris Services', were assisting the Habyarimana government. From 1990 onwards the presence of these two Frenchmen helped bolster defences against both the RPF and internal opposition. A British journalist in Kigali noticed in the windows of the Hotel Diplomates, alongside the usual assortment of CNN, BBC, French radio and environmental organizations' stickers, one with the emblem of the amphibious warfare company of the French paratroopers. Next to it

71

was a label 'bearing the logo of "Groupe Barril"', which had been working for the Habyarimana regime.[46] Advertising his services to a regime
smeared in human rights abuses was of no more concern to the French
mercenary than working for it.

The allegations against Barril and his 'unofficial' Élysée backers were
far more serious than a few ill-judged stickers. Barril was alleged to be
directly training the Hutu militia killers. 'Rwandan military sources
assert that Barril was hired by the Rwandan Ministry of Defence to con-
duct a training program for 30 to 60 men, eventually to grow to 120, at
Bigogwe military camp in the northwest. He was to provide training in
marksmanship and infiltration tactics for an elite unit in preparation
for attacks behind the RPF lines.'[47] Bigogwe was the camp from which
government soldiers and militia carried out massacres in 1991. It was
at this camp that men like Aloys had received their French training in
the art of killing. Journalist Patrick de Saint-Exupéry commented that
there was a 'parallel structure of military command' in Rwanda, and
that the Élysée was treating the country in a 'secret manner'.[48] A French
journalist quoted a high-ranking French officer who became so concerned at Barril's activities in Rwanda during 1993 that he reported to
Mitterrand that such actions could, if made public, be very damaging.
The French president is reported to have replied that Barril had
'received no orders from him'.[49] The inference was that there were
orders from 'someone' in the French military or government, but
Mitterrand was in *Rainbow Warrior* mode – deny everything.

The DGSE also played an important role for Mitterrand in 'spinning'
Operation Noroît to the French public as a humanitarian life-saver for
the African nation. After the RPF's February 1993 attack, the DGSE
informed the media in France that the 'rebels' had burned villages, that
mass graves had been found and that Uganda was responsible for
helping the invasion.[50] The DGSE did not explain how the FAR, in full
retreat, found the time and motivation to exhume mass graves in RPF-
held territory. The point was to show French readers that a 'Ugandan'
invasion was taking place and that France was the good guy helping a
distressed friendly regime to counter this threat. Days later, *Le Monde*
reported a massacre at the Rebero refugee camp. In fact, when priests
went to tend to the presumed injured and dying, they found no one
there, everyone had fled. They then hid for fear that the militia and
Rwandan army would kill them to keep the massacre story alive. For the

DGSE such disinformation made it creditable to send hundreds more French troops and millions of francs worth of heavy weaponry to Rwanda.

On 11 October 1993 Habyarimana flew to Paris on a private visit to see his friend François Mitterrand, while also taking time to meet Foreign Minister Alain Juppé and the head of the French military, Admiral Lanxade. Whatever was said in the state rooms of Paris, Habyarimana returned to his own country in better spirits, and no doubt with words of endorsement ringing in his ears. Less than four weeks later the Rwandan president chaired a meeting on 5 November at Hotel Rebero in Kigali where it was decided 'to distribute grenades, machetes and other weapons to the *Interahamwe* and to CDR young people. The objective is to kill Tutsis and other Rwandans who are in the cities and do not support them' (namely the *Interahamwe* and CDR).[51] Plans for genocide were well under way and arms, including hundreds of thousands of machetes, bought for the purpose, were being imported. One delivery alone of 987 cartons of machetes, weighing 25,662 kilograms, arrived into Kigali via Mombasa in early November.[52]

Warning signs had been glowing warmly since 1990, but had been ignored. The French reaction seemed ambiguous in the extreme. Its ambassadors, including the pro-Hutu Martres, were sending reports back to Paris that genocide was possible. After the RPF invasion in 1990, Colonel Rwagafilita, a close associate of Habyarimana, 'told the general who directed French military cooperation in Rwanda that the Tutsi "are very few in number, we will liquidate them"'.[53] In their daily meetings with their Rwandan counterparts, the French military attached to Habyarimana's army, and police attached to the Rwandan gendarmerie, would have picked up the undercurrents of ethnic tension and hatred, especially as their Rwandan counterparts were often members of the *Akazu*.

Yet Mitterrand and Delaye, his chief adviser on Africa, together with General Christian Quesnot, then head of military affairs for the French presidency, seemed unable to see beyond the hyperbole with which they had bedecked the RPF. Each passing atrocity was blamed on this Anglo-Saxon enemy. Each political assassination, unsatisfactory peace talk or bloody massacre was the result of the 'Khmer Noir' invaders. 'During the three years of the conflict, this perception of the RPF stayed constant and masked the development of the Rwandan regime.'[54]

It was Uganda against Rwanda or on a broader level the United States against France, played out like Fashoda 100 years earlier in one of the poorest nations on earth.

Throughout November and December 1993 reports came in from diplomats and human rights agencies that the militia and civilians were being armed. There were daily calls on the state radio, Radio Rwanda and its 'private' counterpart, RTLM, which was powered by electricity from the presidential palace, to ethnic violence. The Belgian ambassador reported to his foreign affairs ministry on 26 November that the radio was calling for the murder of the liberal prime minister, Agathe Uwiling-iana and her designated replacement, Faustin Twagiramungu. In early December UNAMIR reported suspicious movements by the militia while the *Interahamwe* were being made ready. On 27 December Belgian intelligence reported 'The *Interahamwe* are armed to the teeth and on alert. Many of them have been trained at the military camp in Bugesera. Each of them has ammunition, grenades, mines and knives. They have been trained to use guns that are stockpiled with their respective chiefs. They are all just waiting for the right moment to act.'[55]

On 11 January UNAMIR commander Dallaire sent a so-called 'genocide fax' to UN headquarters warning in stark terms that an ethnic massacre of immense proportions was being planned. According to a source named Jean-Pierre, the *Interahamwe* was in the later stages of readiness to begin wide-scale killing. The informant, a member of the militia and of Habyarimana's security staff, told Dallaire that the UN 'were to be provoked', with Belgian troops especially targeted and killed to produce their withdrawal from Rwanda. Jean-Pierre estimated that the *Interahamwe* could kill 1000 in a 20-minute spell. He had gone to the UN because he disagreed with its plans and asked for protection for himself and his family in return.

The UN commander in Kigali received a fax back that same day, under the name of now UN secretary-general Kofi Annan, who at the time was head of the UN's department of peacekeeping operations (DPKO). It bluntly stated that no action to raid arms caches named by Jean-Pierre could be countenanced. It was against UNAMIR's mandate, as was protecting the informant. Instead, New York told Dallaire to inform Habyarimana of the location of the arms, even though the president had probably ordered them in the first place. The information was also to be passed on to the ambassadors of France, the

United States and Belgium; each was almost certainly already aware of the weapons stores and their possible use by the militia.

France was fully conscious of the increasingly dangerous and explosive situation. The French military attaché, Colonel Cussac, visited UNAMIR on the same day that the fax was sent to ask about evacuation plans in the event of the crisis reaching breaking point. Three days later the Belgian and US ambassadors went to Habyarimana to urge him finally to put the Arusha agreements in place, especially the broad-based government the president had delayed implementing. The French chargé d'affaires accompanied them because Ambassador Marlaud declined to join the delegation. The diplomatic mission to Habyarimana failed to ask for urgent action to be taken on the matters contained in the fax after the French opposed any reference that could antagonize the Rwandan president.[56] While the mission desisted from making diplomatic waves, a DC-10 carrying 90 boxes of 60 mm mortars, probably destined for the FAR and presidential guard, arrived in Kigali from France on the night of 21/22 January. The weapons violated the terms of Arusha and, when UNAMIR discovered them, they were put under a joint guard with the Rwandan army.[57]

In an open letter issued by Human Rights Watch on 25 January Paris came under fire. Directed at President Mitterrand, the letter called for France to reveal the true nature of its military assistance to Rwanda, which it said was 'tantamount to direct participation in the war'.[58] The letter identified France as 'the major military supporter of the government of Rwanda … providing combat assistance to a Rwandan army guilty of widespread human rights abuses, and failing to pressure the Rwandan government to curb human rights violations'. Mitterrand did not respond. UN envoy for Africa Stephen Lewis was blunt in his assessment of French culpability.

> There was diplomatic information flowing in in significant quantities. The French, the Italians, the Vatican, the various governments who had missions in Rwanda, [they] were sending reports at the end of 1993 and early 1994 that signalled an apocalypse. The French government were with the Rwandan government that were planning the genocide, knew everything that was going on and not only didn't complain but did the opposite – legitimized and spoke on behalf of the government everywhere in the world.

So the French government kept giving the killers the conviction that they could get away with murder.[59]

An independent report commissioned into the causes of the genocide also stressed the failure of French intelligence either to make the precarious situation known to its government or to garner information that seemed well known to others in a less amicable relationship with Habyarimana. As one official later said: 'Given its close relations with Rwanda, France had better access than most to obtain intelligence on the extremists. Yet it is striking that senior officials in the Ministry of Cooperation in 1993 regarded Rwanda as the "Switzerland of Africa".' To the extent that human rights violations were noted, they were considered as not particularly bad by African standards. Evidently, DAMI, which is located in the Ministry of Cooperation and reports to it, either did not observe the mounting force of Hutu extremism – which is possible given its preoccupation with monitoring the designated enemy, the RPF – or observed but did not report. Either way, for the ministry most directly and broadly involved in Rwanda, it amounted to a massive intelligence failure.

A 33 year-old Tutsi survivor, Innocent Rwililiza, explained that he felt 'the French knew that a genocide was in preparation, since they advised our army. They supposedly just did not believe it; nevertheless many Whites knew Habyarimana's programme and his character, as they knew Hitler's.'[60] UNAMIR too was struggling. Dallaire found that information discussed between his force commanders seemed to end up with Habyarimana and his advisers. While many of the troops making up UNAMIR were ill-trained and ill-equipped, some of the French military mission remaining in Kigali still saw the force as a threat. When Dallaire left for New York in March 1994 he received news that:

> France had written to the Canadian ambassador to request my removal as force commander of UNAMIR. Apparently someone had been reading my reports and hadn't liked the pointed references I had made to the presence of French officers among the Presidential Guard, especially in the light of the Guard's close link to the *Interahamwe* militias. The French Ministry of Defence must have been aware of what was going on and was turning a blind eye. My bluntness had rattled the French enough for them to take the bold and extremely unusual step of asking for my

dismissal. It was clear that Ottawa and the DPKO were still backing me, but I made a mental note to keep a close watch on the French in Rwanda, to continue to suspect their motives and to further probe the presence of French military advisers in the elite RGF (FAR) units and their possible involvement in the training of the *Interahamwe*.[61]

Diplomats in Kigali also reported observing French officers with *Interahamwe* units in a national park.[62] These were the very killers who were getting ready to unleash the horror in the months to come. The *Interahamwe* 'were easily recognizable from their uniform (*kanga*). It was one of the "open secrets" of Kigali that the militias were training in the national parks.'

Habyarimana continued to delay implementing the Arusha accords, specifically forming a new transitional government. Militants used the delay to continue arming, while the RPF began to do the same.[63] Massacres were becoming increasingly common, with the civilian Tutsi population targeted, another sign of the explosion to come. Dallaire had reported back to UN headquarters of the slaughter on 17–18 and 30 November of around 55 men, women and children. He told his superiors in New York that, given the thorough planning, organization and cover-up that characterized such massacres, 'We have no reason to believe that such occurrences could not and will not be repeated again in any part of this country where arms are prolific and political and ethnic tensions are prevalent.'

On the early autumn evening of 6 April 1994 President Habyarimana walked across the still warm Tanzanian tarmac to his plane for the short trip back to Kigali. He had just attended a regional summit of heads of state in Dar es Salaam, but things had not gone according to plan. The other regional leaders had politically ambushed the 57-year-old Rwandan president. President Ali Hassan Mwinyi of Tanzania, George Saitoti of Kenya, Cyprien Ntaryamira from Burundi and Ugandan leader Yoweri Museveni had been champing at the bit to discuss Habyarimana's failure to put a stable peace agreement into action in Rwanda. Habyarimana not only received the – probably expected – criticism from old rival Museveni in neighbouring Uganda, but also from his own Hutu neighbour, the new president of Burundi Cyprien Ntaryamira. Why, they repeatedly asked, had he not put the

Arusha peace agreement into action in his country? The regional leaders concluded that such a failure was destabilizing the whole Great Lakes area, with refugees fleeing into their countries and militants travelling to Rwanda in search of a new war. Habyarimana faced a 'solid wall of verbal criticism laced with implicit threats in case he failed to comply'. President Ali Hassan Mwinyi of Tanzania implored his Rwandan counterpart to bring an end to the ethnic bloodbath and terror taking hold of his country. 'Now is the time to say "no" to a Bosnia on our doorstep. Now is the time to ensure that hostilities are not passed on to the children of Rwanda and Burundi,' he told Habyarimana. Museveni even accompanied the Rwandan leader to the airport still badgering him to honour his promise to implement Arusha. He described the shell-shocked Juvénal as leaving the conference in no doubt that if he failed to put his own country in order, he would face 'sanctions'.[64]

As he stepped on board his luxury executive jet, a Falcon 50, the gift of the French government, Habyarimana must have been a very worried man. One thing was certain; the Hutu militants would never buy the peace agreement, however it was packaged or whatever public relations effort was attached to it. Near to him sat his personal aide and militant CDR member Colonel Elie Segatwa. What would he be reporting to his *Akazu* colleagues about this Dar es Salaam sell out?

With a show of generosity, even after the verbal battering he had received at the conference, the Rwandan president offered to give a ride to the Burundian president Cyprien Ntaryamira who was feeling tired and wanted to return to Bujumbura as soon as possible. No French jet had been given to him and his old propeller-driven plane promised a far less smooth and speedy ride. Habyarimana invited him on board to enjoy the Falcon's hospitality and perhaps to do a little more diplomatic wrangling over a drink. At 6.50 p.m. the Falcon 50 set off from Tanzania carrying the two presidents, with a view to dropping Habyarimana off in Kigali before going on to Burundi with its guest passenger.

At 8.24 p.m. the Falcon jet began its descent through the night sky towards Kigali airport. Two red streaks of surface-to-air missiles flashed upwards to greet the returning Rwandan leader. They struck the plane with deadly accuracy, creating a fireball that lit up the night sky. The missiles were to trigger an inferno that engulfed not just the ten passengers on the plane, but the whole nation where the wreckage landed.

Chapter 5

Retreat

As the wreckage of the crashed presidential plane lay burning brightly in the dark Rwandan night, ironically in the grounds of Habyarimana's own lavishly equipped presidential palace, the *Akazu* swung its carefully nurtured plan for genocide into action. Within hours of the Rwandan dictator's death, the presidential guard left their barracks and began methodically killing those on pre-planned lists. For France, the major political and military backer of the Habyarimana regime, there followed what seems at first glance to be a seismic policy shift. Instead of rushing more troops to Rwanda as it had over the past three years, Mitterrand's government decided on a near total withdrawal of its military capability. However, this public retreat masked Mitterrand's decision to support the new extremist Hutu government that seized control.

The authors of the attack on the president's plane have yet to be found. The finger of blame was almost immediately laid at the door of Hutu extremists suspected of using the plane crash to initiate their planned genocidal 'final solution' once it was clear that Habyarimana had 'sold them out' by agreeing to implement the Arusha accords. A French inquiry into the crash led by investigative judge Jean-Louis Bruguière,[1] ten years after the event, was reported to have named RPF leader Paul Kagame as its chief suspect, though the inquiry findings were never officially made public. Kagame vehemently denied the charges in April 2004.

The French fascination with the crash is understandable. If Paris could prove that Kagame and the RPF were implicated, then its involvement with the regime would be validated. At one level Paris had every right to be involved with the Falcon-50. It was a French-made plane that had cost 60 million francs from the cooperation budget and was piloted by three French crew members – Jacky Héraud, Jean-Pierre Minaberry and Jean-Michel Perrine, all of whom perished in the crash.

The status and employment of the pilot, co-pilot and mechanic engendered some debate. Despite assurances from Paris that these were civilians hired purely for the specific job of flying the Falcon, some people suspected they were working for the French secret service as well as for Habyarimana. The Ministry of Cooperation paid to return the badly burned bodies of the French crew to Paris for funerals and justified the outlay on the grounds that the three dead men were 'indirect technical helpers' of the French government. Ambassador Martres later admitted that the crew had passed information on to him about the movements of the Rwandan head of state. This was the norm in other francophone African countries like Chad, where French crews working for its president routinely passed on vital information to the French secret services. On 14 June 1994, President Mitterrand awarded the three dead crew members the posthumous Legion of Honour, an unexpected action given the official declaration that these men were 'civilians'. The families of the dead men did not believe the government's 'civilian only' story either. The daughter of co-pilot Jean-Pierre Minaberry, Sylvie Minaberry, took the French government to court in 1997 to find out the truth about her father's duties.

The report by French judge Jean-Louis Bruguière used evidence from the highly unreliable mercenary Paul Barril and three former RPF soldiers, now in exile, to bring a case against Kagame. The allegation was that he shot the plane down knowing that massacres and genocide would follow, gambling that in the ensuing conflict his forces would gain total military and political victory. It is a breathtaking charge, and depends on the reliability of these defectors' testimony. Barril, who was in the pay of Agathe Habyarimana, was quick at the time to go on French television to accuse Kagame. In the days after his excited performance in front of France 2's cameras on 28 June 1994, none of the supposed 'proofs' that he claimed justified his accusations materialized. The missile launcher, tapes of men speaking English with Belgian accents and satellite photographs all remained unseen.[2]

Cooperation minister Bernard Debré reported that French secret service surveillance showed that the RPF was ordered to begin advancing on Kigali on the very day of the assassination, 6 April. The remark showed the effort France was making to tap into RPF communications and its secret surveillance of actions in Rwanda. This makes it even more difficult to believe that Paris was unaware of the genocidal intentions of its Rwandan government partners.

A French military officer, Grégoire de Saint-Quentin, was one of the first people on the crash scene. He lived only 300 metres from the presidential palace where the wreckage of the Falcon-50 lay and had been alerted on hearing gunfire, which he attributed to the panicked reaction of the presidential guard. He reached the scene at 10.00 p.m., about an hour-and-a-half after the disaster had occurred and an unnamed Rwandan officer accompanied him. He searched until 3.00 a.m. for the bodies of the French crew members, and returned at 8.00 the next morning to try unsuccessfully to recover the plane's black box. Over the next two days Saint-Quentin returned to the presidential palace charged with evacuating *Akazu* head Agathe Habyarimana and her family. Four French soldiers were positioned as guards outside Habyarimana's house on the morning after the crash, while the presidential guard escorted the family in and out.[3]

This instant French investigation had the blessing of the presidential guard, FAR and the extremists who controlled the city in the early days after the crash and before an interim government could take over. That the French were close to Hutu extremists like Colonel Théoneste Bagosora was evident from their ability to go freely into such a sensitive area, while Dallaire's UNAMIR force was barred from access to the site, as were the Belgian UN peacekeepers controlling Kigali airport.

In the days following Habyarimana's murder and the consequent start of the genocide, three other French nationals were killed in equally mysterious circumstances. On 8 April, two days after the crash, René Maïer, Alain Didot and Didot's wife were murdered at their Kigali home. The two French sergeants were part of the military and secret service force that remained in Rwanda after Noroît returned in December 1993. Didot was a high-level specialist in repairing radio communications, but did not, according to Colonel Jean-Jacques Maurin, specialize in surveillance. His job was to ensure that the French embassy communications worked, as well as the equipment of the other members of the remaining military force. He was also in charge of training members of the FAR in radio communications and maintaining the radio station of Habyarimana's army. Didot had fitted a large radio antenna onto the roof of his Kigali home and it is this, it was assumed, that led to his murder. It is feasible that the two soldiers were working with secret service operatives on monitoring the RPF. Given Debré's evidence that such surveillance was happening, the French were clearly putting resources into finding out what the RPF – 'the Khmer Noir enemy' – was doing, even after the Arusha accords had been signed. Whether this information was then shared with their partners in the Rwandan government and military, or leaked via 'unofficial' French sources like Barril, is open to speculation. There is no evidence of who killed the three French nationals or of what they were doing to warrant the attack, though in a bizarre turn of events their brutal murders were not reported immediately and when they were French officials put the cause down as 'accidental death'.

The deaths of six French nationals were the trigger for Operation Amaryllis. Less than two hours after the crash, well-prepared and well-organized Hutu militias were on the streets of the capital setting up roadblocks and Colonel Bagosora seized effective control. By midnight, less than four hours after the crash, the first opposition official had been murdered. By midday on 7 April, the presidential guard had killed and sexually mutilated the body of the liberal prime minister Agathe Uwilingiyimana. The 15 UNAMIR peacekeepers sent to protect her were then captured, though the five Ghanaians among them were released. The remaining ten Belgian soldiers were beaten and killed by machetes, bullets and grenades at the Kigali military camp. Rwandan soldiers had been taught by constant propaganda that just as France was 'the saviour', their previous Belgian colonial masters were in league with the RPF and Uganda. By murdering ten defenceless soldiers they planned to get Belgium to do what it had done in autumn 1990, namely withdraw.

On 8 April the French foreign ministry issued a statement. 'In the face of the spread and worsening violence in Kigali', it had been decided to launch a new limited military operation designed to 'provide the security necessary for a possible evacuation of the French nationals' in Rwanda.

Within 36 hours of Habyarimana's death, the French government had decided to fly in a well-equipped armed force of paratroopers – Operation Amaryllis – with the sole objective of evacuating their people from Rwanda, namely French and foreign nationals, members of Habyarimana's family and former government ministers. It was a remarkable volte-face by Mitterrand. In 1990 France had sent in troops to support and keep Habyarimana in power, again at a few days' notice. Yet, after an expensive three-year campaign to keep Rwanda under the former president's control, in a matter of hours a decision came via the chandeliers and velvet couches of the Élysée to abandon past policy and launch a full-scale evacuation.

A number of different interpretations can be given of why this happened. The Élysée's stance was that its priority was to protect French citizens, though it claimed the same thing in 1990 when it sent troops in to stay. Admiral Lanxade, chief of staff to the French armed forces, later defended this new evacuation as the only possible policy. According to him, France could not send in a force to stop the genocide because it did not have the information at the time that it was taking place. He argued that although France could act rapidly to evacuate its nationals, within days of the threat to them, it did not have the means to put in place a deployment to stop the killing, though it later proved able to get such troops together to launch just such an intervention two-and-a-half months later. Lanxade reasoned that those who opposed French intervention in Rwanda would see any mission as a pro-Hutu one.[4]

However, these points do not add up. Given the constant warnings by human rights groups, RTLM hate radio broadcasts, the International Commission on Human Rights, regular intelligence reports from General Dallaire and Belgium, and 'unofficial' sources like Paul Barril working with *Akazu* members, it is difficult to believe that the French government did not know that the planned 'massacres' heralded the start of a wider-scale policy of 'annihilation'. It was this knowledge that decided Paris to withdraw rather than bolster the FAR again. When Roussin was questioned on 13 April about 'the planned and signalled' ongoing massacres, which raised the question of how much the French executive knew about them beforehand, he refused to answer. It is probable that the French government realized that its allies in the Habyarimana government were hell bent on genocide and that Operation Amaryllis was an effort to save France's reputation before the whole country descended into an inferno of killing. By 13 April the RPF was already expressing the view that the killing taking place was indeed genocide, a planned and systematic attempt to exterminate a whole ethnic group. If the RPF understood this, it is difficult to believe that France, which was so involved in the Rwandan situation, did not.

In addition, the speed with which Operation Amaryllis was started showed that they knew that the situation was far graver this time than it had been during the previous years of massacres and civil unrest. With more than 15,000 troops in Africa, France could intervene quite suddenly if it needed to and if there were a political will in Paris to do so. Indeed, when the political will did change two months later, in June, France was very quick to put together just such an intervention force – Operation Turquoise.

A report by an international panel of experts later concluded that 'The French government had unrivalled influence at the very highest levels of the Rwandan government and Rwandan military. They were in a position to insist that attacks on the Tutsi must cease, and they chose never to exert that influence.'[5] It was inconceivable to Mitterrand and the French military that they should now turn on their former Rwandan government allies, with the anglophone RPF the major beneficiary of any such policy. Any return to the Arusha accords would mean a power sharing government with Kagame and his RPF. Paris may have reasoned that it was better to let the renewed civil war, even with its massacres and/or genocide, continue to completion, after which it was likely that the Hutu majority would still hold power. What was politically expedient was to avoid being sucked into the Rwandan carnage, while hoping for and indeed secretly supporting the best-case scenario – victory for its former pupils in the Habyarimana regime.

Lanxade's final argument that an intervention would be seen as bias in favour of the Hutu camp is equally flawed. Mitterrand had ordered French troops to intervene in Africa on numerous occasions in the past and in Rwanda in the previous four years without worrying about how its action would be construed.

Michel Roussin, showing no conceivable embarrassment, told the National Assembly that 'France could not be Africa's policeman'. He insisted that Paris could not and would not intervene in the renewed civil war now under way in Rwanda, with RPF troops in Kigali under attack from government forces and widespread massacres already taking place. Hours after Roussin's announcements in Paris, 190 French paratroopers landed at Kigali airport for the start of Operation Amaryllis. Despite declaring that the intervention would be discreet and strictly neutral, Roussin conceded that Agathe Habyarimana and her family would be airlifted to Paris on 9 April.

At the UN in New York, the Rwandan ambassador got his French counterpart to say that the presidential guard now controlled Kigali airport and any attempt to mount a military intervention, especially by Belgium, would be met by force. However, he added that French troops would be welcome.

Publicly, French government figures suddenly became loquacious about the tiny African country. After barely one speech each year mentioning Rwanda, as France attempted to keep its Rwandan military intervention secret from 1990 to 1993, politicians were now lining up to show their concern about the situation and making five media calls a day. Citing a 'disaster in which violence and hatred have reached unbearable limits', and 'in which horror has no limits', government ministers told their people that France was 'disconcerted'. Foreign Minister Alain Juppé reminded French people that 'we had already done quite a lot for peace to return to Rwanda between both parties' by supporting the Arusha accords and by using a military presence to help bring a peaceful outcome to the talks.[6] This was at odds with the official view the Élysée had pushed since 1990 that its troops had only ever been in Rwanda to protect its own citizens. Juppé now decided the time was right to claim an extra benefit from their presence in Rwanda during the past three years.

The view from the RPF was very different. In his office in the still shell-blasted building housing the Rwandan parliament, Dennis Polisi MP, former RPF ambassador to Brussels, in April 1994 made no effort to hide his disgust at the French attitude.

I was in Brussels when the plane went down. I had been touring East Africa just before, advising the heads of state to [put] pressure [on] Habyarimana to accept Arusha and the peace plan. I was at Uccle in Brussels and, at a press conference on 12 April, we [the RPF] issued a statement that said any French troops staying in Rwanda would be treated as enemies and we would fight them. Kagame made the same statement in Rwanda.

We saw France as being in league with the genocidaire. We certainly did not see them trying to help anyone. France knew all about the genocide, its military intelligence knew about the preparation and the people who must be killed. I think they see the problem for Rwanda and in other African countries as a problem of tribes – so if this Tutsi minority disappeared then so would the problem.

He added, by way of conclusion after a moment's reflection, 'They are cynical, and criminal.'[7]

The French forces that flew into Kigali were bent purely on an ordered evacuation. Indeed, such was their rush to get to Rwanda from their bases in Africa, that the mission did not even inform UNAMIR commander General Romeo Dallaire of its intention.

Dallaire, not surprisingly, was 'livid'. Since UNAMIR had lost control of the airport, he was concerned that the RPF could attempt to shoot the French planes down. Equally, he feared that the Belgian rescue mission, launched like Amaryllis to bring home its nationals, might suffer the same fate as its ten peacekeepers the presidential guard had already butchered. Dallaire also questioned the French motive for Amaryllis. 'Were the French going to get involved once again with the fight or were they really only here to evacuate their expatriates?' he asked himself.[8]

Dallaire was left in no doubt after battling through the corpse-strewn streets of the burning capital.

> My conversation with Colonel [Henri] Poncet [Amaryllis commander] was curt and the French commander showed no interest in cooperating with us. This unhappy exchange was an indication of how the French evacuation task force, Operation Amaryllis, would continue to behave with UNAMIR. ... We had heard from the MilObs at the airport that the French had already evacuated a number of Rwandans and that twelve members of the presidential family were part of this group, but Poncet insisted to me that he was here only to evacuate expatriates and "white people". I told him that within two hours there should be a truce in place but that there was no guarantee from the RGF that they would observe it. At that Poncet asked to be excused and, without waiting for a response from me, simply turned his back and walked off. I decided then that Luc [Marchal] would handle all future dealings with this rude Frenchman.[9]

During the night of 8 April five French C160 transport aircraft arrived in Kigali. The FAR allowed them to land after a French officer asked for vehicles blocking the runway to be removed. The next day *Akazu* head Agathe Habyarimana and 11 members of her family were flown out to a warm welcome in Paris.

In Kigali, Dallaire witnessed examples of Western 'humanitarian' assistance.

> I passed by an assembly point where French soldiers were loading expatriates into vehicles. Hundreds of Rwandans had gathered to watch all these white entrepreneurs, NGO staff and their families making their fearful exits, and as I wended my way through the crowd, I saw how aggressively the French were pushing black Rwandans seeking asylum out of the way. A sense of shame overcame me. The whites, who had made their money in Rwanda and who had hired so many Rwandans to be their servants and labourers, were now abandoning them. Self-interest and self-preservation ruled.[10]

A Belgian journalist, Els de Temmerman, was equally horrified at what he saw.

> I arrived in Kigali on 10 April, with a plane sent by the World Food Program. There were fifty journalists following French and Belgian troops. I was in a French convoy. At some point, we witnessed the murder of six persons in front of us. The journalists begged the soldiers to intervene; we were crying. 'It is not our mandate', one of the soldiers replied. I was so revolted and disgusted … people were laughing in front of the mountain of corpses.[11]

UNAMIR ran into more trouble with the unilateral French operation. A heated row developed after the French used UNAMIR jeeps parked at the airport to evacuate their nationals and *Akazu* members. Dallaire complained bitterly that:

> Seth [RPF liaison officer] angrily told me that the French had been using UNAMIR vehicles to move Rwandans of known extremist background to the airport, where they were flown out

of the country. He also alleged that the French had opened fire on a number of occasions from these vehicles. It was absolutely unacceptable for the French to use UNAMIR this way, putting my own troops at risk and confusing everyone about what our blue helmets meant, and I told them [the RPF] that Luc [Marchal] was arguing this point with the French commander.[12]

The UNAMIR commander registered his disgust to a Security Council adviser who had telephoned him late on 10 April, denouncing the French for stealing his UN vehicles from the airport.[13] Poncet, the French commander, countered that while they had taken the transport they had put French flags over the UNAMIR markings. Eleven years later, Poncet, now a four-star general commanding the French intervention force in the Ivory Coast, was suspended from his position after being suspected of ordering a captured 'bandit' to be murdered by his peacekeeping troops.[14]

The situation in Kigali was one of unimaginable fear and violence. The drunken *Interahamwe* manning the roadblocks stopped, searched and butchered those they took to be Tutsi or on 'death lists' they had been given. The presidential guard drove around the capital breaking into homes belonging to 'political enemies' or Tutsi. Whole families were chopped to pieces and their bodies left where they fell to provide an unexpected feast for the street dogs. By contrast, inside the regal setting of the French embassy, matters were tense but spirits high as the new post-Habyarimana Hutu regime was in the process of being chosen.

It was an incredible event. With representatives of Mitterrand's administration playing host, an interim government was formed in beautifully furnished rooms filled with smiling and laughing Hutu extremists later to be condemned by the UN tribunal in Arusha for genocide. Their French hosts welcomed Froduald Karamira, Justin Mugenzi, Jean-Bosco Barayagwiza, Hassan Ngeze, Ferdinand Nahimana, Jérôme Bicamumpaka, Pauline Nyiramasuhuko and Théoneste Bagosora, as well as other genocidaire who no doubt drank a few toasts to the new regime once the wrangling over their various ministerial portfolios had been completed.[15] Ambassador Marlaud is reported to have told a friend from Belgium that 'it is certainly the first time in my life that I have put together a government,'[16] albeit one that was to organize and carry out the systematic extermination of its own people. Marlaud must also have noticed that, despite the proviso in the Arusha accords for a broad-based government representing all ethnic and political groups, all the members of this new interim government were Hutus and political extremists. While Marlaud suggested that Arusha prime minister designate Faustin Twagiramungu head the new interim government instead of Jean Kambanda, he was quite content to accept the latter.[17]

A Rwandan named Gakumba described the surreal but fearsome atmosphere inside this western embassy when he fled there to escape the killing going on in the streets outside.

> Imagine my incredulity to see the people who were gathered in the French embassy! All the high-ups from the former regime, and their families, the ministers from the President's [Habyarimana's] party, his in-laws. There was the director of Radio Mille Collines and his assistants, well known for their exhortations to commit massacres. ... On the way to the embassy, at dozens of roadblocks, I saw people sitting on the ground, arms tied behind their backs, in the process of being killed. ... I don't know what these powerful people from the [Hutu hard-line] regime had to fear, since I saw them going in and out of the embassy with their FAR escorts to go round parts of the city where the massacres were taking place. In due course they would have meetings in the French embassy to discuss how the situation [the genocide] was developing; they took pleasure in totting up the total number of victims, or complaining that such-and-such a person had not been killed, or that such-and-such a part of the city had not been cleaned [all the Tutsis killed]. They were boasting about the results of their plans and the exploits of the militias. The night I spent there was one of the most agonizing of my life.
>
> The following day the French ambassador [Jean-Michel Marlaud] began the evacuation of all these people to the airport. First on the list of people earmarked for evacuation were certain people well known as heads of militia gangs.[18]

Another witness was Joseph Ngarambe, a 40-year-old member of the opposition PSD. He had escaped to the embassy after running into a

French diplomat whom he knew. On arrival he found around 200
Rwandans, including women and children.

> I was very surprised to meet all the members of the *Akazu*, that is
> to say the entourage of Habyarimana. Certainly, all the poli-
> ticians who had found refuge at the embassy did not have the
> same degree of responsibility – Habyarimana had attacked some
> of them – but those directly responsible for the massacres were
> certainly there; for example, the Minister for Health, Casimir
> Bizimungu,[19] one of the pillars of the regime. And Ferdinand
> Nahimana, MRND ideologue and founder of radio RTLM 'the radio
> of death' which made appeals for massacres. Also there was
> minister of planning Augustin Ngirabatware. In this crowd,
> people who were not part of the intimate group around Habyari-
> mana were small in number.
>
> The ambassador proceeded in the destruction of the archives.
> Dossiers, files, all were burnt before our eyes. Eight Rwandans,
> among them a pregnant woman came to ask for refuge at the
> embassy, which refused to open its doors. It was horrible to see.
>
> On the 12th [April] at dawn, someone came to wake us to
> announce the evacuation. Thirty minutes later, a French soldier
> made the first roll call: it was the names of Habyarimana's key
> men. A group of VIPs presented itself at the final moment to take
> advantage of the evacuation. Among them, ex-Prime Minister
> Sylvestre Nsanzimana, a member of the MRND, and his family.
> They were boarded directly onto the lorry. Around 10 o'clock,
> the minister Casimir Bizimungu went forward at the second roll
> call. We left while the eight Rwandans and about 20 embassy
> guards were asking for asylum. It should be known that generally
> the embassy personnel were Tutsi. But the embassy did not
> evacuate any member of the administrative staff. Of course,
> between them they had worked for a very long time at the
> embassy. They were not considered as friends of France. The plane
> took off from Kigali at 1.00 p.m. and arrived at Bujumbura in
> Burundi at 1.30 p.m. The Burundian authorities gazed with
> hatred as the figures of the Rwandan politicians compromised in
> the genocide disembarked.[20]

Casimir Bizimungu certainly made his feelings plain when he saw Joseph Ngarambe at the embassy, snarling, 'What is he doing here?' All the other leaders of his liberal opposition PSD party had already been murdered. Bizimungu was clearly upset at this lack of completion, quite apart from him turning up in what Prunier called 'an embassy the *Akazu* now referred to as their own'. According to a list André Guichaoua submitted, the vast majority of the 178 people evacuated from the French embassy were members of Habyarimana's regime or Hutu extremist network. Ambassador Marlaud later protested about this but only managed to name two other opposition politicians who sought refuge at the embassy – Pascal Ndengejeho and Alphonse Nkubito.

While ministers of the newly-formed interim government smiled, compared notes on which 'enemies' had been killed and enjoyed traditional French hospitality at the embassy, the story was less rosy for others who were holed up in French property trying to stay alive. Vénuste Kayimahe, a 45-year-old Tutsi, had been a faithful and diligent employee at the French Cultural Centre for a number of years, where he worked as the projectionist and exhibition organizer.[21]

'It was a very big centre, Mitterrand himself visited twice', said Vénuste, 'as well as [former president] Giscard [d'Estaing]. Before the start of the war in 1990, everything went well there and we all got on with each other.' Once the war came things changed for Vénuste. All Tutsis were suspected of being RPF sympathizers and he found himself in constant arguments at work with his French and Rwandan Hutu colleagues and bosses.

When I heard about [Habyarimana's] plane crash on RTLM radio, my first feeling was that things were going to change very badly. I thought the genocide of before [1960s and 1970s] would happen. During that night [6/7 April] I heard gunfire near the centre so I stayed there with my wife, two of our children and a niece. During the following day many journalists telephoned the centre to talk about what was happening but the ambassador was not around and I ended up talking to them instead. All the French staff stayed away on the 7th.

I phoned my French manager, Madame Anne Cros and asked her to send soldiers to take me to where my other children were. She said that it was a period of great insecurity and I would have to try by myself. When I rang Monsieur Cuingnet [head of the civil and cooperation mission], he told me he would send soldiers to get us out. When they arrived they just laughed when I asked them to take us to safety. They told me, 'our mission is not to protect you but the building'. We tried to find a place to hide in the theatre. The French soldiers now occupied the library and conference hall, and they had weapons, including rocket launchers, set up about the place. I helped to cook for them, and shared the food but when I asked again if they would help accompany me to find my other children they refused. It was 'not their mission'.

When the French soldiers came to go they looted all they could, including telecommunication equipment, monitors, even televisions. As I tried to get onto the truck with a friend we were pushed off. The soldiers warned us not to follow them. Later that afternoon Belgian soldiers arrived at the centre led by a French captain, who showed the soldiers where to set up guns. Then he left. The Belgian soldiers, led by a Colonel, promised not to leave us there. Their mission I heard afterwards was to collect the Belgian foreigners to take to the airport. They took us to a French primary school, then on to the airport in the Belgian convoy, with UN and Belgian soldiers accompanying us.

I think the French were criminals. They abandoned me to my enemies. I begged them to bring my children to me here or to a safe place.

A key allegation Vénuste made concerned French troops rearming the *Interahamwe*. 'At one point the *Interahamwe* asked the French soldiers for more grenades. They said, "we have finished our food [grenades] will you give us some more?" And they did.' This was perhaps not surprising given the huge airlifts of munitions from Paris to Rwanda over the past three years, but to restock the very killers who were currently roaming the streets murdering at will was appalling. Such behaviour goes beyond the genuinely friendly relations the two sets of armed troops showed to one another and that Vénuste also witnessed.

At the roadblocks there were friendly greetings exchanged in French between the *Interahamwe* and the French troops – "how are you" and "how's it going?" A young Russian woman who managed to get airlifted to Nairobi told me the French trucks just went over the bodies of those massacred and made no effort to go round them. Only two young French soldiers seemed to be affected by what was happening. They told me they were frightened by the massacres going on.

Vénuste, a kindly, intelligent, well-spoken man, had worked for the French for 20 years. His reward was to be abandoned, along with his family, to the militia and their machetes. He suspected this was purely because of his ethnic background.

Charles, another Tutsi worker at the cultural centre, lived several hundred metres from his work. On the morning of 7 April he rang his French employers several times pleading for help. After watching from his window as women and children were shot and hacked to death at nearby roadblocks he was in no doubt that the same fate awaited him if he stayed. His employers told him to 'make do'.

At the entrance to the apartment block, fifty of his neighbours were lying in a pool of blood. He managed to make it to the cultural centre, only to be told by French paratroopers on the morning of the 12th that they were leaving 'because we've got all the French people out'.

Charles and the other Rwandan employees at the Centre were left to fend for themselves. The French paratroopers had gone as far as to smash a hole in the false ceiling of the library, in which they told the Rwandans that they could hide. Outside, on the streets of Kigali, there were militia roadblocks every 200 metres: hundreds of drunk, drugged, screaming Hutu gang members were slaughtering every Tutsi they could find, and any Hutu suspected of sympathizing with them.[22]

Like Vénuste, Charles was rescued by Belgian troops, who came to use the centre as a base for their own evacuation. Crouching under tarpaulins in the back of trucks, he was smuggled out to the airport.

Ambassador Marlaud's defence was that he had never been asked at any time about what to do with employees at the embassy and cultural centre, so no decision was made on the matter.[23] Cuingnet, who told

Vénuste at the time that he had no power to intervene to save him by evacuation, declared that 'we were not put in charge of saving the Rwandans'.

On 11 April a telegram arrived from Paris confirming that Rwandan nationals who were recruited locally and were part of the embassy staff should be evacuated. Yet, despite this order, Pierre Nsanzimana was the only Tutsi employee to be evacuated with his family; all the others were abandoned, which suggests that the French staff and members of Operation Amaryllis discriminated against them.

The later 1998 French National Assembly inquiry into the matter concluded that 'the treatment given to the family of Habyarimana was far more favourable than that given to the Tutsi employees at the French representative offices, the embassy, the cultural centre and the Cooperation Mission.'[24] Despite this admission, the inquiry stopped short of asking why a bias was so apparent, and why French soldiers and diplomats ignored the pleas of their longstanding Tutsi work force. Were the French soldiers and staff 'too rushed' or concerned about lack of space in the lorries and planes? Or did it betray a lack of sympathy and even racism towards the Tutsi?

Some of the more gung-ho French soldiers' attitude certainly betrayed a bias towards their former comrades in the Rwandan government. Colonel Jean Balch, while recognizing the danger that justified the evacuation of foreign nationals, declared that closing the embassy was 'a little hasty'. He stated that the RPF was not necessarily going to win at that moment and that the FAR were resisting well the attack of the *Inkotanyi* (RPF).[25] Balch felt it would take only a few more French military advisers to reverse the situation, so that 'June 1992 and February 1993 could be "replayed" exactly again in April 1994. In effect, instead of running, the French should do as before – and repel the RPF.'[26]

Ambassador Marlaud had one last important job to do before locking up the embassy and heading for home – to shred and burn all documents and paperwork gathered over the previous decades. Those entering the embassy afterwards spoke of two rooms filled with destroyed evidence of the French role in the Habyarimana regime. Some of the last footage of the operation showed three concerned French soldiers carefully placing Marlaud's dog in the evacuees' plane. It was obviously not a canine of Tutsi origin.

As the new interim government was being formed in the French embassy, Amaryllis commander Colonel Poncet sent troops to a local orphanage to rescue the children and their helpers. St Agathe's orphanage, which the president's wife founded for the children of FAR soldiers killed in the war had, according to the French pressure group Survie, been subject to some important 'personnel' changes before 6 April. Hutu militants and members of the president's entourage had been put into the orphanage as 'helpers' and were now ready to be evacuated as 'staff members'.[27]

The orphanage driver was alleged to have helped in the ethnic 'whittling down' of the children's original carers. The day after the plane crash all female helpers had been gathered in the orphanage common room. Militiamen entered and the driver went from one carer to another pointing out who was Hutu and who was Tutsi. The Tutsi women were then taken outside and killed – in one case a woman called Alice suffered a horrifically slow death after she was deemed not to deserve a quick end.[28] Seven Tutsi helpers at the orphanage were murdered. They were quickly replaced by 'killers' who now wanted to head into a luxury exile in France and the West.

Five days later the French troops arrived; 94 children were evacuated, plus 34 adults, now mostly men betraying a very high 'care to child' ratio. When the refugees arrived in France on 12 April the male 'carers' disappeared. It is difficult to believe that the French did not know who these men were, given the thorough checks that took place before anyone was allowed to embark and that the men did not seem to know the children. The French military's response was that they were told that some of the children were to be adopted in France, but they did not have time to sort out which children this applied to and which were staying. Given that every place on the plane was at a premium, it is surprising that more checks were not made on carers and children and that the orphanage 'staff' were allowed to disappear on landing in France. According to pressure group Survie, the only possible reason such children were evacuated was as a front to save the adults – whom it alleged were heavily implicated in the genocide.

By contrast, the attempt to evacuate the children of Prime Minister Agathe Uwilingiyimana, who had been murdered at the very beginning of the genocide, raised other concerns about French impartiality. The children had hidden after their mother was killed and, despite militia and presidential guard efforts to find them, they were rescued by UNAMIR Captain Mbaye Diagne and taken to the Hotel Mille Collines. The problem then was to get them out of the country. On trying to board a French plane at the airport they were denied political asylum and told to go away. It was left to French Africanist André Guichaoua to hide the terrified and emotionally traumatized children and smuggle them on board a plane after distracting French officers overseeing the evacuation.

Tutsis throughout Kigali fled to places where they felt they could gain safety and protection; the Amahoro stadium on the outskirts of Kigali, which UNAMIR soldiers guarded, was one such refuge. Many thousands were stopped on the way and peremptorily slaughtered. Another 2500 refugees, including 400 children, fled to the École technique officielle (ETO), a technical school run by Catholic Salesian priests a few kilometres southeast of Kigali and considered safe because a detachment of Belgian UNAMIR troops was billeted there. While most of those who fled were Tutsis, a few opposition politicians or critics of the government also came. They were confident that UNAMIR, given its peacekeeping mandate, would protect them.

The ETO consisted of a number of buildings surrounded by a fence. Under Captain Luc Lemaire, the UNAMIR force of 90 had pitched camp in its grounds. But the foreign soldiers were as anxious and afraid as those who had come to be protected by them. After the murder of ten Belgium UNAMIR troops on 7 April they realized that they were possible targets for the militia, which surrounded the ETO the following day.

The position of the Rwandans inside the ETO's fences was far worse. Many were refused entry to the actual buildings by the Belgian peace-keepers and had to camp outside. The situation became more desperate after 8 April when the Belgium government decided to evacuate its nationals. On 11 April, a French contingent from Operation Amaryllis arrived at the ETO to prepare the expatriates to leave. A priest noted that the French came because their relations with local people were good while the Belgians were afraid of local hostility, but the French troops, in red berets and with tricolours emblazoned on their vehicles, caused the Tutsi refugees much anxiety. Some felt they had come to replace their Belgian UN counterparts. Others felt that they were there merely to evacuate foreign nationals. Many feared they were in league with the genocidaire.[29] The troops from Amaryllis were certainly able to go to and from the site without any objection from the surrounding *Interahamwe* who were baying for blood.

The French troops brought expatriates from the nearby area to the ETO site ready to evacuate them *en masse*. However, no one told the frantic Tutsi refugees inside the ETO that they were to be left to a certain, horrific death. Slowly the truth of what was happening dawned on the watching masses.

Yves, a survivor of the massacre, related:

> We saw the French soldiers come back at about 12.00 or 1.00 p.m., in about five jeeps and three Hitachi minibuses. It was clear that something was going to happen ... the French and UNAMIR soldiers began piling these [white] people into the lorries. When they had finished they came and told us to go and eat. We refused, because we had just realized it was a trick to distract us, so that they could get away quickly without our knowledge.[30]

Except for some Rwandan clergy and nuns, those evacuated were white.

> It was difficult to ascertain what the criteria for inclusion might have been. For instance Boniface Ngulinzira, who was an immediate target of the extremists, had been under UNAMIR guard since before the 7th [April]. He was brought with his family to ETO by the peacekeepers, but they offered him no further protection. He was not taken, although he asked the French troops to evacuate him, and was killed in the massacre later that day.[31]

The journey for those few who did manage to get on one of the trucks in the French convoy was still filled with danger. Emmanuel and his wife, both Rwandans working for UNDP, eventually managed to convince a UNAMIR officer that they should be evacuated. 'ETO was occupied by Belgian soldiers,' Emmanuel wrote later,

> but we were evacuated by the French. The streets of Kicukiro [in Kigali] were already littered with corpses as we left. As we drove past, cries of '*vive la France!*' rang out from the crowds lining the

roads. We'd been divided into two convoys. The first convoy went via Rubirizi to the airport. The second, our convoy, went to the French *lycée*. When we got there the soldiers, probably French, wouldn't let us in. We stayed outside under the amused gaze of the soldier guarding the entrance. Not far from there, at the entrance to the Kigali sports centre, there was an *Interahamwe* roadblock. They came to threaten us, saying they were going to kill us in the night.

In the evening at around 6.00 p.m., the soldier guarding the entrance came up and told us to 'clear off'. I answered, 'I'd rather be shot than killed with a machete.' He burst out laughing and left. It was as if they were mocking us.

Emmanuel and 12 other terrified refugees spent the night in hiding; the next day, as ten more lorries of evacuees arrived, they took advantage of the confusion to slip into the *lycée*. They were later evacuated.[32]

The French military returned to the ETO around 1.00 p.m. and the Belgians seized their chance of a 'safe' escort provided by the red berets to pull out of the area. The *Interahamwe* waiting nearby began shouting and blowing their whistles once news of UNAMIR's withdrawal came through. They knew their killing spree was only minutes away. In a desperate bid to keep the Belgian force and their French compatriots at the ETO, many Rwandan refugees threw themselves onto the road in front of vehicles or tried to clamber on board. The soldiers hit them to make them move and fired into the air, terrifying the already traumatized crowd.

One survivor of the later massacre told African Rights investigators, 'There was already a group of *Interahamwe* beside another exit dancing, shouting and beating drums while UNAMIR soldiers [and their French escort] were going through the main gate. They were delivering us into the hands of the *Interahamwe* who intended to massacre us.'[33]

Those who had fled to the ETO were, even at the last moment, unprepared for the sudden withdrawal. None had a chance to flee, for *Interahamwe* invaded the buildings even before the dust from the European convoy's vehicles had settled. Militiamen armed with machetes, clubs, spears, grenades and guns attacked the helpless crowd of Tutsis. The killers taunted their victims with jibes such as 'Where's your UNAMIR? They've abandoned you, haven't they?'

Thousands were hacked to death in the resulting carnage. The French and Belgian UNAMIR force could have escorted the refugees to the Amahoro stadium where UNAMIR peacekeepers were still in place protecting those who had fled there; or, given that the Belgian force had been ordered to withdraw from UNAMIR, other peacekeepers like a Ghanaian or Bangladeshi contingent could have taken their place guarding the ETO. At the very least, those fleeing should have been warned so that they could try to escape before the *Interahamwe* sealed all the routes around the area.

The French force held the key to this situation. Clearly popular with the Hutu militants who cheered them as they went about their evacuation, the French also had vital lines of communication with members of the new interim regime and military figures like Bagosora. If they had explicitly stated, given what they saw when reaching ETO, that the refugees were not to be harmed, it is difficult to believe that such would not have been the case. That no account seems to have been taken of the consequences of the withdrawal is incredible.

Belgian priest Father Louis Peeters condemned UNAMIR's withdrawal as full of 'ridiculous excuses', arguing that Dallaire should have taken stronger action. 'The soldiers were well aware that they were going to leave. The French and Belgian soldiers could have done something. The French were quite influential in Rwandese politics. As they were there during the evacuation, they could easily have escorted the refugees to the Amahoro stadium. Unfortunately they did not.'[34]

Apparently no French commander radioed back to his headquarters about the situation at the ETO, asking for new orders to help save the refugees. More than 2000 died at this location.

According to Human Rights Watch:

> The French were in a position to save Tutsi and others at risk with relatively little difficulty, and yet they chose to save very few. French troops moved easily around the city, even when transporting Rwandans. Militias cheered them and gave them the thumbs up sign, while they greeted the Belgian soldiers with a gesture of cutting their throats. In some cases, Belgian soldiers even removed insignia that identified them as Belgians, and passed themselves off as French. In at least one case, French embassy personnel made no response to pleas for help from a

Tutsi employee and in another they refused assistance to a Hutu prosecutor [François-Xavier Nsanzuwera] well known for his opposition to Habyarimana. French soldiers on one occasion baulked at escorting some Rwandan clergy to a safe haven but in the end gave in to pressure from UNAMIR soldiers and did so.[35]

Investigators later asked an unnamed French government official whether pressure from Mitterrand's government had brought about changes in the policies of the genocidal interim regime. He replied, 'What pressure? There was no pressure.'[36]

The French authorities proved that they could influence and stop the *Interahamwe* killing when they intervened to save refugees at Hotel Mille Collines in Kigali in mid-May, a story given prominence by the Hollywood film *Hotel Rwanda*. The four-star hotel had become a place of sanctuary for more than 1000 terrified people after the genocide began, with bloodied militia surrounding the building anxious to 'finish off' the 'cockroaches' inside. These included Tutsi and notable Hutu moderates such as the aforementioned former attorney-general François-Xavier Nsanzuwera, who had previously initiated an investigation of Hutu Power murder squads. Hotel manager Paul Rusesabagina used desperate tactics to stave off the mob of *Interahamwe* who surrounded the place. Cellars of beer and wine were used to bribe the militia and army leaders not to attack the hotel, with FAR chief of staff Major General Augustin Bizimungu a regular 'guest' whose influence was bought in champagne and fine claret. Vitally, Rusesabagina had use of an outside phone line that the militia had failed to discover, and with this he spent long hours making increasingly desperate phone calls to any influential Western former guests and contacts he knew. He contacted the French foreign office and sent numerous faxes to President Clinton at the White House. One refugee, Thomas Kamilindi, gave an interview to a French radio station on 29 April in which he described the desperate state the traumatized hotel occupants were in, including having to drink water from the swimming pool after the *Interahamwe* cut off the hotel's water supply. The interview was broadcast in France the next day, but clearly made little impact on the government in Paris. Mitterrand was too busy laying out the red carpet for the visit of two prominent members of the interim regime to worry about such 'technicalities'.[37]

An abortive UNAMIR attempt on 3 May to escort 62 refugees from the hotel to Kigali airport ended in near fatal results for those trying to flee. Rusesabagina was informed 12 days later that all the refugees were going to be killed later that night. He immediately called the director-general of the foreign office in Paris, pleading for his help. 'Mister, if you want these people to be saved, they will be saved. But if you want them to die, they will die today, and you French people will pay in one way or another for the people who are killed in this hotel today.' The result of the call was almost immediate. Bizimungu came to the hotel to assure the frantic manager that those residing there would not be touched.[38] Libération journalist Alain Frilet was quick to point out the incongruity of the action by Mitterrand's government. 'Paris, of course, declared itself powerless in the face of the killings. But it's not contested that the head of the Élysée's African Cell, Bruno Delaye, succeeded ... in personally intervening with the head of state officer of the Rwandan armed forces to prevent the Hutu militiamen slaughtering the refugee personalities at hotel Mille Collines.'[39] A disgusted civil servant at the Quai d'Orsay commented that the 'prompt intervention ... showed to what extent Paris can still influence the unfolding events.'[40] Despite Rusesabagina's efforts, it was clear that 'the life-and-death decision lay, as always, with the killers, and, tellingly in this case, with their French patrons.'[41]

While such life and death situations became the daily norm in Rwanda, *Akazu* leader Agathe Habyarimana arrived in Paris to a warm welcome from Mitterrand's government with bouquets of flowers and a cheque from the Ministry of Cooperation for $40,000, money designated for 'urgent assistance for Rwandan refugees'.[42] She still had President Mitterrand on her side. Bernard Debré, former minister of cooperation, asserted that Mitterrand remained 'very attached to former President Habyarimana and his family, and to everything that was part of the old regime.'[43]

In an interview on Belgian television channel RTBF on 25 April, an emotional Agathe Habyarimana condemned the RPF, which she alleged had shot down the presidential plane. 'I am sure that the Good Lord will avenge our family,' she added.[44]

Chapter 6

Arming the Genocide

As the giant French C-160 transport planes curved away from Kigali airport carrying soldiers from Operation Amaryllis and a cargo of foreign businessmen, aid workers, ex-Habyarimana officials and *Akazu* members, the land underneath them was bathed in blood. The Rwandan genocide was fully under way. The carefully laid plans were being dutifully carried out. The day the *Interahamwe* militia had waited for had arrived; the West had literally 'flown away' leaving them free to carry out their terrible *umuganda*.[1]

The world's media, along with its politicians, had eyes at this time for only one African nation, South Africa, where the first post-apartheid elections were being held. On 10 May Nelson Mandela was sworn in as the new president, with his inauguration bringing together the largest number of heads of state since the funeral of US President John Kennedy in 1963. Politicians, journalists and businessmen swarmed to the hotels of Cape Town and Johannesburg, seeking vital alliances in the 'new' situation. Rwanda, a tiny, insignificant country with, it would seem, insignificant people, was by contrast the victim of appalling Western apathy.

Gitarama, a small, dusty, faceless town 45 kilometres from Kigali, was the first haven for the interim government set up after President Habyarimana's death. It was a government of murderers with a twofold objective: to repel the RPF advance now threatening Kigali, and to initiate and carry out the planned genocide to annihilate an entire ethnic group. An ageing and infirm Théodore Sindikubwabo was declared president and ambitious Jean Kambanda prime minister. The new ministers, appointed days earlier in the French embassy, now held meetings with local government officials to encourage, threaten or delight in the Tutsi genocide. Heading this group of killers and pulling the strings of the new government and militias was Colonel Théoneste Bagosora. The architect of the genocide was linked to the family of Agathe Habyarimana's but had ambitions of his own to take charge of Rwanda one day. Using his position at the ministry of defence, Bagosora, an intelligent and ruthless individual, who had already acquired the nickname 'the Colonel of Death' for his role in the killing of Tutsis,[2] had been able to monitor and set up networks for the 'final solution' during the two years prior to the genocide. He had returned from the Arusha talks in February 1993, where he had been supporting the extremist CDR party, proclaiming, 'I come back to declare the apocalypse'.[3] Now he was enacting it. These were the men the French government would spend the next three months legitimizing and supporting, politically and militarily.

The bright and busy corridors of the UN building in downtown New York were full of their usual complement of suited diplomats, fax machines and secret memorandums. While each day in April and May Security Council representatives picked up their coffee, croissant or breakfast bagel on the way to their office or debating chamber for another hard day of meetings, the lives of small children, pregnant women and terrified elderly Tutsis were being ended by laughing killers in Rwanda. The cynical disregard by Clinton's America and its client British government of John Major for the lives of these 'black Africans' in a country of no economic importance has been well charted. Unlike Iraq, where evidence for armed intervention was either dubious or non-existent, in Rwanda satellites were showing the mass killings and masses of dead bodies. Even the Vatican, without any such spy system, was able to call the nightmare 'genocide' three weeks after it started. This was no 'secret' slaughter. By the end of April around 200,000 people had already been killed in Rwanda.

Besides its client francophone states, France had several important allies on the Security Council, as well as the amiable diplomacy of the UN head, secretary-general, Boutros Boutros-Ghali. The former Egyptian minister was a known francophone who had worked closely with all parts of the French government and, indeed, owed the government in Paris a debt of thanks because its support had been vital in gaining his current position. Boutros-Ghali had trained as a lawyer at the Sorbonne in Paris and France presented him as a candidate of impressive intellectual and diplomatic credentials when elections for the new UN secretary-general came around in November 1991. A personal friend of François Mitterrand, he commented that the French president 'seemed to feel a personal victory in my election'[4] – not surprising given that the anglophone countries, including the USA and Britain, had supported a different candidate. Three years after the genocide, in November 1997, Boutros-Ghali, with French backing, was elected general secretary of the International Organization of the Francophonie.[5]

In a UN vote on 21 April France followed Boutros-Ghali's lead by backing Resolution 912 to reduce Dallaire's UNAMIR force by 90 per cent to a meagre 270 peacekeepers. This effectively weakened UNAMIR so much that it would be almost impossible for it to give even humanitarian help to victims or assist those who sought UN protect-tion. Other countries, including Russia and Britain, also voted for this option, but the difference was that France was deeply involved in Rwanda and knew the substance of events on the ground. It meant that the interim government and militia now had a free hand to continue the carnage knowing that no Western force would intervene. Bago-sora's apocalypse was safe to continue.

Prime Minister Balladur justified the French stance on the grounds that his country could not take an initiative to send troops to stop the massacres as this would look like a 'colonial operation', especially if they stopped the RPF advance. By contrast Operation Noroît, or the later Operation Turquoise, were, it seems, not deemed to have 'colonial' hallmarks.

The Rwandans' plight managed to attract some media attention in France in the spring of 1994, and with it the views of the political establishment. From the original intervention of Operation Noroît in October 1990 to the plane crash on 6 April 1994, the occasional article in the French press had led the public to believe that Paris was stand-ing by a country in distress. It was defending a fledgling democracy, pushing for a diplomatic solution, carrying out humanitarian work and protecting its own hard-working nationals. The genocide, with stories of the unfolding horror starting to appear in the press, especially in *Le Figaro*, *Libération* and *Le Nouvel Observateur*, shattered this cosy image with detailed evidence of the French government's complicity with the Hutu regime. The earlier French presence was now questioned; Rwanda finally came onto the French political and public agenda. By

12 June *Libération* was even suggesting that France had trained the militias that were carrying out the bulk of the killings.

On 10 May Mitterrand went before the television cameras to defend his policy, stating that French soldiers could not intervene in every war, or be 'international referees' in the rivalries that split so many countries. Given his constant military interventions throughout franco-phone Africa during the previous decade, his words sounded particularly hollow.

The government's defensiveness was well illustrated by an interview former minister for cooperation Michel Roussin gave to French radio on 30 May. When pressed about Operation Amaryllis leaving staff at the French embassy to be killed, and its relations towards the RPF, he lost his cool, shouting at the startled female interviewer, 'What are you interested in? What are you interested in, madame? Is it the fate of these people, horrific pictures of whom we see every day, or is it a political analysis which is no longer topical?' He then exploded at questions over French training of the FAR.

> No, first of all the figure is wrong, it is – the figure is totally wrong, and, and also [pauses] I do not. ... Even if it were seventy instructors, it is not these people who started [pauses] the slaughter we have been witnessing ... [pauses]. We have not, we have cooperation ... [pauses]. It was very limited because as soon as the Noroît operation was dismantled and UNAMIR took over from it we no longer had any role apart from traditional cooperation. Therefore I believe that again these are groundless accusations.[6]

Inside the UN, the 15-member Security Council, its decision-making body, continued to discuss the Rwandan crisis. But as ill luck would have it, one of the countries whose turn it was to be represented was Rwanda, in the form of Jean-Damascène Bizimana, its odious ambassador who represented the interim government. He used his position to make a series of highly inflammatory speeches maintaining that the killing was due to the civil war and that both sides were responsible. In a letter of 2 May to the president of the Security Council, Bizimana alleged that since 6 April 'several tens of thousands of people have been killed by the Rwandan Patriotic Front (RPF)', and they were carrying out 'large-scale massacres'. He demanded the UN put a force into Rwanda to cause an immediate ceasefire.[7] This constant confusion between the RPF and FAR fight for control of the country and who was carrying out the genocide was carried over into the media. Papers like the *New York Times* and *The Times* (London) failed to differentiate, with reports of wide-scale ethnic massacres and war, and a failure to analyse those organizing and implementing the genocide.

Publicly, French foreign minister Alain Juppé was giving out the same message as Bizimana. 'Since the international community cannot and is not willing to interfere physically in the country [Rwanda] … the only remedy is democracy. The African countries are committed to get more deeply involved in resolving this country's conflict.' Thus, the French were making 'all possible efforts' to make this happen. Juppé, like the Rwandan interim government, constantly referred to the need for a 'ceasefire' and a return to the Arusha accords to stop the killing, so further increasing the diplomatic smokescreen.

On 28 April, Juppé told the National Assembly in Paris that the large-scale massacres were part of a vicious 'tribal war', with abuses by both sides.[8] Later that summer Bruno Delaye told a human rights group that, though the Hutu had committed terrible crimes, it was because they were frightened for their lives. 'It was regrettable but that was the way Africans were.' It was more than a little akin to Mitterrand's comment to an aide in spring 1995 that '*dans ces pays-là, un génocide, ce n'est pas trop important*' (in countries like that genocide doesn't really matter),[9] revealing an inherent racism at the heart of the Élysée. Human Rights Watch noted that 'France continued its campaign to minimize the responsibility of the Interim government for the slaughter.'[10]

The interim government wanted UNAMIR to stay, for it recognized early on that without it the militarily superior RPF would be unhindered in pushing for absolute victory. France, backed by its UN francophone votes, made sure pressure was increased behind the scenes to keep the UN vacillating. Czech ambassador to the UN Karel Kovanda summed up the French diplomacy on Rwanda at the UN as being about making any number of aspersions about this or that faction, with the aim of creating sufficient confusion to stop action being taken. Kovanda described how the francophone Djibouti ambassador had never spoken a word in French in the two years the Czech diplomat knew him at the UN. 'Then suddenly he comes out with a whole speech in fluent French when the Rwandan debate begins.' The fact was that France was pressing its 'client' francophone African states in the UN to back its pro-Hutu policy in Rwanda. With the backing of francophone nations such as Oman and Djibouti, together with Rwanda, France made no attempt, despite its inside knowledge of events, to clarify the need for immediate action to stop the genocide. It received backing in this political stance from the USA, which wanted no action for a different set of cynical reasons. Clinton was afraid the spectre of body bags returning from Rwanda would badly affect his poll ratings. The 'black hawks down' fiasco the previous year in Somalia had been highly criticized from all sides in the USA. For both Mitterrand and Clinton the 'do nothing' solution as a short-term answer to the unfolding genocide suited their individual political aims.

Mitterrand reaffirmed his support for the genocidal interim government at the end of April when two of its most extreme representatives were given an official welcome on a state visit to Paris. Foreign Minister Bicamumpaka and Hutu militant leader Jean-Bosco Barayagwiza had the traditional red carpet treatment when they met Bruno Delaye at the Élysée Palace on 27 April. Mitterrand himself was away in Turkmenistan.[11] Foreign secretary Alain Juppé then received them at the Quai d'Orsay and they later had talks at the cooperation ministry.

While they were wined and dined in Parisian splendour, in Rwanda Claudine Kayitesi, a young Tutsi girl was hiding in the Kinkwi forest. 'On the 30th April they [*Interahamwe*] attacked from all sides ... they had a vast programme of killing that would go on all day without a midday break. That evening, there were thousands of corpses and dying people, in the bottom of the ponds, all over the place.'[12] That same evening, Mitterrand's guests Barayagwiza and Bicamumpaka were rather more agreeably entertained at an official banquet in Paris.

The symbolism of these genocidaires' official visit to France was vital because to the interim government it meant recognition by a permanent member of the Security Council. To the French people, it looked as if the new Rwandan government was indeed composed of 'good guys'. Certainly, interim president Sindikubwabo was delighted at such a positive show of support from the French government and military. He called up French chief of staff General Quesnot on 4 May, leaving a message 'to thank [Mitterrand] for all that you have done for

Rwanda' and for the advice given by Paris to his government representatives on their recent visit.[13]

When asked about the wisdom of giving an official political reception
to two exponents of genocide in Paris, Delaye replied that he must have
'received 400 assassins and 2000 drug traffickers in his office. You
cannot deal with Africa without getting your hands dirty'.[14] The same,
many Africans might reasonably respond, could be said of dealing with
the Mitterrand government.

The French intimated the importance of keeping diplomatic channels
open with both sides in the conflict. Mitterrand, avoiding references to
the previous French support for the FAR, spoke on 15 May about the
need to facilitate dialogue between the two parties, the need for 'international leadership' through 'big diplomatic efforts'. He reiterated the
need for 'humanitarian' help, voting 200,000 francs for this purpose.
Mitterrand also sought to involve other African countries in resolving
the Rwandan 'conflict', chief among them Mobutu's Zaire. Behind the
scenes, Paris supported the Zairian dictator in scuppering a regional
summit on Rwanda that had been scheduled for 'anglophone' Tanzania
at the end of April. On 9 May, Bruno Delaye – Mitterrand's African
counsellor – reiterated this stance, saying, 'We won't have any of these
meetings in Tanzania. The next one has to be in Kinshasa [in Zaire].
We cannot let anglophone countries decide on the future of a Francophone one. In any case, we want Mobutu back in, he cannot be
dispensed with and we are going to do it through this Rwanda
business.'[15]

A confidential newsletter, reputed to be from French government
circles, showed the cynical disregard with which some, at least, of the
French military and political establishment viewed the ongoing genocide. Entitled 'considerable political and geostrategic interests are
hidden behind the Rwandese heap of corpses', it argued that the
francophone country held a key to the region, and could not be 'lost' to
anglophone influences. These included Museveni's Uganda, with the
spectre of the 'Great Satan' itself, the United States, in the background.
The article finished by taking an uncompromising stance.

The region cannot be left in the hand of an English-speaking
strongman completely aligned to American views and interests.
This is why, since 1990, France has supported the late President

Juvénal Habyarimana in order to fight the RPF. It did not work out, so now the only choice left to us is to put back in the saddle the Zairian President Mobutu Sese Seko, the one man capable of standing up to Museveni.[16]

French aid workers who had flown back home with Operation Amaryllis had tried to put pressure on their government to intervene to stop the genocide. Jean-Hervé Bradol, from MSF (Médecins Sans Frontières went to the Africa Cell at the Élysée to plead for action.

We went there to ask them to intervene, and because they have a strong link with the militaries in Rwanda, we guessed they could have an influence and stop the killings. The first answer that we got was that they had difficulties in reaching the Rwandese by phone. When they told me that it was impossible for them to reach the Rwandese by phone I was completely depressed because I realized that they were not ready, they did not have the will to stop the killings.[17]

The French were aware that a ceasefire was highly unlikely, but continued to push for it. With the RPF slowly but surely pressing back the interim government's forces, a ceasefire became the only way Bagosora and his henchmen could hold onto power. Yet to expect the RPF leadership to sit down calmly and discuss ministerial portfolios with members of an interim government that had massacred up to half a million people by the end of May was quite fantastical. The Czech ambassador at the UN, Karel Kovanda, found the whole concept of a ceasefire ridiculous. 'It is rather like wanting Hitler to reach a ceasefire with the Jews,' he exclaimed. General Quesnot wrote privately to Mitterrand to say that any ceasefire was highly unlikely: 'the process is from now on irreversible, Paul Kagame wants a total military victory.'[18]

On 15 May France was the first country to call the actions in Rwanda genocide, but deliberately confused the reality of the carnage by calling on both the *Interahamwe* and the RPF to end the terror and killings. Mitterrand later repeated this 'double genocide' fallacy. However, until the beginning of July, France continued to recognize the government that was carrying out the 'genocide' it had now named. It was akin to witnessing the work of the extermination camps while giving recognition to the Nazi government whose policy it was to use them. Equally, France made no public declaration calling for the interim government to halt the organized killing, though it was clear by May that the slaughter was happening in the area controlled by the interim government and not by the RPF.

In New York, France continued to back the interim government spokesman when discussion took place on the need for an immediate embargo of arms being sent to Rwanda. Mel McNulty, an analyst on the Franco–Rwandan situation commented:

> At the UN Security Council on 17th May, France [in the person of its permanent representative Jean-Bernard Mérimée] made common cause with the ambassador of the Rwandese Interim government, who was trying to oppose the voting of an embargo on arms destined for Rwanda – on the pretext that this embargo would only penalize 'government' forces. France was opposed to it because the flow of arms deliveries was continuing, with the support of most of the [French] military personnel, who were hostile to the embargo.[19]

France eventually voted in favour of the embargo, mindful of the public outcry if it had stood against it, with the lone vote against it coming from the Rwandan ambassador. In reality, the embargo was for public consumption only because the arms deals were to continue, but in secret.

On the same agenda and day the UN voted through Resolution 918, which agreed to send a new 5500-strong force, UNAMIR II, to Rwanda acting under a newly-defined mandate that allowed it to take action against persons or groups that threatened protected sites and populations. During the debate the Security Council members had to listen to a speech by Rwandan foreign minister Jérôme Bicamumpaka in which he detailed alleged RPF atrocities, including the allegation that they tore out and ate the hearts of their Hutu enemies. It was, by all accounts, an extraordinary performance, made worse by the grim silence with which it remained unchallenged by its listeners. As the UN representatives sat back in exhaustion after an eight-hour debate to wring out this new resolution and mandate, it became clear that without money and resources being volunteered, the new force, UNAMIR

II, would not see Rwanda or help its Tutsi victims for months to come. Like the embargo, it gave a public impression of action, though the reality was of no consequence to traumatized Tutsi still hiding out in the marshes and swamps away from their *Interahamwe* killers.

Dallaire, the UNAMIR commander in Kigali, had to face the effects of the world-power political manoeuvring. Stuck in the Rwandan capital with a decimated peacekeeping force, after repeated denials of assistance, he came to the conclusion that

> self-interest dominated. I mean casualties overruled. I had one person come into my headquarters during the genocide asking for statistics on how many people were killed last week, and how many yesterday, and how many do you expect to be killed today, and how many weeks of this killing you think is going to go on. And my staff officers brought him to me and I said, 'Why these statistics?' He said, 'Oh, you know my country is assessing whether it will come in and the government believes that the people, the public opinion, could handle for every soldier killed or injured an equivalent of 85,000 dead Rwandans.'[20]

At the end of May Dallaire heard reports of a speech by the French minister for human rights, Lucette Michaux-Chevry, to a special UN commission of diplomats at a meeting in Geneva. 'As requested by France, the Security Council has significantly expanded UNAMIR [Resolution 918 on 17 May]. Without delay France had provided exceptional assistance to the victims of the conflict.' Dallaire commented wryly, 'Yes, I thought, to the French expatriates who wanted to flee and to members of the Habyarimana family. She patted her nation on the back shamelessly.'[21]

Two days after the vote at the UN, on 19 May, the French magazine *Le Nouvel Observateur* published a four-page report entitled 'Rwanda, journey to extreme horror'. It subtitled the piece, 'the tragedy that has transformed Rwanda into a battlefield, the towns and roads into burial sites, is not an ethnic war between hostile tribes but an organized and systematic extermination of those who opposed a government armed and supported by France.'[22] At least someone in France knew the truth.

While Juppé and Delaye defended the French response to Rwanda politically, the French military was far more proactive. For many of its senior figures the spotlight was on stopping the RPF victory rather than the genocide. Most influential of all were Generals Huchon and Quesnot. The latter, with his daily briefing session with Mitterrand at the Élysée, was able to push his own anti-RPF agenda. Huchon, as head of the Military Cooperation Mission, had the power to put such theories into action. It was, as Franco-Rwandan expert Mehdi Ba asserts: 'like Huchon was an arm and Quesnot the brain' behind French policy in Rwanda.[23] In the three years preceding the genocide only two people were prepared to stand up and offer an alternative view to Huchon's pro-Hutu bias. One, it was thought was 'somebody in Tanzania – maybe the young chargé d'affaires who sat through the Arusha process, with the other at the Ministry of Cooperation'.[24]

From April to July Huchon welcomed visits from Lieutenant-Colonel Cyprien Kayumba, director of financial services in the Rwandan ministry of defence, who was shuttling between Rwanda, Paris, Kinshasa, Nairobi, Cairo, Tunis and Tripoli. The interim government's representative was on a tour of francophone dictators and arms dealers. The object of his 27-day stay in Paris was to gain funding for urgent arms deliveries to the interim government. He noted, 'it is necessary without delay to provide total proof proving the legitimacy of the war that Rwanda [the FAR] is involved in, in order to regain international opinion in our favour and to be able to gain bilateral cooperation. In the meantime, the [French] Military [Assistance] Mission of Cooperation is preparing to make emergency actions in our favour.'

On Monday 9 May Lieutenant-Colonel Ephrem Rwabalinda, adviser to the Rwandan chief of staff, arrived for a secret meeting with General Huchon at the MAM. His four-day stay until 13 May was designed to bring pressure on the Rwandan army's French 'allies' to acquire vital combat equipment. In a two-hour meeting, Rwabalinda 'spelled out the FAR's urgent needs: munitions for the 105 mm artillery battery (at least 2000 rounds); completion of the munitions for individual weapons, if necessary by passing indirectly via neighbouring countries friendly to Rwanda; clothing; transmission equipment'.[25] According to a report of the meeting later recovered by Belgian journalist Colette Braeckman, Huchon realized that the French army was 'tied hands and feet' by public opinion. The order of the day was secrecy, with open arming of the FAR as in 1990–93 now clearly not possible. However, the MAM gave the go-ahead for a 'secure telecommunications system to allow

General Huchon and General Bizimungu of the FAR to communicate without being overheard.'

Some 17 radio sets were shipped from Ostende to the FAR. These were capable of communicating on seven different channels in secure mode, thus allowing Huchon to speak to General Augustin Bizimungu and other Rwandan military and political leaders without fear of their private conversations being overheard. It also allowed French secret service agents to remain in constant touch about what was happening in Rwanda and to plan their own actions. Huchon is said to have promised that the 'urgent needs' Rwabalinda described would be evaluated in a 'detailed and concrete' way once the secret telephone contact was established between him and Bizimungu.[26]

Huchon also told Rwabalinda that an airfield was needed at which to land aid in 'complete security', with all spies driven out of the area first.[27] Such a strip was available at Kamembe, near Cyangugu in the southwest corner of Rwanda. Huchon promised that the French military was 'preparing measures to save us' [interim government and its armed forces].

According to Human Rights Watch 'Rwabalinda reported that Huchon returned several times to this point – that the "French government would not put up with accusations of helping a government condemned by international opinion if that government did not do what was necessary to defend itself. The media war is urgent and all subsequent operations depend on it".[28] The inference was, according to Human Rights Watch, that 'Huchon and his aides were more concerned about the public perception of the killing than about the killing itself. The condition for important renewed French assistance was not to end the genocide, but to make it more presentable to the international press.'[29]

Human Rights Watch asked for a meeting with Huchon to discuss a letter it uncovered in which Rwabalinda described his meetings with the French general. Unsurprisingly, Huchon was unwilling to discuss this evidence. The details in the letter are corroborated by a Rwandan military source.[30]

Rwabalinda's meetings with Huchon showed how desperate the interim government was to get its major backer onside and fully involved. Without French help, the RPF was set to defeat the FAR within weeks. The Rwandan officer pleaded with Huchon to let French troops intervene and to put pressure on the international community to stop the RPF offensive. While he mooted the use of 'indirect' military assistance (mercenaries) Huchon 'urged the creation of a zone under secure FAR control, where deliveries could take place safely'.[31] Ephrem Rwabalinda was shot dead in a Zairian refugee camp in 1995 – an act, according to investigative researcher Jean-Paul Gouteux, that bore all the hallmarks of the French secret services eliminating a witness to this murky affair.[32]

Neither the French media, parliament nor the later National Assembly inquiry ever looked into the secret meetings between the Rwandan and French military representatives in Paris or the encoded radio sets 'given' to the FAR. General Huchon's diary, payment details and other factual identification could have been used to testify to the validity of the report Braeckman made public. Instead, the French military and political establishment's official 'silence' on this matter speaks volumes about the truth of the allegations.

On 30 April Boutros-Ghali condemned the ongoing slaughter in Rwanda and appealed for states to stop arming the protagonists. 'The Security Council warns that the situation in Rwanda would be further seriously aggravated if either of the parties were to have access to additional arms. It appeals to all states to refrain from providing arms or any military assistance to the parties to the conflict.'[33]

Two weeks later the appeal was reiterated as part of Resolution 918. Paragraph 13 declared that 'all States shall prevent the sale or supply to Rwanda by their nationals or from their territories or using their flag vessels or aircraft of arms and related *material* [sic] of all types, including weapons and ammunition, military vehicles and equipment, paramilitary police equipment and spare parts.'[34] It called on all states to give information on how the embargo could effectively be implemented, give information on any violations and recommend 'appropriate measures in response to violations'. However, a number of very credible witnesses point to France, officially and unofficially, continuing its arms deliveries to the Rwandan military throughout the period of the genocide.

Two days after Habyarimana's death, a UN Senegalese military observer reported to his Belgian commander Colonel Luc Marchal, that he had seen arms being unloaded from two French planes at Kigali airport. The French flights had arrived two hours earlier than expected.

Marchal later told a journalist that the armaments were not for Operation Amaryllis but for the Rwandan army. 'They [the ammunition] just remained a few minutes at the airfield and immediately after, they were loaded in a vehicle and they were moved to the Kanombe camp' where the government troops were based.[35]

The commander of the French operation rubbished this account and said his troops had requisitioned Rwandan army trucks to take the cargo away, and that anyway it was not mortar ammunition. This raises two further points: the ease with which the French were able to liaise with the FAR on the ground and the question of whether it was ammunition for different weapons, if not mortars.[36]

The interim government made contact with international arms dealers and shippers, and used its French army connections to obtain supplies that bypassed arms-control regulations and the UN embargo. A host of dealers in various countries assisted the deliveries, including the UK, South Africa, Albania, Belgium, Bulgaria, Egypt, Israel, the Seychelles and Zaire. None of those responsible has been convicted of the crime of 'assisting genocide'.

From mid-May onwards, arms supplies were delivered via Goma in Zaire, just across the Rwandan border. Journalists, the United Nations International Commission of Inquiry (UNICOI) set up in 1995, and human rights organizations pieced together the trail from the 'unofficial' arms dealers to the banks that financed the deliveries. This complex path involved several governments, though each in turn denied any official participation.

Two 40-ton arms deliveries arrived on the nights of 15 and 18 June on Air Zaire flights to Goma from the Seychelles. The weapons were then transferred to the embattled FAR across the Rwandan border in the northern town of Gisenyi. They included anti-tank missiles, fragmentation grenades and ammunition. The trail for financing the deal was detailed and well hidden, and included payments to an arms dealer from the Banque Nationale de Paris on behalf of the Banque Nationale du Rwanda in Kigali.

It was alleged that the use of the Banque Nationale de Paris was an intrinsic part of the deal, and that it was no coincidence where it was based. According to an investigation by the French paper *Le Figaro*:

The inventory of the weapons bought from the Seychelles government closely resembled a list the exiled interim Minister of the Interior of the Rwandan government had sent to the French government in May 1994. Both Bagosora and Ehlers [the arms dealer] were well-connected in France. Bagosora had been the first Rwandan officer to be admitted to the French war academy in Paris. Ehlers, a former member of the South African navy, had received military training at French submarine bases in Toulon and Lorient in 1970 and 1972.[37]

The complex gunrunning operation continued throughout May and June, with the last delivery to the interim government made on 18 July. The choice of route for financing and shipping the arms, via Goma, suggests a need both for secrecy and for the perpetrators to 'cover their backs' now that the UN embargo had been enacted.

An investigation into the illicit arms dealing by British journalist Christian Jennings, aired as a documentary called 'The Gunrunners' in November 1994 concluded, 'Efforts to investigate … bank accounts and find out which private French security company was contracting aircraft to fly weapons into Zaire, was blocked.[38]

French state enterprise Sofremas (Société française d'exploitation de matériels et systèmes d'armement) was also heavily involved, despite coded denials. It acted as a go-between selling arms manufactured in France, South Africa, Israel and former eastern bloc countries to regimes willing to buy them. According to Human Rights Watch, based on correspondence recovered from the Rwandan ministry of defence, 'Sofremas wrote to Kayumba [chargé d'affaires at the Rwandan embassy in Paris] on 5th May at his Paris address stating they were prepared to ship $8 million worth of ammunition of South African manufacture as soon as they received a payment of 30 per cent of the price and necessary EUC/Zaire.'[39] The EUC (end user certificate) related to the country in which the arms would be used. By putting down Zaire, the real destination of Rwanda could be hidden and no awkward questions asked.[40]

On 5 May, the same day this deal was agreed, the French cabinet suspended all arms deals to Rwanda, confirming a provisional suspension in place since 8 April. The director of Sofremas, Germaine Guell, stated that the 5 May deal never took place or at least that the company made no further deliveries to Rwanda after the embargo of 17 May.

This carefully worded statement, like those of the [French] government ministers, did not exclude deliveries to Goma. In fact Guell explicitly conceded that 'it is possible and even probable that Mobutu's government agreed to have Goma serve as a conduit for material meant for Rwanda.' He admitted that his company had been asked to deliver arms this way ... but he declared they did not do so. ... He remarked, 'It would be a pretty unscrupulous government to deliver *matériel* to Zaire that it knew would end up in Rwanda.'[41]

Jennings's investigation was damning in its conclusion of French complicity in rearming the Hutu militants and militia.

These arms shipments were either going directly from a French parastatal [Sofremas] and being shipped by a French company [DLY Investments Ltd], or were being subcontracted by a series of French middlemen and front companies. All were going to a regime that had left such legacies as the mountain of corpses in the church at Ntarama. The FAR and the *Interahamwe* were being re-supplied.[42]

Franck Johannes, a journalist on the South African French language paper, *Journal du Dimanche*, said deliveries of weapons to Rwanda had been taking place 'every evening since mid-April' in unmarked Boeing 707s.

When questioned about these illegal arms deals the French government issued a number of denials, though many of them were in guarded and ambiguous language. Bernard Debré, for example, admitted that arms deliveries had continued for 'between five and eight days, perhaps ten days after the massacres started ... because we didn't immediately realize what was happening'. Yet, within two days, France had known enough to send in Operation Amaryllis and embark on a total evacuation of its nationals.

The French consul in Goma, Jean-Claude Urbano, justified five arms deliveries in May and June, which were taken across the Rwandan border to Gisenyi, by telling reporters from Human Rights Watch Arms Project that they were simply honouring contracts negotiated with the Rwandan government before the imposition of the embargo. French paper *Libération* noted on 4 June that 'all sources on the spot [in Goma] – including well-placed French ex-pats – have expressed their "certainty" that these arms deliveries were "paid for by France".'[43]

On 12 June the MSF president and director, Philippe Biberson and Brigitte Vasset, met foreign minister Alain Juppé.

> We asked him, 'people say there are deliveries of weapons to the Rwandan government or to the Interim government or to the government in flight – is it true that France continues to deliver weapons to Goma?' Juppé answered: 'Listen, all that is very confused, there were some agreements of cooperation or defence with the government, there were some hangovers maybe, but with regard to my services, I can tell you since the end of May there are certainly no deliveries of weapons to the Habyarimana regime.' While he was saying this he looked at the other side of the [river] Seine, towards the Élysée [Palace]. 'But what happens over there, I don't know anything about it.' The implication that the Élysée was countenancing continued arms deliveries was far from subtle.

The two aid workers concluded that 'it was pathetic'.[44]

Meanwhile, foreign secretary Juppé, while not beneath pointing the blame for the arms deliveries at his political rival François Mitterrand, was making sure that his reputation stayed clean. An unnamed defence attaché at a French embassy in the region denied that there had been official deliveries of arms from Paris, but added, 'an under-the-counter assistance, by parallel circuits, is always possible. You know, I could tell you a story or two about shady arms traffic deals in Paris.'[45] While the arms deliveries were a political matter in the West, in Rwanda they meant more misery, suffering and death.

At Michel Roussin's office in the Ministry of Cooperation, former secret service man Philippe Jehanne confided that on 19 May, two days after the embargo began, we were 'busy delivering ammunition to the FAR through Goma. But of course I will deny it if you quote me in the press.'[46] On 22 May, President Sindikubwabo wrote to Mitterrand to plead for more help, with the situation in Kigali now desperate. The official head of this genocidal government composed a moving testimony to the appreciation he felt for all Mitterrand had done. 'Monsieur le President [Mitterrand], the Rwandan people express to you their sentiments of gratitude for the moral, diplomatic and material support that you have given them from 1990 to this day.' He signs off assuring the French leader of his 'highest consideration'. It is a truly remarkable letter from the president of a nation that had planned and carried out the genocide of around 400,000 by this point in late May.[47] A month later, Admiral Lanxade, chief of staff of the French armed forces, robustly defended the French military and government against its many critics in a radio broadcast. He told listeners to Radio Monte Carlo at the end of June, 'we cannot be reproached for having armed the killers. In any case, all those massacres were committed with sticks and machetes.'[48]

French mercenary Paul Barril was at the heart of French efforts to maintain links with the Rwandan army and give support on the ground to the Bagosora regime. He was now working as part of the 'parallel network' of unofficial French operatives linking the interim government with the Élysée. Barril claimed to have been in Rwanda throughout the period of the genocide, April to July 1994. In fact, as already seen, he arrived in Paris to appear on French television on 28 June to accuse the RPF of shooting down his employer's plane.

Barril, dressed like a Gallic James Bond, smiling and self confident in military gear, appeared rather appropriately in the French version of *Playboy* magazine in March 1995. Here he happily boasted that he had been Habyarimana's 'counsellor' for years and that after his death the new Rwandan interim government's defence secretary had naturally turned to him. 'I arrived by helicopter [in Kigali] … my first decision was to hurry to the French embassy and to raise the flag. … For the [Hutu extremist] Rwandans, to declare that my home was in the embassy would have a strong psychological meaning.' It was an attempt to show that although he was now employed in a private capacity, the Frenchman and his country would not abandon those who spoke the same language.[49] Indeed, Barril was happy to have 'holiday snaps' that later appeared in the French press taken of him standing heroically outside the French embassy and lolling next to an artillery gun.

Several Rwandan officers testify to Barril's appearance in Rwanda during the genocide. His work for the interim government included training 30–60 men, later up to 120, at the Bigogwe military camp, the same base from which the Rwandan army and *Interahamwe* had carried out massacres of Tutsis earlier in the civil war. Barril was charged with operation 'Insecticide' – a direct reference to the Tutsi whom Hutu militants nicknamed *inyenzi* (cockroaches). The recruits were to be given commando-style training with the aim of infiltrating and destroying RPF groups behind the front line. According to French journalist Patrick de Saint-Exupéry, interim foreign minister Jérôme Bicamumpaka gave the former Élysée policeman a free hand and a $1,200,000 budget to help the genocidal regime stay in power. Barril had no moral qualms about working for a government that was butchering its people.

Sébastien Ntahobari, the military attaché at the Rwandan embassy in Paris, reported that Bizimana, the interim government defence minister, had transferred the money from Nairobi to the French capital in June 1994. Barril was to be paid for his 'services and assistance' to the regime and an associate of Barril's came to the embassy to collect the money.[50] On top of the mandate to train Hutu military personnel for field operations against the RPF, on 6 May Agathe Habyarimana gave Captain Barril another mission – to investigate and research the plane crash. For this detective work Barril was again to receive ample financial recompense.

The Belgian lawyer who publicly defended Barril in the French press, Luc de Temmerman, was also Agathe Habyarimana's lawyer and he told those who were interested that Barril had worked for the Rwandan government but had not done anything illegal to his knowledge and that his men had only participated to a small degree in the war. Augustin Bizimungu (head of the FAR) told Temmerman that the war was fought fairly and that the militias had carried out some massacres, but this was a 'normal enough situation' in a war that had gone on for four years.[51]

Barril was not the only French operative working in Rwanda before the arrival of Operation Turquoise in mid-June.

> UNAMIR, Rwandan army officers and RPF sources all reported seeing several white men in military uniform in Rwanda, and not part of UNAMIR, in early April and again in mid-May. Three or four French-speaking white men in military uniform ate at the Rwandan army officers' mess for several days in April and then left Kigali by helicopter for the northwest.[52]

In mid-May a Rwandan army helicopter flew French-speaking soldiers with large amounts of equipment to Bigogwe. The helicopter pilot, according to witnesses, was white. Elsewhere, UNAMIR officers reported seeing whites in military uniform driving rapidly through Kigali on two occasions,[53] as well as at the Hotel Meridien in Gisenyi, the interim government's headquarters. Other witnesses reported seeing French-speaking soldiers in the south of Rwanda. A French officer told journalist Patrick de Saint-Exupéry that these men were probably mercenaries. The question then arises: were they working with Barril or other agencies, and with the official or unofficial support of the French government or Huchon's MAM?[54]

Military sources had tried to raise 100 mercenaries to help the Rwandan army secure the southern Rwandan towns of Butare and Kigoma, and in doing so keep open the arms routes from Zaire and Burundi. 'This was supervised by DGSE parallel agents close to a retired French officer.' A mercenary recruitment office had even been opened in Brussels.[55] The French officer was also said to be responsible for introducing Agathe Habyarimana to Lebanese and Belgian arms dealers.

Meanwhile, in Rwanda the daily killing continued. Innocent Rwililiza, a 38 year-old Tutsi teacher who fled to the countryside remembered hiding behind a ruined house.

> Some *Interahamwe* walked inside and found a [Tutsi] family. I heard the blows striking bones, but I could barely hear any lamentations. Next they discovered a child behind a well. It was a little girl. They set to cut her. From my hiding place I could listen to everything. She did not ask for pity ... only murmured before dying 'Jesus' ... then little cries.[56]

In market stalls in neighbouring Uganda, laughing traders yelled out in Luganda, '*Lelo tulide mututsi*' – 'Today we shall eat a Tutsi'. It was an allusion to the hundreds of bloated corpses that had flowed down the Akagera River into Lake Victoria. Eating fish had become a joke for eating Tutsis.[57] While arms dealers, mercenaries, politicians and presidents exploited the ongoing genocide in whatever way was most conducive to them, the 'little cries' of the victims went unheard.

Chapter 7

Operation Turquoise

I t was a typical summer day in Paris. While tourists ate homemade
dairy ice creams outside Notre Dame Cathedral and sipped coffee
in brasseries by the Seine, senior politicians shuffled from their
offices and drawing rooms into the black limousines that would take
them to the Élysée palace for a routine inner-cabinet meeting. Prime
Minister Édouard Balladur, Foreign Secretary Alain Juppé and Defence
Minister François Léotard sat comfortably in antique chairs as
President Mitterrand, ageing and ailing, trundled through the various
policy points assigned for discussion. Then, under 'any other business',
as if announcing another mediocre spending review or Bastille Day
entertainment, Mitterrand sprang his announcement. France, he had
decided, was going to send a large intervention force into Rwanda.
Operation Turquoise, as it was later named, would, he told his startled
colleagues, take place as soon as possible. Balladur and his right-wing
henchmen, shell-shocked by their Machiavellian president's sudden
about-turn, no doubt spluttered into their Perrier water.

The initial response was for Mitterrand's political rivals to oppose any
such action, fearing that France would get sucked into an African war
it could not control. But opposition cabinet members, after looking for
ways to stop the intervention, soon decided on a change of tack. The
right-wing opposition could not be seen to allow Mitterrand the moral
high ground of announcing he was in favour of helping Rwanda while
they opposed it. Equally, they did not want a damaging split at the
heart of the French political system.[1]

Juppé saw his opportunity to clamber onto the Rwandan bandwagon
and gain plenty of 'moral' points by showing his concern. Despite
Mitterrand asking his ministers to keep the decision to themselves,
presumably so he could be the first to announce and take credit for it,

the race was on to secure maximum political acclaim from the news.[2] Within 48 hours of the cabinet meeting, Juppé had appeared on television to broadcast the forthcoming operation, before writing in the left-wing paper *Libération* on 16 June that:

> we have a real duty to intervene in Rwanda. The time to watch the massacre passively is over, we must take the initiative. ... France is ready with its main European and African partners to prepare an intervention on the ground to put an end to the massacres and to protect the populations threatened with extermination. ... France will live up to its responsibilities.[3]

It was an astonishing piece of spin by Juppé. African analyst Gérard Prunier was unimpressed: 'having spent the last 40 days silently watching its former pupils and protégés commit a massive genocide, the government discovered it had a conscience just as media pressure became irresistible and when South Africa threatened to intervene militarily.'[4]

Each part of the French government and military establishment had its own reasons to back the intervention. Mitterrand had already conceded privately by mid-June that the interim government was 'a bunch of killers'.[5] Turquoise gave him a chance to play the 'humanitarian' card so beloved by the media and show a sceptical French public and international audience that France 'cared'. Moreover, it proved that France could still mount an impressive military expedition at short notice, which would bolster its flagging reputation with other worried francophone dictators who feared their own civil unrest.

Across the political divide, Mitterrand's Gaullist opponents were pragmatic in their assessment of the intervention. Juppé and his ally Chirac were aware of the immense media bonanza such an ethically caring intervention could bring them. Balladur, the prime minister, and his defence minister François Léotard were less enthusiastic, recognizing the high stakes involved. If Turquoise went wrong the headlines would be unbearable and his job would be on the line. His reasons for reluctantly backing a scaled-down limited intervention were, according to a letter sent to Mitterrand on 21 June, because the situation happened in Africa, happened in a francophone country and because of the moral aspect.[6] All three reasons had been true since the genocide began two months earlier.

Balladur also pushed for the operation to meet various conditions, the first being to gain a UN Security Council mandate for it. He argued that any attempt at a unilateral intervention, like the earlier Operation Noroît, would be catastrophic for France. Equally, the operation needed to be limited in time to 'a few weeks' until UNAMIR II, which had been authorized way back on 17 May, finally entered the country. As it stood, the UN operation was still months away from deployment in terms of preparation of troops, equipment and finance.

Generals Huchon and Quesnot, like other military 'hawks', had always been keen to intervene, arguing that France should never have left Rwanda but used its troops, as in 1993, to keep the RPF at bay. To the more gung-ho French military, Turquoise could enable the Rwandan army to re-form and counter the RPF advance. Gérard Prunier, the African expert, who surprisingly given his 'liberal' credentials had been drafted in to help plan the intervention, ran into such officers who were 'grumbling in aisles about "breaking the back of the RPF"'.[7]

A mere nine months earlier the French military command had been involved in stopping the RPF dead in its tracks. It was unsurprising then that 'many soldiers interpreted their Turquoise brief to imply a rearguard action in support of their beleaguered Rwandan allies, to allow them to retreat in good order and regroup.'[8] A US military officer, who spoke frequently with several Turquoise officers, reported that many had seemed resentful of the pull-out ordered in 1993 under the Arusha agreement and were now determined to 'kick butt' when it came to meeting the RPF.[9]

The reality was that any intervention needed to take place without delay. By 13 June the RPF had advanced through the central town of Gitarama and was besieging the northern Hutu stronghold of Ruhengeri. Military analysts expected Kagame's army to sweep through the rest of Rwanda within a month, with the towns of Butare and Cyangugu in the south and Gisenyi in the north, to which the interim government had fled, the only major obstacles. Any French operation needed to happen fast if it was to gain credit for 'saving' Tutsis from the genocide or stopping a total RPF victory. With the aid of the encrypted communication system sent from France, General Huchon was well aware of the timeline working against him.

Criticism of the impending intervention was not slow in coming. Amnesty International called on the French government to explain its links with the Hutu extremists. A group of Tutsi priests wrote in a letter to their superiors that Turquoise was to them not a 'humanitarian' operation but merely a 'cynical enterprise'. Why, they asked, had France done nothing in the two months the genocide ripped apart Rwanda, even though it was better informed about what was happening than others? Why had it failed to exercise the least pressure on the interim government when it clearly had the means to do so? 'For us, France has arrived too late for nothing,' the letter concluded.[10] The OAU condemned what it saw as a blatant attempt by France to rescue its power base in Rwanda. Belgium condemned the planned operation, while the UN special representative in Rwanda called Turquoise a 'political intervention' that was 'not helping matters'. Former rightwing president Giscard d'Estaing, no doubt anxious to pour scorn on his socialist successor Mitterrand, described Turquoise as purely an attempt to protect 'some of those who had carried out the massacres'.[11]

Even the French media, significantly analysing their country's involvement in Rwanda for the first time in four years, expressed reservations about the motivation for the coming intervention. Le Monde examined the government's record and wondered why it had been

> satisfied with selfishly repatriating French nationals in April and approving, like everybody else, the withdrawal of the 2000 UN troops in Rwanda just as one of this century's worst massacres is taking place? Why this belated wakening that is happening, as if by coincidence, just as the RPF is gaining the upper hand on the ground? France will find itself once again accused of coming to the rescue of the former government, but its initiative will effectively shore up African regimes that are just as corrupt, like that of Zaire's General Mobutu.[12]

However, the French media were still content to print 'good news' stories they were fed by their government. Some days before Turquoise was announced, Bernard Kouchner, a founder of aid charity MSF and a former French health minister, had arrived to see Dallaire at his UN Kigali headquarters. He told the UNAMIR commander that:

> he wanted to save a bunch of orphans in Interahamwe-held territory. He wanted to fly them out of the war ... [and that] the

French public was in a state of shock and horror over the genocide in Rwanda and was demanding action. I told him I was totally against the export of Rwandan children, orphaned or not. They were not a means for some French people to feel a little less guilty about the genocide.

Kouchner then went off to see the genocidaire, accompanied by a 'coterie of journalists, and managed to persuade Bagosora that letting the orphans go would be good "PR" for the Interim regime'. Dallaire commented, 'I already didn't like the idea of exporting Rwandan children, but to do it to give the extremists a better image made me ill.'[13]

However, when persuaded that it might make a ceasefire between the RPF and interim government troops more likely, Dallaire agreed. Bagosora was particularly keen on the transfer, seeing it as a chance to impress the French authorities, the public and the world.[14] Some 50, mostly sick, children were eventually flown to Paris on 5 June, arriving to a waiting media circus anxious to witness French 'humanitarianism' in action. The 'rescue' of the orphans certainly made good PR all round – for Paris and Bagosora.

In mid-June Dallaire left for Nairobi and meetings with NGOs and UN officials. While on a two-day break, he received a phone call from the French ambassador asking for a meeting about orphans. 'I wondered what it was with the French and their obsession with orphans: what did it mean that they were now approaching me directly rather than going through Kouchner? When I sat down again, I told Beth [his wife] that I thought the French were up to something and I needed to figure out what.'[15] He commented that he never envisaged Paris planning an intervention 'under the guise of humanitarian relief', with the support of Boutros-Ghali and the Rwandan army, the FAR.

Three days after Mitterrand announced to his cabinet on 14 June that an intervention in Rwanda would take place, Kouchner was sent to see Dallaire again to get his cooperation for the French operation. The UN commander had just returned from his Nairobi trip and received the Frenchman, not knowing 'when or if his humanitarianism masked the purposes of the French government'. Kouchner immediately told Dallaire he was there as an interlocutor for his government and, after recounting how appalling the present situation had become and the lack of any international action, went on to drop a bombshell.

The French government, he said, had decided that in the interests of humanity, it was prepared to lead a French and Franco–African coalition force into Rwanda to stop the genocide and deliver humanitarian aid. They would come under a Chapter VII UN mandate and aimed to set up a safe haven in the west of the country where people fleeing the conflict could find refuge. He asked me for my support. Without a pause, I said, "Non!" – and I began to swear at the great humanitarian using every French-Canadian oath in my vocabulary. He tried to calm me with reasons that probably sounded high-minded to him but, considering the track record of the French in Rwanda, struck me as deeply hypocritical: surely the French knew that it was their allies who were the architects of the slaughter.[16]

Being called out of the room to be told that another UNAMIR 'peacekeeper' had just been killed did little to lift Dallaire's mood. He returned to fire another savage barrage at an uncomfortable Kouchner, telling him that he could not believe the effrontery of the French in planning to use a humanitarian cloak for an intervention that could enable the Rwandan army to remain in power in part of the country. He argued that France should have reinforced UNAMIR if it were so keen on sending help, not set up what looked suspiciously like a 'rival' UN force that was far better equipped and with a precious Chapter VII mandate allowing it to use force if necessary. Not surprisingly, Dallaire complained that the French government had spoken to everyone, including the Hutu militants and RPF, but had told him nothing. 'I had been kept in the dark like a mushroom – and fed plenty of fresh manure,' he countered.[17]

The first draft of the plan for Operation Turquoise envisaged French troops entering Rwanda through Gisenyi, the northern heartland of Hutu extremism. With the imminent arrival of RPF troops in this area, there was the possibility of an early firefight with them, as well as the embarrassment of militants welcoming the French with open arms. Yet, if the idea were to take the credit for saving Tutsi lives, then Gisenyi was the wrong place, as they were all dead. A Hutu trader in the area had told a French journalist, 'We never had many Tutsi here and we killed them all at the beginning without much of a fuss.' The plan was quickly shelved.[18]

In the end, the only feasible entrance to Rwanda was through Goma in Mobutu's Zaire. The French mission would enter Rwanda through the southern town of Cyangugu before spreading north to include the regions of Gikongoro and Kibuye. The clinching argument for this route was that at Nyarushishi camp, near Cyangugu, there were many Tutsi who had managed to flee the genocide and they would make ideal fodder for Western TV crews anxious to see 'humanitarianism' in action.

At the UN Secretary-General Boutros-Ghali 'personally intervened in support of an authorization of Operation Turquoise.'[19] In a letter to the president of the Security Council dated 20 June, Boutros-Ghali estimated that another three months would be needed to get UNAMIR II under way. 'Meanwhile, the situation in Rwanda has continued to deteriorate and the killing of innocent civilians has not stopped.' The letter recommended considering France's offer to lead a multinational operation in Rwanda under a Chapter VII mandate to 'assure the security and protection of displaced persons and civilians at risk' – by 'all necessary means'.[20] This was despite Dallaire's current UNAMIR force, and indeed UNAMIR II that was to follow, having only Chapter VI mandates. The following day, the French ambassador to the UN, Jean-Bernard Mérimée, wrote to Boutros-Ghali promising a French operation with assistance from francophone Senegal that could step into the gap caused by the delay in sending UNAMIR II, while adhering to the same objectives. The ambassador assured the UN secretary-general that 'The objective naturally excludes any interference in the development of the balance of military forces between the parties involved in the conflict.'[21]

On 22 June, Resolution 929 gave France UN backing for its intervention, which it was agreed should last a maximum of two months. The vote for the resolution was far from unanimous. New Zealand, Pakistan, Nigeria, Brazil and China abstained. The New Zealand ambassador, Colin Keating, who along with the Czech Karel Kovanda had taken the greatest interest in the Rwandan situation and had attempted to initiate an earlier UN intervention, called for UNAMIR II to be urgently sent instead. The OAU also opposed Turquoise on the grounds that one of the parties involved in the conflict, the RPF, was unhappy about the French intervention. 'For several African leaders, it was additional evidence that a major European power could manipulate the UN and humanitarian operations to demonstrate its own power in the region.'[22]

To divert criticism that it was once again launching a unilateral intervention for its own reasons, Paris was anxious Turquoise should be a 'multinational' operation. In fact, Senegal and Chad were the only countries to send troops and this only after pressure from France, which paid for its francophone allies to join the operation.[23]

In wartorn Kigali crowds of exuberant Hutu militiamen and Rwandan army soldiers openly celebrated the news of the French intervention as if their saviours were coming to keep them in power. Hutu mobs waved the French tricolour signifying 'liberty, equality and fraternity'. Dallaire, cooped up under mortar fire at his headquarters in the capital, reported that '"Vive la France" was heard more often in Kigali than it was in Paris. RTLM continued to tell the population that the French were on their way to join them to fight the RPF.'[24] He added, 'It seemed to me that for every life that Operation Turquoise would save, it would cost at least another because of the resurgence of the genocide.' The real fear for those Tutsis who had survived nearly three months of the genocide was that the twin push of the RPF and French would force the militia 'into a final killing spree'.

The Canadian UNAMIR force commander left his bosses at the UN in no doubt that he was against any French presence in Kigali, threatening to resign from his post and even shoot down French planes if they landed at the airport in the capital.[25]

In the event France did not wait for the UN mandate to be passed before Operation Turquoise moved into action. An armada of giant air cargo planes, including an Airbus, Hercules, Transall, Antonov AN-124 and Illuyshin IL-76 flew equipment and crack French troops into Goma in Zaire. It had been impossible to find enough transport planes to carry the expedition's equipment. The USA turned down a French request to use its planes, and in the end Lanxade had to do a deal with Russia and Ukraine to make use of their old Soviet transporters to fly in the bulk of the men and armaments. It was finally agreed it would be tactically foolish to attempt any landing of French forces in Kigali, given the certain fight against the RPF that would follow. Zaire became the main base from which the operation would move forward. In total, the French forces mustered 2924 troops and 510 support staff, as well as air and logistical cover. Paris also decided its soldiers would not wear the blue helmets of the UN but the green and red berets of the French elite paratroopers and marines.

French special forces had already been involved in reconnaissance for the move across the border from Zaire to southern Rwanda and had made contact with their Rwandan army and *Interahamwe* counterparts. Janvier, a leading militiaman testified,

> In June 1994, the French arrived in our country. They came in through the Congo [Zaire]. They put up at the Hôtel Résidence which was where I saw them for the first time, on the occasion of a meeting with the prefect and the commander of the region to organize for their entry into the country, via this town. This hotel is on the Congo side, at Bukavu.
>
> More precisely, I went to the Hôtel Résidence with Yusufu Munyakazi [an *Interahamwe* leader] in a Suzuki jeep. We left the car there and took a minibus, accompanied by the prefect and the military commander as well as the député [MP] Félicien Barigira. They had a small meeting at the hotel.
>
> We went back in the evening with two Frenchmen who accompanied us to the bridge that marks the border. It had been decided that they'd enter the next day, but they didn't wait for the next day. They returned that night, at around 8 p.m., with knitted Ninja masks over their faces! These are a type of black mask that covers the face, with holes for the eyes and mouth. It's black in colour. They [the French] entered at night over the bridge with their jeeps and equipment. They said there wasn't any equipment left [for our work]; they supplied us with rifles, ammunition, grenades and all the rest.[26]

The intervention force was comprised of some troops that had already taken part in the earlier campaigns in Rwanda from 1990 to 1993. However, the French paratroopers were, for public purposes anyway, meant to ignore the Rwandan army (FAR) and presidential guard with which they had spent three years training, fighting alongside and socializing, as they headed for certain defeat to an anglophone 'Ugandan' invader. It made for an uncomfortable test of loyalties.[27] If Janvier is to be believed, such sympathies between the French and their 'pupils' resulted in the Rwandan army, now desperately short of ammunition, being rearmed by some of Turquoise's men.

Turquoise had more than 100 armoured vehicles, a battery of 120mm mortars, Gazelle helicopters, four Jaguar fighter-bombers, four Mirage F1CT ground attack planes and four Mirage F1Cs for reconnaissance purposes. A whole array of transport planes flew in the arms and troops ready for immediate deployment.[28] The troops included elite special forces not normally seen in such 'humanitarian' roles. Detachments from the 1st RPIMA (Régiment parachutiste d'Infanterie de Marine d'Assault) in Bayonne, were joined by commandos from Trepel de Lorient, a force of EICA (Escadron d'Intervention des Commandos de l'Air) air force commandos based in Nimes, plus secret service police from the GIGN and special service operatives from CRAP. It was an extremely powerful force for a mandated peacekeeping operation.

Yet, this much heralded and impressively armed 'humanitarian' mission had very few trucks with which to move the displaced people or survivors it had supposedly come to rescue. Armoured personnel carriers, which could move the odd two or three survivors, were no good faced with the dozens who came out of hiding when they sensed the French might save them. As a result, many more Tutsis were killed in remote areas because Turquoise did not have the resources it needed to take them to safety. It was a failure that commanders in the field did not attempt to redress even after initial reconnaissance had shown the scale of the problem with which they were dealing. Unlike Operation Amaryllis, when trucks were taken from UNAMIR to help move survivors out of the conflict, this time there was no other transport to requisition or, indeed, were there any plans to fly in such vehicles.

Hutu crowds and *Interahamwe* killers received the troops from Turquoise with unabashed joy as they passed through villages, and drove along the potholed red dirt roads. Journalist Scott Peterson was shocked at the welcome given to the Turquoise troops:

> The French ... were met as liberators. They were heroes to the Hutus. The welcome party was outrageous, because it was clear that these European soldiers were saving the killers from all the demons that their violence and murder against the Tutsis had stored within their psyches. Freshly made *tricolores* waved from every hand; men chanted and danced with their machetes and bottles of beer. The crime had been committed, and now it was being absolved; they would be safe. Banners proclaimed 'Vive la France!' and praised President Mitterrand for his mercy and care.

Militia checkpoints evaporated when the convoy of troops passed. Confetti was thrown. I was jostled by the crowd, as they tried to humour me and ply me with beer.[29]

Guardian reporter Chris McGreal passed through 24 roadblocks on the stretch of road from Gisenyi to Kibuye, each guarded by a motley collection of militiamen armed with the occasional gun, but mostly clubs and machetes. He found any white person was usually regarded as a French soldier and given a warm welcome.

The barricades are frequently decorated with hastily fashioned French flags and signs praising President Mitterrand for intervening. Others denounce Belgium and Uganda for supporting the rebels. In areas where French troops have passed through they have often met with a rapturous reception from people who believe the soldiers are not there to rescue the remaining Tutsis but to shield the Hutu majority from the rebel Rwandan Patriotic Front.[30]

Journalist Patrick de Saint-Exupéry described the welcome as having the ambience of a football match as tricolours were waved and crowds screamed their support for the paratroopers. He reported a pickup truck, crammed with militia killers shouting 'Vive la France' and 'Vive les Français'. It was, 'as if the Americans had been welcomed by a fanfare by the [Nazi] guards at Treblinka in 1945'.[31] In Gikongoro, scene of some of the worst butchery, the prefect even had his employees rehearse their warm welcome by practising 'spontaneous' cheers, while in the Hutu heartland of Gisenyi the authorities deployed entire schools of children to wave little French flags.

One young Hutu priest called Étienne summed up the feelings of many of his fellow extremists.

In Rwanda you are not able to choose your side, after lulling the fears of the international community, France must fight on our side. She must not become the toy of the RPF as the blue helmets of UNAMIR have. It is known that national reconciliation is not possible and that only a military solution is possible to put an end to the conflict. We have gone too far.

He justified the genocide of the Tutsis by saying, 'they were preparing to kill all of us; they had lists ... if the French army betrays us the country will sink even further into catastrophe.'[32]

Aloys Mutabingwa was certain the French were there to help the Hutu stay in power – after all during the previous three years he had been taught by his French trainers how to kill, a message he then relayed to his own *Interahamwe* recruits.

In 1994, when the genocide took place, the *Interahamwe* put into practice what we had taught them, and what we ourselves had learned from the French. They set about killing the Tutsis. They didn't stop killing them. Eventually, the French came to our aid. The men in charge locally had told us this would happen; they'd asked us not to worry, as they'd summoned help, and the French were going to come to our aid since they'd learned that the Tutsis were otherwise going to take over the country.

It was towards the end of June. We learnt that the French were on their way; the men in charge told us as much and urged us to prepare a warm welcome for them. We went to Russizi; it's not at all far from here. We really celebrated their arrival in style, as was only proper! There were all the leaders, Manishimwe and the prefect, Bagambiki. There was also a shopkeeper, very active on the *Interahamwe* side: his name was Édouard Bandetse. They made it clear they were very satisfied. We said 'thank you' to the French, as they were going to come and save us from the Tutsi menace.[33]

The crowds that flocked round the French APCs and jeeps had been encouraged to give Turquoise an enthusiastic reception by both the official Radio Rwanda and Hutu hate radio RTLM, which began broadcasting in July 1993.

Transcripts of RTLM's broadcasts, obtained from the 'media' trial in Arusha of Ferdinand Nahimana, Jean-Bosco Barayagwiza and Hassan Ngeze in 2003, showed how much control DJs exercised over the Hutu population. Witnesses at the trial in Arusha said that the two main objects the killers had at roadblocks were weapons and radios. Mixing current pop sounds with damning indictments of all the interim regime's enemies, RTLM was more responsible than anything else for fixing in the minds of ordinary Rwandans the need to take an active role in the genocide for the 'good' of the nation. Constant references aimed at dehumanizing the *inyenzi* and *inkotanyi* Tutsi and their sympathizers contrasted starkly with the praise heaped on the great friend of the regime – France.

Habimana Kantano, one of the leading DJs, specialized in whipping up anti-Tutsi hatred. On 28 May, eight weeks into the genocide, he proclaimed on air that

> if you are a cockroach you must be killed, you cannot change anything; if you are *Inkotanyi* (RPF) you cannot change anything. No one can say that he has captured a cockroach and the latter gave him money, as a price for his life, this cannot be accepted ... don't accept anything in exchange [for his life] he must be killed.[34]

The radio presenters went into particular overdrive when news of the French intervention became known. Kantano announced on 19 June that:

> 2000 men [French troops] will be coming and this is not [a] negligible number of soldiers. The French troops were here before; they came to support us or rather help us restore peace in the country, and then thanks to the *Ibyitso* [Tutsis living in Rwanda, literally 'traitors'] governments, the *Inkotanyi* of course said: 'the French must leave the country'. The French went packing and left for good. And this was beyond comprehension, but that was a trick by the Belgians to replace them. ... Therefore it goes without saying that the *Inyenzi* do not want those French troops; but this changes nothing; whether they like it or not, the French will come to Rwanda at all costs.
>
> We should be ready to welcome them [the French]. Let's be ready ... prepare to welcome our French guests; there is no other way to get about it. I think that we should smile when we meet them in the street ... if necessary, we should offer them flowers, extend a cordial welcome to them ... and then later, even some of our *Sederikazi* [Hutu women/girls] should approach them and chat with them, talk to them and then er ... if necessary, they also will get foreign currency from the troops. You know that

when the French were here, the RPF-*Inkotanyi* told the very beautiful Tutsi girls to accost the French and poison them. From then, the French started discovering what the Tutsi women were; I saw it myself. When the prostitutes went to expose themselves near the hotels, the French first asked, 'is that one not Tutsi?' Upon discovering that a girl was Tutsi, they abandoned her. We want those French troops; they should come and arrest those criminals [the RPF]. Let them come and prevent those wicked fellows from killing Rwandans.

I believe the French troops will be here by Wednesday at the latest. Let us prepare a rousing welcome for them. We have no conflict with them. They are our fellow men coming to help us stop the *Inkotanyi* from pushing us around. We must therefore receive the French cordially, embrace them and chat with them, especially as we share the French language. Even if someone tries saying '*bonjour*' to them, it is different from the *Inkotanyi* who do not even know how to say '*bonjour*'. Let us take the example of Corporal Kagame who cannot even say '*bonjour*'. So, be ready to welcome the French troops properly; where possible, prepare sorghum wine for them, coconut banana liquor for them; get Primus beer with which to welcome the French troops. This will make them happy and they will feel at home.[35]

Even as the RPF surrounded the capital, Kantano was still putting his faith in a French intervention to save the interim government. He implored his listeners:

I am asking you to get ready to welcome the French. How can we get ready to welcome them? We have to start writing on clothing and on any material we can find … we have to write nice words to welcome those French. We will write this: 'Long live the humanitarian action!' 'Long live France!' 'Long live Mitterrand!' 'Long live the UN!' '*Inkotanyi* = assassins', 'Inyenzi = animals' … every writing that can show the French how things should be conducted. This can be written on mother's traditional crowns. It can be written on big placards that we will use to welcome those French. Where there are flowers we have to search for them and throw them in their cars. Children should also prepare dances for

them. And there are words to be used like: 'bonjour', 'merci'. ...
Our young women should try to approach them [the French]
and lift their spirits.[36]

So, as the French troops moved along into the south of the country at
the end of June they were left in no doubt that they were both wanted
and needed. It was indeed after Operation Noroît, the much anticipated
'second coming', to bail out the Hutu extremists yet again. First up for
the French was the immediate 'rescue' of 8000 Tutsis at Nyarushishi
camp near the southern border town of Cyangugu. This was the
necessary 'media gift' showing the 'humanitarian' nature of the
operation and proving that French President Mitterrand was indeed a
man of heart and deed. The truth was much less pleasant.

The pro-Hutu stance of many French officers now in the field was
obvious. Colonel Didier Thibault, a senior officer in the Cyangugu
area, gave vent to the frustration many Turquoise troops felt about
their supposed 'neutral' role. Thibault was an alias for Tauzin, a French
secret service operative who had previously worked as a military
adviser to Habyarimana and was credited with having 'spectacularly
saved the situation' in holding up the RPF offensive in February 1993.
Not surprisingly, his loyalties lay with the Rwandan army and he was
unsympathetic to an RPF victory. He had a close working relationship
with the local prefect Emanuel Bagambiki who was in charge of the
refugee camp at Cyangugu stadium to which 8000 Tutsis had fled for
protection. Tauzin told the waiting media that he had no authority to
disarm the militia or dismantle their roadblocks, which the French
intervention force found were there to greet them and which were still
in place every kilometre or two to catch the remaining Tutsis.

The media were told that Bagambiki was a key organizer of the
killings and enjoyed choosing his victims with Nazi-style 'selection
squads'. Genocidaires under his command would sporadically enter
the stadium to drag off to their deaths people regarded as traitors or
dangerous to the local authority. One witness, Pierre Canisuius, said
that at one such selection Bagambiki had picked out his father and 14
others to take away and kill. When questioned about working with a
man who was directly implicated in the killing, Tauzin replied, 'we
are not at war against the Rwandan [interim] government or the
Rwandan armed forces [FAR]. They are legal organizations. Some

members might have blood on their hands, but not all. It is not my task and not my mandate to replace these people.' He went on to say that in his opinion these were 'political' questions and not for him to consider.[37]

Allegations that individual French troops were not only in league with the *Interahamwe* but also raped, murdered and stole Tutsi cattle make salutary reading. The refugee camp at Nyarushishi was surrounded by militia who had arrived too late to massacre its terrified inhabitants without outraging the media scrum that accompanied the newly arrived French force. Inside the camp conditions were appalling. There was very little food and the inhabitants were totally dependent on people outside, including the French, for sustenance and water. One 15 year-old Tutsi, Beatrice, had fled to the refugee camps to escape the massacres in the surrounding area, along with her young brother, Gilles Rurangangabo.

> Then, one moment, the French arrived. [Gilles] ... went to work for the French. We liked to go and see him where he was working for the French – they paid him in canned food and he gave us some to eat. Some of us children would go over in groups to the French to pick up the cans they'd thrown away. At other times, they didn't give them to us, they threw them to us as if we were dogs – we'd stand there and gaze enviously at them. When they threw the stuff to us, we'd go back home.

One day Gilles did not return home. When Beatrice went to enquire what had happened to him, she was told that he had gone to work for other French troops further north. After further questioning, which clearly annoyed the French, they admitted that the Tutsi child had been handed over to the *Interahamwe* who had killed him. Then:

> [T]hey chased us away with teargas, telling us that they were well aware of the deceitfulness of the *Inyenzis*. We ran away, and they pursued us, insulting us and throwing stones at us.
>
> When they realized they weren't going to catch him [the boy who had enquired about Beatrice's brother], they were really put out, and they started to take it out on other children who were going to fetch water for example. They chased them away and

refused to grant them access to the water. They shut off the water and forbade anyone to go looking for kindling wood. So eventually we no longer had anything to eat, since we didn't have any water or wood to do the cooking. In the end, the men got together and decided they should accompany the little groups of children who were going to fetch wood or water outside the camp. The women and girls couldn't risk going outside. If a girl dared to venture out she was rapidly spotted, shackled and forced to sleep with them; she was raped.

We realized that this couldn't go on, that those men hadn't really come to rescue us or protect us. The [Tutsi] men got together and it was decided that from now on they would be the ones who carried out the chore of fetching wood and water. No women or young boys would dare to do it any more. The men gathered and set off in quite a big group to fetch wood. After that, we didn't dare ask the least question and we never found him [Gilles], not even after the French had gone. We don't know how he died; we haven't any idea of what became of him or where he fell.

That's what I can tell you about the French right now – they brought us nothing but grief, and I certainly can't say that they did anything positive for us at all. They didn't come to our aid. Furthermore, if someone dies when he's in your care, it's only right that you should explain everything you know about the matter!

We thought that they'd come to protect the people who were in danger, but in fact they watched the *Interahamwe* enter the camp and seize people they led off to kill. But they were there. Another thing: even when the *Interahamwe* didn't enter, the French entered and they would beckon over a person they then took away, as if that person was going to come back. They left with the *Interahamwe* and the people they'd taken away never did come back.

The *Interahamwe* accompanied the French when they came into the camp. They didn't kill the people in the camp – they took them away and went off to kill them in the military zone, where no civilians were admitted. That's where they killed the ones they'd taken away. Even when people ran after them to try and do something, they were stopped by the barrier, so they couldn't go any further and were helpless.

There's another girl I know who was raped by the French in the camp, a girl called Clémentine; she'd be able to tell you a great deal about the French. She went to live in Kigali, and she drives someone's car – I don't know whose. But I've forgotten her surname.

What they did, from what I've heard, was this: they went outside the camp to look for cows to slaughter; it was there that the *Interahamwe* carved up the cows they'd taken from the Tutsis. But I know one case of a cow that the French took from a peasant who was living near the camp, promising they'd pay him the day he went to get his money. But when he went to the camp, he was chased away and they never paid him. The only answer he got was that this cow was Tutsi property and that nobody paid for Tutsi property.

I'm also one of those who went round begging for meat to grill, but in vain. The French were happy to open the barrier and those who went across into that zone were then obliged to come back to our camp as fast as they could, but those who entered their [the militia's] encampment didn't usually return. They were never seen again; they must have been killed immediately, right where they were.

In my view, I'd say the French came to kill along with the *Interahamwe*; they were there to kill. I can cite the example of my brother whom they killed while he was working for them, so they were responsible. There's another case of a man from Mibilizi who had gone to work for them – he suffered the same fate as my brother.

What I would demand from France is that, seeing that they brought immense grief to Rwanda, like the gaoled *Interahamwe* who acknowledge their actions – Rwanda should bring these French here to acknowledge what they did together with the *Interahamwe*. They'd led the whole world to think that were coming to rescue the people here, they'd signed an agreement saying as much; but instead of rescuing us, they came from outside the country to kill us, together with the *Interahamwe* from inside.

The *Interahamwe* acknowledge their crimes and some of them are coming out [of prison]; why shouldn't they [the French] acknowledge what they have done, as the *Interahamwe* have? They should have protected us and on this point, like Bagambiki our killer, they refuse to admit a thing. It's worse than the *Interahamwe*. They should have stopped those *Interahamwe* from killing us, they were their bosses. The French were responsible for the *Interahamwe*, they need to explain themselves.[38]

Beatrice was not the only survivor to testify about the French troops' actions. In 2005, 11 years after the genocide, a French army investigation was launched when six Rwandans filed charges of 'complicity to genocide and/or crimes against humanity' against the French forces. Auréa Mukakalisa, who was 27 years-old at the time, testified that the *Interahmawe* at Murambi refugee camp raped her while French soldiers controlled it.

'Hutu militiamen came into the camp and pointed out the Tutsis who the French soldiers then forced to leave. I saw the militiamen kill them – I saw French soldiers themselves kill Tutsis using gleaming big knives.'[39]

Janvier, a 25 year-old member of the *Interahamwe* testified that the 'worst' of the French soldiers

seized the surviving women and forced them to become their wives. They took them into the camps and did what they wanted to them. Of course those women were forced into it. What do you expect a woman survivor to say? Everyone had abandoned the survivors; their only hope of rescue lay with those whites! A Frenchman would make her an object of his pleasure, and then, shortly after, he'd abandon her and take up another. That often happened at Nyarushishi, in our area too in Bugarama, wherever they went. When you were a Tutsi, you had to die, and that was that.[40]

When the French arrived, we greeted them as our longstanding allies, people we knew really well. It's true, they proved as much to us – they never forbade us to do or say anything on this point. As for them, they were pleased with us and never did anything to hinder the work of those who were doing all those things. Who was the enemy? They too knew that the enemy were the Tutsis. When they came to a place where there were Tutsis ... and at that time the Tutsis were starving, some of them had gone for many days without eating, as they hid out in the bush. ... The French had some fortified biscuits, canned food. Instead of giving it to those starving people, no, they gave it to the Hutus and the *Interahamwe*. When they left those places, they would fire into the air – this was the signal that the coast was clear and we could go in and kill them.

One example I can give, you see, is this: the first jeep to arrive at Mibilizi, the first place they came to a halt was Mibilizi; this was where the first Frenchmen stopped. There were Tutsis who had survived there. But as a result of what had been decided at the meeting – which I myself did not attend – when the French left Mibilizi to return to Kamembe, those people were immediately killed. There were almost 3000 people there. They were all killed.

At that period, there were a lot of corpses in the country; it was yet again the French who advised us to throw the bodies into the water or to bury them instead of leaving them there in the open for everyone to see. At that period, people were killed and abandoned where they lay. It can be awkward if you leave bodies out in the open, the French asked us to bury them or to throw them into the water. We threw them into the river Rusizi. At home in Bugarama, the bodies were all thrown into the waters of the Rusizi, and they were swept away.[41]

Aloys, now in prison charged with genocide, testified to the collaboration between the *Interahamwe* and Operation Turquoise at Nyarushishi camp.

The French came, and at the border they discussed the situation with Bagambiki and Manishimwe, the lieutenant in command of the region. Eventually, the French went straight to Nyarushishi, a place where they'd brought the Tutsis from the Kamarampaka stadium. Two days after they arrived, we received a message asking us to get the *Interahamwe* together so they could go to Nyarushishi to kill the Tutsis.

So we assembled the *Interahamwe* and went up to Nyarushishi
and encircled the camp. We'd just encircled it when a Frenchman arrived, I don't know if he was the superior officer of the
others, but he said to us that, 'given that there are many people
gathered here, the satellite photos must have picked them up, the
international community might well have detected their
whereabouts, it's no longer possible for you to kill them here. But
you can flush out and liquidate all the ones that are hiding.' As
we came back down, we systematically burnt and destroyed the
houses that had so far been unaffected. When we came across
anyone with a bit of a long nose, we killed them without even
checking their identity; 'even the French have signed your death
warrant,' we told them. This is what we told them everywhere,
that even the French had given us a licence to kill.

Before leaving Nyarushishi, the French had given us grenades
and combat rations. We came back eating, feeling really cheerful.
The events carried on. At the border, we continued killing people
and throwing them into Lake Kivu. Under the eyes of the French,
of course! At one moment the French told us, 'you Rwandan
Hutus aren't very bright! You're killing people and throwing
them into the water and not doing anything else! Don't you
realize they'll eventually float up to the surface and they'll be seen
by satellites? You really don't have a clue!' It was the French who
taught us how to slit their bellies after we'd killed them and throw
them into the water without there being any risk of them rising to
the surface. We learnt our lesson and started to put it into practice.

Even afterwards, when they found us destroying and looting a
house, they asked us if we knew where the owner of the house
was. If you were so unwise as to say that you'd heard he'd fled
and that you didn't know what had become of him, they'd
practically kill you themselves. They'd lay into you, call you
stupid. 'So instead of first eliminating the owner before attacking
his house, you're doing things the other way round! What do you
think you'll have to say to him later? This is the ethnic group
you're fighting, right?'

They said this to us looking us right in the eyes and wondering
why we were so stupid. 'First you begin by eliminating the owner
and then you can see to the destruction of his house,' they said.

They were the ones who taught us all this. So, the truth of the matter is that the French came along to help carry out the genocide, clearly and visibly so, since they supported us in various ways.[42]

On 30 June Dallaire travelled to meet Turquoise commander General Lafourcade at his Goma headquarters to hammer out a 'French zone' beyond which the French operation would not progress. He was impressed with the operational readiness of what he saw, all the more poignant given his own threadbare UNAMIR resources of a handful of poorly armed, little-trained troops in Kigali, ferried about in much-repaired APCs.

> The French had obviously not skimped on their own logistics, billets and military equipment, and had carefully deployed around the airfield and in the town [Goma]. Witnessing the size and level of the outfitting of the camp vividly put into relief my own lack of support. Money and resources were no problem when the full weight of a world power is put behind the effort ... [the] elite units ... [from] the French foreign legion, para-troopers, marines and special forces ... were equipped with state-of-the-art weapons, command and control communications, HQ assets, over one hundred armoured vehicles, batteries of heavy mortars [and] a squadron of light-armed reconnaissance and medium troop-lift helicopters.[43]

The smartly dressed French officers, in their grey-green field uniform, reacted curiously to Dallaire's opinions on how the two UN forces should work together. It became obvious that there was a split in his French military audience, betraying underlying tensions and sentiments within Turquoise itself.

> While I was talking about stopping the ongoing genocide, his [Lafourcade's] staff were raising points about the loyalty France owed its old friends. ... They thought that UNAMIR should help prevent the RPF from defeating the RGF (FAR), which was not our job ... my French interlocutors continued to express their displeasure with UNAMIR's poor handling of the military aspects

of the civil war. They refused to accept the reality of the genocide and the fact that the extremist leaders, the perpetrators and some of their old colleagues were all the same people. They showed overt signs of wishing to fight the RPF. Some of these officers came from the colonial tradition of military intervention in the domestic affairs of former client states; they saw no reason to change their views over what they billed as one more interethnic squabble.[44]

Dallaire's impression was that 'the French never did reconcile which attitude was supreme in Turquoise.'

While the official Turquoise mission continued to move up from Cyangugu in the south, the situation in the northwest, homeland to Habyarimana and the Hutu extremists, was kept from the prying eyes of the droves of media now alerted to the 'newsworthiness' of the Rwandan plight. According to the one foreign reporter who covered this 'undercover' campaign, 200 elite French troops arrived near Gisenyi to carry out reconnaissance operations. Supplies were brought up from Goma and camps made around Gisenyi and 15 miles east at Mukamira, a former French training base in previous years. Barril was nearby at Bigogwe camp, training recruits for his 'insecticide' programme. Tauzin even declared the French were prepared to advance to Ruhengeri, which was besieged by the RPF.

Certainly, there was a growing air of desperation in Gisenyi among interim ministers who knew that without immediate French support they risked ending up alongside President Habyarimana, whose corpse Hutu extremists were hiding in the fridge of a local café. Human Rights Watch concluded that this operation by the French in the northwest was part of the 'military secrets' going on in parallel with the public mission of Turquoise.[45]

At the UN and in diplomatic and press circles, French government representatives were working overtime to justify the operation. Mitterrand had embarked on a high-profile tour of South Africa to meet newly installed President Nelson Mandela. The visit was important, with big economic stakes to play for in the new post-apartheid country and massive financial contracts that scores of French commercial and cultural representatives were eyeing amid fierce Western competition. Mitterrand hoped to persuade this typical anglophone country to do business with France and to get important media credit for appearing with one of the icons of the twentieth century. Mandela ensured that the controversial Rwandan policy of his guests remained on the agenda, telling reporters,

> If it is no longer possible to solve things peacefully, that is a decision that should be taken by the United Nations as a whole and not by one nation individually. Problems of this nature, which happen in other countries, should not be the subject of unilateral action as far as I am concerned. ... I neither condemn nor approve what has been done [in Rwanda]. I have my own views, but I will express them to the OAU.[46]

At the G-7 summit on 9 July in Naples, Mitterrand delivered a speech calling for 'a development contract, based on a new international ethical-moral code' between the West and the 'developing world'. The aim, the French president preached, should be to get the poorer countries 'off the fringes' and into the midst of countries that had a greater amount of the world's riches. The *Financial Post* commented:

> Under normal circumstances Mitterrand's little lecture might be expected to drag out of the G-7 some ringing declaration of intent which – like so much that emerges from their annual get-togethers – will turn out to be absolutely meaningless. But coming as it does from a statesman who is currently showing his concern for the travails of the Third World by a highly 'question-able' intervention in Rwanda, Mitterrand's proposal may provoke only hollow, if concealed, laughter.
>
> It's true, of course, that French troops in Rwanda have rescued a handful of nuns and taken under their protective wing a few pathetic Tutsi survivors straggling out of the bush to escape their French-armed and, some of them, French-trained Hutu attackers. But overall, their actions have tended to confirm that their over-riding objective is exactly what sceptics suspected all along – to protect and preserve their client Rwandan government of Hutu extremists.[47]

Chapter 8

Bisesero and Withdrawal

T he road that winds slowly upwards by the side of Lake Kivu, through the small pretty lakeside town of Kibuye, is one of the most scenic stretches in Rwanda. One's eyes are held by the incredible greenery of sorghum, banana and mango groves, and the steep-sided ravines that drop down precipitously to the blue-grey waters of the lake. In 1994 this area, known as Bisesero, became a major killing field and, by July, it was difficult to move more than a few yards without stumbling across a badly decomposing or half eaten body, left to the elements and scavenging dogs. It had been a particularly wet period, with incessant and torrential rains lasting for days. For Tutsis who were still alive in late June, sheltering in holes and hiding amid the soaking green foliage of the plantations, life was made even worse by being attacked by swarms of mosquitoes and insects.

Of the 70,000 Tutsi inhabitants of Bisesero at the start of April, fewer than 2000 were left three months later. This hilly region had seen massacres before. Some remembered the 1959 pogroms when Hutu killers stalked the region and hundreds were beaten to death. But unlike in the rest of Rwanda, in Bisesero the Tutsis fought back. There they had a reputation for being warriors who would not allow an enemy to force them from their lands.

When Habyarimana's plane was shot down on 6 April many Tutsis from the surrounding areas fled to the hills of Bisesero, including Anastase Kalisa, a 21 year-old labourer at the nearby Gisovu tea factory who took refuge on the slopes. 'The *bourgmestre* of Gisovu, Alfred Musema,[1] who was the director of the Gisovu tea factory, together with

146

local teachers drove around everywhere in their cars, making Hutus aware that their President had been killed by the Tutsi and that they had to start taking revenge. They also said that the Tutsi intended to exterminate the Hutus.'[2]

The massacres began once the militia had taken many Tutsis' machetes, clubs or spears from them at gunpoint. Houses were burnt and cows slaughtered. Vans brought killers along the two-hour trek by road from Kigali. Three respected local officials and businessmen, Clement Kayishema, Dr Gérard Ntakirutimana and Obed Ruzindana,[3] used their authority to organize and lead the genocide. Like an immense game of cat and mouse, attackers – 'as many as the grass in the bush' – mounted repeated operations to hunt down families and individual Tutsis taking refuge in the hills.

The Tutsis fought back. Unlike elsewhere in Rwanda where they sought refuge in their homes, churches or local community buildings and were slaughtered with little resistance, at Bisesero they used what weapons they had kept from the militia to counter the *Interahamwe*. However, after living in the open, being soaked by the rains, with insufficient food and drinking water, under constant fear of attack and without any facilities to treat machete and bullet wounds, by June the survivors were in a desperate state.

With more than 65,000 decomposing bodies on the hillside, the exhausted survivors had to endure the daily nightmare of seeing dogs and crows slowly devour the bodies of their murdered kin. As the survivors fought desperately through April and May, the killers, who came in buses and were paid for their 'labour' by men like Obed Ruzindana, became increasingly concerned to finish the 'work.' Genocide made good business sense; it took away rivals and a fat profit could be made from seizing Tutsi homes, possessions and money.

For the 2000 survivors left hiding in holes, mine shafts and amid the heavily wooded slopes, the news on the radio at the end of June that French soldiers from Operation Turquoise had arrived in the Kibuye area to stop the genocide was both unexpected and immeasurably welcome. It is difficult to imagine how it must have felt to be hunted for two months, to be on 'death row' waiting for a machete or club to end your life in the most brutal way and then hear an announcement on the radio of your salvation. It was the same feeling the Jews inside the gates of the remaining concentration camps must have had in the summer of 1944 as rumours of the advance of the Allies reached them. There was a glimmer of light in the form of the green and red berets of the Gallic soldiers. Anastase said:

> We had a horrific time from April to June. It was the first time I learned how terribly hard life can be. We had nothing to eat or to drink. I had no one to protect me and was very frightened what would happen. It was the first time I had ever seen a man kill another. I was alone and there was no one to help me. The three months were like 100 years. The first time I saw the French soldiers, I felt at last some hope, as if I was not dead after all and that there could still be a new life.[4]

On 27 June a well-armed advance party of Operation Turquoise discovered the survivors. Its base was only a matter of minutes away in Kibuye, which on 17 and 18 April had been the scene of two appalling crimes when, at the church of St John and in the town stadium, a large group of killers, directed by local government officials, had slaughtered crowds of Tutsi civilians who had fled there for safety. Afterwards, the Hutu authorities brought in Caterpillar trucks to move the 13,000 mutilated bodies into mass graves.

The foreign troops were easily spotted making their way up the hillside. Witnesses speak of four to six vehicles, with 20–25 troops. Megaphones were used to call the Tutsis from their hiding places with promises of food and safety. When the French stopped, wounded, ill and frantic Tutsis began coming out of hiding towards them.

According to another survivor, Damascène, 'The French arrived, but we saw when we came out that they were accompanied by some of the militia killers – men like Alfred Musema, Nzarora, Mika and others whose names I did not know. The French soldiers seemed aggressive and not pleased to be here.' Charles Seromba told the same story. 'There were about 20 French soldiers, who seemed ill at ease and not happy to be here. We asked for food and drink. We saw them arrive with the militia, but though this made us very anxious we still came out of hiding to meet them. We were desperate and at the very end of our strength.'

François witnessed the French force using helicopters that kept an eye on what was happening on the ground.

They were the ones who summoned us with microphones, asking us to reveal ourselves and come out of our hiding places – we'd been hiding in some of the mine holes in Bisesero. They told us we had to come out since they were coming to rescue us, and intended to transport us to a place of shelter, in zones occupied by the [Rwandan] Patriotic Front where there was no risk of us being killed.

Some people came by helicopter with the French, there were, among other things, three helicopters, three that I saw with my own eyes. The others arrived by jeep, there were three of them also, I didn't see another one – they were jeeps that belonged to the French with *Interahamwe* who were disguised in clothes from the Red Cross. This was a trick to stop us recognizing them; they were with some soldiers in the jeeps.

As regards those who arrived by helicopter and those who arrived by land, they used the microphone to tell us they were coming to rescue us, that this was an opportunity the French were giving them to rescue us. 'Show yourselves so that the French can take you to a safe place.' They spoke to us in Kinyarwanda, since the French don't speak that language.[5]

Anastase continued:

The French soldiers did not look happy, instead very military and aggressive. All we [survivors] were armed with were bows, arrows, some lances and clubs, but no guns. The French road-block meant we survivors came out to see them, but we had to give them our arms. But they had come with the militia. I recognized Jean Baptiste Twagirayezu [a known *Interahamwe* killer] there with them.

Eric Nzabahimana was another survivor who came out of the bush where he had been hiding to speak to the soldiers and to persuade them to help him and his fellow survivors. He was aware that the French were with Twagirayezu who assured the troops that the victims here were the Hutus, and that they alone were threatened. Eric said:

As I could see that these French men were really listening to this

149

teacher (Twagirayezu), I called out to the Tutsis who were in the bushes. I even showed them the Tutsis who had received machete blows and who had been shot. I also showed them the corpses that were there. After that, the French listened to me. The soldiers looked at us and asked us to continue hiding. They told us that they would come back in three days.

Colonel Jean-René Duval – known as 'Diego' – led the French special service commandos. They discovered the survivors after two nuns at a convent further down the slopes had alerted them to the fact that terrible events were happening in the hills. The French soldiers had picked up a guide from a village to take them to an area where the survivors were expected to be found. Unknown to them, this guide was himself a well-known killer whose appearance with the French caused panic, fear and confusion when they reached the survivors.

The French troops took photos of the nightmare scenario in front of them. Even for most of the soldiers, not used to the ravages of Africa, it cannot have taken too much common sense or initiative to know who was telling the truth: those who came out from the bushes, emaciated, fatigued beyond reason, cut, wounded and with desperation written on their faces, or the *Interahamwe* in their own convoy, dressed in clean clothes, or disguised in Red Cross uniforms, looking well fed and watered. The fear of the survivors was palpable.

However, having come across the desperate Tutsis and having heard their tales of daily death and slaughter at the hands of the militia, Diego decided to leave and return in 'two or three days' time' to recover those who were in mortal danger. It is unclear why this specific period of three days was decided upon if in fact help could have been sent earlier – within hours or certainly within a single day – had the will been there. Journalist Patrick de Saint-Exupéry, who accompanied Diego on this initial mission, states that the entire Turquoise operation was put together – men equipment, aircraft and supplies – and flown several thousand miles to Rwanda in a mere nine days.[6] It is scarcely believable that it would then take a further three days to move a few kilometres unless there was a lack of will to do so at a higher political and military level. It seems that Diego had expected to return earlier than the stipulated two or three days, but in the event had been prevented from doing so by orders from superiors.

The result of the three-day French withdrawal was as predictable as it was terrible. The waiting militia, who had been searching for surviving Tutsis, suddenly found them in front of them. Anastase commented: 'When they [the French] said they were going my life again became a nightmare. The militia returned the next day.' Another survivor, Jérôme, recalled how 'immediately after their [the French] departure Dr Gérard [Ntakirutimana] came with his militiamen; they wiped out many of the people who had been hidden before the arrival of the French.'[7]

Vincent Kayigema, who was eight years old at the time, testified that the French had assembled around 200 Tutsis who had come out of hiding on a hill; facing them were crowds of armed militia. When the French then turned their armoured vehicles round and left, the militia stepped in 'and killed more than half of the Tutsis who were there'. In the intervening three days before the French returned about 1000 Tutsis were slaughtered. Damascène put the figure at 2000. Many Tutsis were too exhausted to run and hide again. Emotionally, too, many gave up. Their last hope of salvation had proved a ruse – a cruel Gallic joke.

While the militia resumed its 'work' with enthusiasm, the French patrol went back to base. According to Patrick de Saint-Exupéry, Diego spent the next three days making numerous calls on his satellite phone to Paris to alert higher command about the imminent danger to the hundreds of Tutsis they had seen on the hills. At the later 1998 inquiry, a clash of different dates for the eventual rescue of the survivors hints at some form of cover up. While Saint-Exupéry is clear that the initial discovery was on 27 June, the French commanding officer, Marin Gillier, told the inquiry that his men came across the 'Rwandan tragedy for the first time' on 30 June, which would have meant no delay before the rescue came, rather than the three-day wait, which was the reality.[8] In fact, on 26 June, the day before Diego and his men discovered the survivors, three journalists – Hugeux, Kiley and Bonner – had informed Gillier that massacres were taking place. For the next three days Gillier, like Diego, made repeated calls to his superiors to ask for action to be taken to assist those at risk, but failed to receive clearance. Gillier's testimony to the 1998 inquiry smacks of an attempt to cover up his own failure to act – when action was taken it was by his troops 'on their own' initiative against specific orders not to intervene – and to protect those senior military figures who had refused Gillier permission to mount a rescue.

Diego eventually tired of talking to superiors in Paris who, despite Turquoise's alleged humanitarian mandate, seemed inclined to resist intervention. After waiting around for orders to move that never came Diego, according to Saint-Exupéry, set off back into the hills with his men. This time Colonel Jacques Rosier, head of the special force attached to Turquoise, directly intervened to stop him. This veteran of Operation Noroît landed his helicopter on the road in front of Diego's troop convoy. Signalling to Diego to come over, the two officers had then been involved in a 30-minute discussion before Diego ordered his troops to turn round and return to their base. Rosier, who had been in Rwanda from June to November 1992 as head of the pro-FAR military cooperation operations in Kigali, had told him that they could go no further.[9] He still seemed to regard all Tutsis as possible RPF 'enemy', even if in this case they were desperate genocide survivors.

The fact was that army chiefs did not see this rescue mission as a priority. Instead, they fell back on the formulaic response that possibly 'the hills were alive with RPF infiltrators' as the reason for not taking the initiative in allowing a rescue mission. This was despite reconnaissance patrols having found no evidence of the RPF and, although they had flown over the Bisesero survivors, overhead aerial operators had received no orders to try to spot alleged RPF movement in the area.[10] Rosier and other commanders in Paris were refusing to countenance a rescue mission even though the French had a base full of special service commandos, the equivalent of the British SAS, ready and willing to return to help the survivors and stop the genocide. Moreover, Operation Turquoise was trumpeted as a UN-mandated 'neutral' expedition, so any meeting with Kagame's RPF should now have made no difference. The French foreign office was in contact with the RPF through Dallaire and it would have been perfectly feasible to have negotiated an expedition to rescue the survivors. This was not 1992 and the French were not 'at war' defending the FAR and Rwandan government. The continued antipathy towards the RPF in the minds of some senior officers who had served in Rwanda during Operation Noroît, however, and their failure to delineate what was now a totally different situation was a real Achilles heel in the ability of Turquoise to fulfil its 'humanitarian' remit. At Bisesero this attitude allowed the genocide to continue and the genocidaires to stroll around unhindered.

152

On 29 June Defence Minister François Léotard visited the area on a public relations mission to ensure that the media gave full coverage to the 'humanitarian' operation and that Mitterrand's government received all the plaudits it deserved for its Rwandan intervention. Léotard's officers had fully briefed him on the likelihood of the killing nearby continuing, for the journalists with Operation Turquoise had asked for action to be taken to help those they had seen being massacred on the hills. According to Raymond Bonner of the *New York Times*, 'Léotard rejected any operation to evacuate or protect the embattled Tutsi at Bisesero saying that the French "did not have enough troops to protect everyone".'[11]

Under continued pressure, Léotard gave in before he left, though the subsequent mission, which Captain Marin Gillier was detailed to provide on 30 June, was first and foremost aimed at rescuing a French priest from a church near Bisesero. In fact, after learning of the plight of the survivors on 29 June, Sergeant-Major Thierry Prungnaud told Gillier, his commanding officer, that he and his companions in the 13th RDP (Régiment des dragons parachutistes) would be heading into the hills to rescue the survivors the next day. Gillier made no effort to stop them, even although they were effectively breaking a direct order not to leave base. Once the Tutsi survivors were rediscovered, further help was sent for and the rescue began in earnest.[12]

The Tutsi survivors greeted the belated return of the French troops with a wide range of emotions. Many wondered if they were in league with the killers. After all, they had previously arrived with militiamen and then left, perhaps to allow the genocide to continue. When Damascène saw the French returning, he feared they would face imminent death. 'We asked them to kill us instead of continuing to side with the *Interahamwe*. And we felt hate towards them and feelings of wanting vengeance on them and their *Interwahamwe* compatriots.'

This time the French used drums to persuade the survivors to come out again from hiding and, as before, it took place in front of groups of armed militia who stood watching on a nearby hill. The survivors, now fewer than 1000 in number, were put into a group and given biscuits, water and medical attention. Most were in a terrible condition.

One woman, Anathalie Usabyimbabazi, who had lived in the undergrowth for two months and kept herself alive by eating raw potatoes, had to endure seeing dogs ripping up and eating the mutilated bodies around her. She was so emotionally disturbed that the French at first refused to take her on the grounds that she was a 'mad woman'. Eventually, persuaded that she had been normal before the genocide, she was taken away for treatment. Prungnaud described coming across a valley in which 10,000 people had been killed and in which the survivors were in a truly 'lamentable condition'.[13] French troops had then combed the area for more survivors among the scattered debris of mangled, machetted, decomposing and half-eaten bodies. The French force found no evidence of RPF infiltration.[14]

Charles Seromba remembered the French action well. 'They did not apologize even when we showed them the bodies of those killed when they left three days before. But we were so hungry and thirsty we had to come out of hiding again even though we were unsure what would happen.'

With other traumatized Tutsis, Damascène was taken down the steep slopes to the bottom of Muyira hill at the centre of Bisesero. The survivors did not speak to the soldiers, partly because many could not speak French and partly because many who could did not want anything to do with them.

The traumatized survivors were given a choice. They could depart for the RPF-controlled area or be moved into the self-declared 'safe zone' held by the French. Not surprisingly, given the previous actions of the French and their continuing open ambivalence to the killers who walked about with the foreign troops and were clearly still anxious to 'finish the job' of killing the remaining Tutsis, the survivors opted for the former.

Anastase said he had seen Alfred Musema twice at Bisesero while the French were there.

> He [Musema] told the French soldiers that there was no need to protect these Tutsis because the country was safe … I was there when he came the second time. Every one [of the survivors] screamed and told the French that he should not be allowed to come into the camp. Despite our shouts that he was a killer the French let him go.

Other witnesses said he asked the French to hand over the survivors to them. Eric testified:

The French protected us but they did nothing to punish the *Interahamwe* who had killed us. On the contrary, these assassins had many conversations with the French. He [Musema] told these soldiers to leave and not to protect the people who were the cause of insecurity in the region. He was in a red Peugeot. The survivors who saw Musema wanted to attack him but the French calmed the situation and Musema left.

Seeing the killers of your family and neighbours driving around the French camp and talking to the foreign troops, it was perhaps not surprising that the survivors opted to be taken to the RPF zone rather than stay in the French SHZ (safe humanitarian zone). This sparked an angry reaction from their French 'saviours', which many of the survivors witnessed.

Damascène said, 'For the first days they treated us very well, but later they reacted badly against us because we asked to be moved to the [RPF] area that was close to us. They refused us food to eat and drink, as well as the clothes they had promised us.' Philimon Nshimiyimana described the soldiers as angry 'so much so that they stopped giving us food', while seven survivors, with Anastase acting as spokesman, commented:

> While negotiations went on with the French and RPF as to whether we would be allowed to go to the RPF zone, we were not allowed food or drink for long periods. The French were not happy when we said we wanted to go to the RPF zone. To make their point the kids and adults were chucked into the back of trucks for the journey to the RPF zone like things that don't matter.

Today, inside a corrugated metal shed on a Bisesero hillside, only metres away from where the French convoy arrived, are several long wide tables. Layed out on each table are line upon line of skulls, perhaps 2000 in all, of all sizes, from those of tiny babies to elderly adults. At the far end, 15 metres away, are more piles of bones. The light filters through holes in the metal ceiling and rudimentary walls. Each skull, each head, each person, all with a tale of calamitous suffering, all with a story of anguish and pain they can no longer shout

out. The empty eye sockets look blindly out into the dark. Ten years after the genocide bodies are still uncovered each week on the mountain and the remains brought here to this grim carnal house.

Charles commented, 'I feel nothing towards the French now. I think the French soldiers are like the *Interahamwe*.' For the only time in our conversation he raised his voice in anger and emotion, a voice that up until then had remained soft and low despite the appalling story he offered. 'If a French soldier stood in front of me now I would accuse those soldiers of being criminals. They killed my family.' Charles's brother was murdered during the three-day period when Turquoise left the Tutsi of Bisesero to their fate.

Anastase said he wished the paratroopers had never arrived, for with the RPF rapidly approaching the survivors could have been saved.

> If the French soldiers had not come here we would have stayed in hiding and only come out when the RPF arrived, which would have been soon. Because of the French many came out and were killed. I'm sure more would have survived if they had not come. I think of the French like I do the *Interahamwe* – that is together.
>
> They came up, after all, with the militia, and they travelled together with them to Gikongoro, Kibuye and Cyangugu. The French have a great responsibility for what happened here.

The 1998 inquiry into France's role in Rwanda devoted a meagre 20 lines to the incident at Bisesero. It put the lack of action firmly down to Gillier, although, as we have seen, the real reason for the failure to intervene was that Diego and Gillier were given direct orders not to mount a rescue mission. That such a rescue eventually came at all was because individuals like Prungnaud had enough courage to break ranks and disobey orders to put humanity before politics and military pride.

***

Bisesero proved to be a watershed for many French soldiers, especially those drafted in from bases in Africa or serving on the continent for the first time. Prungnaud later described how, at the five-minute briefing session the troops were given when they initially arrived at Turquoise headquarters in Goma, they were specifically told that Tutsis were killing Hutus. This deliberate disinformation about the genocide clearly came from high up in the French military from those who still wanted to 'beat the RPF'. Prungnaud reckoned that the officer who gave the briefing to his men was unaware of who was killing who and was just reiterating what higher command had told him. It took most of the soldiers several days, indeed weeks, to recognize that this was a deliberate falsification. With Hutu crowds and militia cheering their arrival in the country, and orders to work alongside the Hutu police, prefects and *bourgmestres*, most of whom were genocidaire, it was not surprising that ordinary soldiers with no previous experience of Rwanda or any axe to grind about continuing the fight against the RPF, assumed that they were the 'good guys'. The legionnaires at first also took the vast swaths of Hutu refugees as a sign that they were the victims of some appalling RPF/Tutsi terror.

After events like Bisesero, the truth of who was killing who became all too evident, leaving men like Prungnaud to feel that they had been deliberately manipulated by both the Hutu killers who had warmly welcomed them and fed them lies and by their own higher command. He complained, 'We thought the Hutu were the good guys and the victims.' Another soldier spoke with disgust of how he had had enough of 'being cheered by murderers'.[15] French journalist Thierry Cruvellier commented that many of the soldiers he saw were sickened and upset by the slaughter into which they had stepped.[16]

It was as if there were several different French armies in the area during Operation Turquoise. There were the brothers in arms with the FAR during Noroît in 1990–93 as well as those that had recently arrived in Rwanda with no preconceptions. The approaches of men like Diego and Marin Gillier were totally different, for example, from that of Tauzin who headed the 1st RPIMA. Unsurprisingly, units that had previously fought alongside the FAR, such as Foreign Legion regiments like the *regiments étrangers parachutists,* or the RPIMA, were more hostile than others to the RPF and its 'Tutsi sympathizers'. They found it difficult to accept that their FAR allies had been defeated and were now in retreat. The war against the RPF took precedence in their minds over the ongoing genocide. It was as if Turquoise was still an extension of Noroît and its aim to repel and undermine the RPF was paramount. Colonel Rosier and others who shared his hardline anti-RPF stance in Paris, such as Generals Quesnot and Huchon, along with mercenaries and secret servicemen already in the country, were working to an agenda far removed from the UN-mandated intervention that was publicly lauded by the Élysée. The sole objective was to defeat Kagame.

Equally, many French troops acted with immense courage and integrity to help save Tutsis and to make the horror of the genocide fully known. Some like Prungnaud, who had helped train the presidential guard in 1992 and was horrified to learn of its involvement in the genocide, chose to disobey orders to help the survivors at Bisesero.[17] Others, with no previous involvement in Rwanda, were soon able to dismiss the disinformation they had received about who was killing who and got on with the practicalities of saving life and feeding refugees.

Captain Gillier, for example, is said to have urged a media cameraman to film the site where hundreds of corpses were found when the French returned to Bisesero on the grounds that 'people must see this'. He described the killing as 'intolerable'.[18] Though criticized for being a 'desk man' who was afraid to take risks, Gillier's reaction to the difficult situation in which he was put at Bisesero was understandable. Caught between soldiers who wanted to save life and his commanders who had a different agenda, it is not surprising he 'froze'.

Lafourcade, like other officers in the command structure, did his best to pull the various strands of his mission together, but there was always a political and military extremist bandwagon in the French camp that made Turquoise an uneasy mix of views and action.

Near Cyangugu, in the south, a journalist described how

> bodies of Tutsis, no more than two hours dead, lie among the banana groves. The houses they once lived in stand half empty, looted even while the life drained from their owners' veins. French soldiers from the Special Forces, the first of 2500 troops ... arrive at the scene. There is little the reconnaissance team can do. They are two hours too late. Nearby, Hutu militiamen armed with modern automatic rifles and Stone Age clubs, the sort of men, if not the very ones, who have carried out massacres like this, stand about smiling and waving at the French soldiers. Many wear bandanas in the red, white and blue of France. A Rwandan army jeep races through the countryside similarly decked out.[19]

Such French troops cannot have taken long to realize that their briefing on who was killing who had been a complete fabrication.

***

Throughout Rwanda the genocide and chaos continued into July. The RPF advance continued to quicken, to deny any advantage to the incoming French force. The Rwandan army and militia sustained their killing spree and the tactic of pushing the Hutu population into retreat with them. Up to 300,000 refugees began moving towards the borders in an attempt to flee the RPF advance.

On 1 July Jean-Bernard Mérimée, the French representative at the UN, sent a letter from Mitterrand's government to Boutros-Ghali informing the secretary-general of the need to establish an SHZ in southwest Rwanda. It cited earlier Resolutions 925 and 929 as authorizing such a zone.[20] This was despite Prime Minister Balladur telling the world before Turquoise began that France would on no account become a 'force d'imposition'. Yet, the area of the proposed zone, which precluded any RPF presence, was clearly one of demarcation, cutting Rwanda in two and depriving one side of total victory.

However, the Security Council showed no will to readdress a debate on Turquoise. While internationally the new SHZ was perceived as a way the remnants of the Hutu army, militia and government could escape RPF retribution, no country wanted to get politically involved in the UN Security Council by contesting its setup. Instead, it was silently permitted.

Bastille Day, 14 July, provided Mitterrand with an excellent opportunity to justify the French action in Rwanda with some impressive-sounding 'spin'. In a televized interview on Channel France 2, he claimed that Habyarimana had been a real advocate of the 'La Baule principles' that France could not intervene in Rwanda during the genocide because this was the job of the United Nations and that if the present Rwandan crisis restored the power of President Mobutu Sese Seko (in Zaire), this was due to unforeseen circumstances. According to Prunier, any informed observer of such 'machiavellian statesmanship' would have 'hesitated between involuntary admiration for the President's constructive capacity for lying and disgust at the degree of contempt it implied for the citizen-spectator'.[21]

With the fall of Kigali on 4 July and the setting up of the SHZ, Operation Turquoise entered its second stage. After further negotiations with Kagame, using Dallaire and UN representative Shaharyar Khan as intermediaries, General Lafourcade withdrew his forces to an area of 70 square kilometres in southwest Rwanda. It included the town of Cyangugu, the district of Gikongoro and reached up to Kibuye on Lake Kivu.

Such a zone was only made possible after the finalization of talks with the RPF. According to newspaper reports, an agreement between the two forces was reached on 6 July.[22] A day earlier, Turquoise had withdrawn from the Hutu heartland and the interim government HQ at Gisenyi, a signal that the northwest was finished as a base for the FAR. It was also an acceptance that Kagame had won the war. An uneasy peace came into effect between the two sides, with the RPF tolerating the SHZ, while the French in turn restrained the more belligerent members of their staff who wanted a crack at Kagame's men. At the start of July, Colonel Tauzin had announced, from his position near Gikongoro, that if the RPF challenged the 'line in the sand' the French had drawn, he would 'open fire against them without any hesitation … and we have the means'.[23] Lafourcade issued a statement rebuking the gung-ho Tauzin, declaring that 'we will not permit any exactions in the HPZ [SHZ] against anybody and we will refuse the intrusion of any armed elements.'[24] For the sceptical Kagame, the question was which of Lafourcade or Tauzin best represented the true sympathies of Turquoise.[25] Lafourcade, wisely sensing that Tauzin was a liability to this immensely sensitive operation, had him replaced as head of his unit and returned to Paris.

Other French officers were in agreement with Tauzin and complained 'off camera' about the role they were playing. Prunier overheard a senior officer moaning after the fall of Kigali, that 'the worst is yet to come. Those bastards will go all the way to Kinshasa now. And how in God's name am I going to explain to our friends [francophone heads of state] that we have let down one of our own.'[26]

Aloys, the Rwandan army recruit and *Interahamwe* trainer, was certain about what he witnessed.

They [the French] told us they were heading off to Gikongoro and Kibuye to bar the route to the RPF, so they wouldn't set foot in Gikongoro. They assured us it was inconceivable the RPF could come and find us in Cyangugu. They asked us to ensure we found all the Tutsis still in the region so that we could exterminate them. They promised that our zone would, thanks to them, become a Turquoise Zone. It was Frenchmen who spoke in those terms. Then they told us it was too late, the RPF had forces they hadn't suspected; we'd waited too long before appealing to them; it was too late.

They were telling us all this when things were taking a turn for the worse for them and they'd started exchanging fire with the RPF at Gikongoro. They told us there was no other way round it; we all had to escape to the Congo without exception. Anyone who tried to stay behind would be considered to be a cockroach himself. It was the French themselves who said all this.

They asked us to flee wherever they went; in the small trading centres they urged people to flee from the RPF. Like in those small centres, they asked everyone they encountered, 'Tutsi or Hutu?' If you answered 'Hutu', they gave you the thumbs-up, saying 'Yes!' But to recognize a Hutu, they relied on this sign: the fact he was carrying a cudgel. Some of the cudgels had studs in them – we called them 'no possible ransom to redeem an enemy's life'; this had really impressed the French. They told us that, on this point, they recognized that the Rwandans had a sense of creativity and that they would never have imagined such a weapon for killing with. We'd killed with those things several times, right in front of their eyes, and they did nothing to prevent us.

Frankly, if they'd come to save people, they'd never have let us continue killing the Tutsis in front of them, let alone given us some of the equipment that we were using.

Another thing, if the French hadn't lied in saying they were coming to save them, there wouldn't have been so many Tutsis killed from among those who had survived up until then. When the French arrived, the surviving Tutsis had every chance to get away, first and foremost since the RPF was coming up fast. And what did the French do? They advanced so as to hold up the RPF troops and prevent them coming to rescue the Tutsis who were still in Cyangugu. This is what aggravated things in that prefecture.

Yes, once the RPF were held up by the French, we found the time and the patience to flush out the ones who'd managed to hide. We'd already been doing that but we were frightened of encountering an RPF soldier. We knew they were going to arrive from one day to the next and we'd seen some of our soldiers running away. You told yourself that if you risked nosing around in the bushes, you also risked finding an *Inkotanyi* who wouldn't forgive you.

But once the French had told us 'don't worry, we're on our way!' we felt secure and we started to go deeper into the bushes to flush people out – we were full of confidence and determination since we had the blessing of the French and knew we were even going to reconquer the whole country.

Not only did they advise us, but they even ensured we had enough food. And they took the initiative and came to us. Sometimes they would meet the prefect, Manichimwe, who sent a soldier called Bikumanywa, a sergeant major in charge of the stocks at the Karambo camp. He would come and give us the instructions that he'd received from the French. 'You can go wherever you want, without fear – we've got the French supporting us, and they certainly don't want to see the country in the hands of the cockroaches.'

As for the roadblocks, there too the French weren't exactly complimentary about our work. They told us the barriers would give us away and they advised us to remove them and inspect everything by the roadside. We took away the tree trunks that were blocking the road and we kept an eye on everything, at least along the road. They explained to us that when the international community keeps things under surveillance, if the satellites see barriers, it creates a really bad impression; so they advised us to keep watch on the road without erecting barriers.

No, there was never the slightest problem or misunderstanding in our relations with the French. They distributed weapons even outside Nyarushishi [a refugee camp just inside the Rwandan–Zaire border] at the customs post for instance, when they entered the country.[27]

In some areas of the Gikongoro sector, French forces had set up their own roadblocks to stop not Hutu militia, Rwandan army and interim government ministers and officials from entering the SHZ, but the perceived real 'enemy' – possible RPF infiltrators.

French paratroopers at one such roadblock stopped Alphonse, a Hutu from Butare, as he was travelling back to his village near Gikongoro. They insisted he remain with them to help spot possible RPF infiltrators trying to get into the SHZ. Alphonse remembered,

> the biggest problem at the roadblock was them wanting me to point out who people were. 'Even you could be an RPF member' they said to me. 'How do we distinguish them?' They said they had come to help but could not distinguish now who to help. By this time the government troops [FAR] and militia had changed into civilian clothes. The RPF were infiltrating the safe zone by using FAR and militia uniforms to get into the zone for reconnaissance purposes. It was almost impossible for me to distinguish the RPF and FAR from each other. But I was left in no doubt that the RPF were still very much seen by the French as 'the enemy'.[28]

While in Butare, Alphonse said he had seen the genocidaire Georges Rutaganda, vice-president of the *Interahamwe*, leaving Hotel Ibis with French troops to go to Gikongoro, before the RPF arrived in the town.[29]

> The French troops said what was happening was just 'trouble among the people' and that it was Rwandans fighting Rwandans, even though they must have known genocide was happening. I think they knew what was happening but did not care. They just called it 'killings'. There were journalists from the BBC and other media also around to research and see what had happened, but no soldiers seemed interested.[30]

The fear of RPF infiltration and destabilization of the SHZ was a pressing concern for the French troops. A cartoon published in *Le Canard Enchaîné* during Operation Amaryllis summed up the phobia French soldiers now felt towards the RPF and Tutsis. It depicted a furious and exasperated looking French officer looking from one Rwandan to another shouting, 'Have you ever tried to distinguish a big

Hutu from a small Tutsi?'[31] It was a near-impossible task. Even native Rwandans could not tell their ethnic group by just looking at a person, hence the killers' need for identity cards.

Pierre, a member of the retreating Rwandan army commented, 'It was said that the Inkotanyis [RPF] were coming in civilian dress but were still armed. So they [the French] disarmed all civilians so as to stop any Inkotanyis getting past. I don't know what they might have done to an Inkotanyi they caught. I'd left beforehand and up until I left they hadn't caught a single one.'[32]

***

A vital decision faced the Turquoise leadership once the SHZ was declared at the start of July – namely how to deal with the armed militia, FAR members and interim government ministers now fleeing into the zone. As the RPF swept across the remaining area of Rwanda, Hutu peasants decided on flight away from both the conflict zone and any RPF repercussions. RTLM played on the fear and guilt, putting out messages that the RPF was slaughtering whole villages and committing genocide against the Hutu population. The prefect in Ruhengeri warned that anyone who stayed would be massacred.[33]

For the interim government now preparing to flee from Gisenyi the best possible outcome was for Kagame to inherit a deserted country. With the fall of Kigali, around 1.5 million refugees fled with what belongings they could muster towards 'safety' in the SHZ. With the fall of the northern towns of Ruhengeri on 13 July and Gisenyi a few days later the southern French zone became a magnet for both the innocent and guilty.

UNAMIR commander Dallaire commented,

> as predicted, the creation of the HPZ (SHZ) lured masses of displaced people out of central Rwanda and into the French zone. This was the terrible downside of Operation Turquoise. Having made public pronouncements about their desire to protect Rwandans from genocide, the French were caught by their own rhetoric and the glare of an active international media presence, and now had to organize the feeding and care of them … the trap the French had rushed into would inevitably begin to close.

Either they would pull out as soon as they could – even before the sixty day limit of their mandate – or they would be cast in the role of protectors of the perpetrators of one of the most severe genocides in history.[34]

Despite its public banner of humanitarianism, the problems Operation Turquoise faced were largely political. Should its officers disarm the militia and FAR contingent in the SHZ? Should they arrest and imprison, to await later investigation, those who were named as carrying out the genocide? And should they arrest the architects of the slaughter, the members of the interim government now fleeing into the SHZ? As with so much French policy on Rwanda, the answers that came from politicians in Paris and military leaders on the ground were confused. Judging from the solitary sheet of paper on which the initial plan for Turquoise had been written, it did not look as if the matter had been given much thought.

The need to please the world's press and uphold Turquoise as a great French success meant statements affirming the capture of genocidaires and the disarming of the militia were vital for the operation's 'humanitarian' credibility. Politically, however, such a strategy could badly damage French influence over other francophone African dictators, would fly in the face of its previous policy of complete support for the Rwandan army and interim government, and was deeply unpopular with hardened French Africanist politicians and military figures.

The result was confusion. Even before Turquoise began, Foreign Minister Juppé declared in mid-June that 'France will make no accommodation with the killers and their commanders … [and] demands that those responsible for these genocides [note plural] be judged.'[35] The deputy director of African and Malagasay affairs at the foreign office, Yannick Gérard, advised cutting off French support for the interim government. 'Their collective responsibility in calls to murder over Radio Mille Collines during these months seems to me to be well established. Members of this government cannot, in any case, be considered valid interlocutors for a political settlement. Their usefulness lay in facilitating the good operation of Operation Turquoise. Now they will only try to complicate our task.'[36] He added that such 'discredited authorities' were useless and harmful. The only statement the French government should now give to them should be to 'get lost as fast as possible'.[37]

Elsewhere the message was far more supportive of the genocidaires. On 11 July General Lafourcade welcomed the interim government ministers fleeing to the SHZ as Gisenyi fell, telling them they could seek asylum in France.[38] By 15 July, realizing what a public outcry this statement was causing, the decision was reversed, with the foreign office in Paris declaring that such ministers entering the SHZ would be arrested.[39] The reality was that France had dealt with this 'band of killers' for several years. To arrest them now was both to fly in the face of friendship and loyalty and to admit publicly that it had supported men it now knew were mass murderers.

Dallaire received a memo from Lafourcade confirming that the French commander and his government 'had no mandate to disarm the RGF', though he would prevent it from taking action in the humanitarian zone. His memo stated that

> Turquoise was not going to disarm the militias and the RGF in the HPZ (safe zone) unless they posed a threat to the people his force was protecting. As a result the extremists would be able to move about freely in the zone, safe from any interference from the French, and also safe from retribution from, or clashes with, the RPF.[40]

On 15 July, having learnt that several members of the interim government were now in Cyangugu in the south of the SHZ, Ambassador Gérard wrote to Paris of his concerns: 'Since we consider their presence undesirable in the secure humanitarian zone and knowing as we do that the [interim government] authorities bear a heavy responsibility for the genocide, we have no other choice, whatever the difficulties, but arresting them or putting them immediately under house arrest until a competent international judicial authority decides their case.'[41]

Instead, in the confusion of the mass of humanity now crowding into a tiny area of southern Rwanda, the interim government's prefects, mayors, ministers and militia continued to go about unchecked. Lafourcade found he needed to talk to such ministers to try to resolve the refugee crisis because the militia and Hutu radio still effectively controlled the mass of people fleeing towards Zaire. Dallaire, along with UN envoy Shaharyar Khan and Lafourcade, went to Gisenyi to meet interim foreign minister Jérôme Bicamumpaka, FAR leader

General Augustin Bizimungu and other ministers. Dallaire suspected the genocidaires were planning to re-form over the border in Mobutu's Zaire, and were even now making bargains with local power dealers in Goma and the surrounding area 'to retain their weapons and political structure, thus setting up to come back into Rwanda in force within a couple of years and start the war all over again'. The UNAMIR commander also made a tacit reference to 'sympathetic senior French officers inside the [refugee] camps', where the mass of displaced people had settled, colluding with such deals.

On 16 July Lafourcade met Bizimungu again at the French HQ in Goma.[42] The French general asked Dallaire to keep the meeting private, fearing media embarrassment if his conference with this genocidaire became known. On his return by helicopter to Bukavu, a major French base for Turquoise, Dallaire became increasingly aware of quite how much human misery now swarmed around the border area between Rwanda and Zaire. 'I was surprised at the lack of NGO or UN agency presence in the town, but I already knew that Turquoise did not have a solid humanitarian plan. There had been major looting in Cyangugu under the noses of the French. This was not looking good at all.'[43]

The wrangling over the possible arrest of the genocidaires continued. The French government decided to ignore the advice of its ambassador Gérard about the genocidaire problem. Bruno Delaye, Mitterrand's African adviser, commented that the French mandate for Turquoise 'does not authorise us to arrest them on our own authority. Such a task could undermine our neutrality, the best guarantee of our effectiveness.'[44] On 18 July Admiral Lanxade reiterated that 'France has no mandate to arrest the members of the former government.'[45] Though keen to change the mandate to allow the safe zone to be set up, Mitterrand was less than keen to push for it to allow the arrest of the leading killers.

The OAU surmised that France was failing to arrest the genocidaires for political and highly cynical reasons. First, to claim that it would harm French neutrality to arrest the perpetrators was nonsense. France had never been neutral in Rwanda and even now was resettling *Akazu* members in Paris. Second, France had never asked for the mandate to be modified, which it could have done if this were a sticking point. No mandate was ever set in stone – witness the setting up of the safe zone. Third, France tended to act unilaterally anyway; it had not bothered with mandates for Operations Noroît and Amaryllis, and had started

Turquoise without waiting for UN 'permission'. Finally, the real mandate was the Genocide Convention, which France had signed up to in Geneva on 12 August 1949. Under Article IV, 'persons committing genocide ... shall be punished, whether they are constitutionally responsible rulers, public officials or private individuals.' The French government was keen to announce that it registered the happenings in Rwanda as genocide before the rest of the world wanted to use the word. Now it backed away from enacting the convention, where the mandate to arrest and bring to justice those who had committed such horrific crimes was obvious.

The French arrested just nine alleged genocidaires, but even they were not handed over to UN custody, as originally promised.[46] Two other suspects, known as 'Prima' and 'Sebastial', were arrested by local officials and given to the French. They were later escorted to Zaire in French vehicles when Turquoise pulled out of Rwanda, and released.[47] Journalist Sam Kiley reported that on 2 July the French military evacuated Théoneste Bagosora, the Rwanda genocide's chief architect, to safety from Butare along with other 'persons'.[48] His information came from a high-ranking French officer who knew Bagosora well. In an article entitled 'France's killing fields', *The Times* accused the French of using the SHZ as a place that was 'safe from the advancing RPF and thus safe for the murderers'.[49] Former President Giscard d'Estaing reinforced this view when he condemned the zone for merely protecting some of those who had carried out the massacres.[50]

Former *Interahamwe* Janvier was blunt in his appraisal of what he witnessed.

> The French came to finish off what had been prearranged in agreement with Habyarimana, even if he was now dead. They gave no assistance to the victims. If they claim that they did, let them show us a single killer who they arrested. They killed maybe between one and five *Interahamwe*. If this was the objective, why didn't they kill Munyakazi for instance, since he was the commander of an entire battalion of killers? This simple question requires an answer from them, so ask them on our behalf. Why didn't they arrest Yusufu our [leading *Interahamwe*] commander?[51]

Disarming the militia and Rwandan army as they retreated was another problem Turquoise needed to address. In practice, in the rare event it happened, it meant collecting antiquated rifles while the real killing weapons of the genocide – machetes, hoes, axes and clubs – were left in the killers' hands. Colonel Tauzin insisted that up to 7 July he had collected around 100 weapons, but that most of the other armaments had already been destroyed in fighting with the RPF. A later French inquiry concluded that it was 'uncertain' if any methodical and systematic disarmament had taken place. As a result, militia and FAR activity was 'not stopped completely in the SHZ'.[52] According to Pierre, who was fighting with the FAR as they retreated towards Zaire:

> Turquoise was aimed at containing the *Inkotanyis* [RPF] and preventing them crossing over and coming here to Gikongoro. On one occasion, for instance, they'd tried to pass through Mwogo to enter Gikongoro. That time they fought them and the *Inkotanyis* had to beat a retreat under heavy French fire. The French had prepared their attack but the RPF must have lost a lot of their men.
>
> When the French saw men fleeing, they took special care to protect the fugitives fleeing for the Congo. The ex-FAR were in cahoots with the French. For instance, when the FAR crossed the border with their weapons, the French didn't disarm them; they let them through without hassling them.[53]

Turquoise also failed to close down RTLM, the hate radio station that, though continually having to move its broadcasting centre, managed to stay on air propagating its mission to see the killers 'work' harder and faster to fill the graves with Tutsi dead. Dallaire had protested for some time about RTLM, but his words fell on especially deaf ears. Francois Léotard alleged that jamming the radio's frequency or destroying its transmitters was not part of the mandate given to the French by the UN.[54] The issue was one of free speech, and while the interim government was still recognized as 'legitimate' the radio station should be allowed to express its opinions. This again was despite Article IIIc of the Genocide Convention, which made punishable any 'direct and public incitement to commit genocide'. Bruno Delaye also claimed that the French operation was unable to find the transmitters

RTLM was using, despite the impressive air reconnaissance power, satellites and modern ground surveillance systems in use.

Any enthusiasm to jam RTLM was not helped by the friendship of its founder, Ferdinand Nahimana, with members of the French government. Indeed, former ambassador Georges Martres was even alleged to have described Nahimana as 'a fine little Frenchman'.[55] This former history professor and Hutu extremist propaganda chief, whom Operation Amaryllis had airlifted to France in early April, later returned to Rwanda to ensure that his radio station was still in robust health and continuing its killer broadcasts. Nahimana also acted as an emissary between the interim government and Turquoise.

The French safe zone had, by mid-July, become a stepping off point for terrified Hutu peasants aiming to cross into Zaire, where refugee camps were already being set up. For the interim government the policy was to get to Zaire to re-form and rearm. To make this possible it needed the collusion of the French operation. While Hervé Ladsous, the French chargé d'affaires, issued a statement prohibiting any armed people from entering the SHZ, it was obvious that this applied only to the RPF. French troops allowed, and even actively assisted, the retreating Rwandan army and militia to cross into Zaire with their equipment and weaponry intact. Human Rights Watch reported one foreign soldier who testified to seeing Turquoise military refuelling Rwandan army trucks before they left for Zaire with looted goods.[56] As it was, FAR troops walked about openly in the safe zone with their weapons, many the gift of previous French assistance. The OAU reported that Rwandan army soldiers were receiving whole cargoes of weapons in the camps, organizing military exercises and recruiting new troops to prepare to return for a final victory in Rwanda.

Not surprisingly, RPF commander Paul Kagame was unhappy about genocidaires re-forming a few kilometres the other side of the Rwandan border. The RPF expressed disquiet to Lafourcade about this, while shelling Goma airport on 17 July from positions inside Rwanda, with explosives hitting the runway while planes loaded with equipment came and went. The effect on the refugees piling into the town from Gisenyi across the border was, according to Dallaire, 'debilitating'. French commanders accused the RPF of attacking its forces near Kibuye and a statement was issued from Paris to say that Turquoise would no longer tolerate intrusions into the SHZ.

On 18 July, the day after taking control of the Hutu stronghold of Gisenyi, the RPF announced it was calling its own ceasefire. On 19 July a new broad-based government was sworn into office in Kigali with Hutu moderate Pasteur Bizimungu as president and Paul Kagame as vice-president.

***

Diogène, a former FAR member, sat and sipped his Primus beer by the hotel pool where we met. It was a humid day and Diogène, now a high-ranking officer in the new unified post-genocide Rwandan army, spoke of the events he had witnessed ten years before in the spring and summer of 1994. As a FAR battalion commander in Kigali from 1991 to 1993 he made many trips to the northern Volcano region where the RPF attacks were most acute.

I knew some senior French officers, for example Colonel Chollet, who taught tactics to the FAR in Rwanda, and had been appointed special adviser to the Rwandan army staff. He seemed to be both a military man, but also a politician. I saw him often on the ground advising the commanders about operations, especially when fighting in the northern Volcano area.

The French officers were sure that the RPF would never win. They were disappointed in 1994 by the RPF victory. They wanted to bring in military support on the ground but it was too late. By this time half the territory was in the hands of the RPF and the FAR soldiers had lost morale.

When Operation Turquoise entered Rwanda via Zaire both the [interim] government and [Hutu] people were unsure if they had come to fight the RPF. But in fact the only firefight was near Butare, when two French soldiers [later released by the RPF] were captured in an ambush. France did not stop the genocide near Gikongoro, which continued despite the French presence.

French soldiers provided the FAR with help with the heavy artillery and mortars. Ammunition also had to be replenished from French stocks, but lack of money often meant weapons were taken back to the armoury as there was no ammunition for them. The French seemed happy to be here but shocked by the amount of death. The army [FAR] and [interim] government disappeared when the French didn't fight. It was very important what the French did – the Rwandan government was lucky that for the past seven years the RPF could not win the war or advance [because of the French military presence].

Everyone saw that politically France was supporting the interim government. When the French arrived in Gikongoro [during Operation Turquoise] they were very well welcomed – with flags and happy sentiments as if the war was now over.

My family and I and other families were taken to Zaire in helicopters in July, along with other [FAR] officers – about five in total; when we got there, after about three or four days we issued a statement condemning the genocide. After that we had our guns taken off us; we were escorted at gunpoint from our tents by French soldiers and thrown out of the camp, which was near the airport. We were accused of being against the [interim] government and working for the RPF. We had issued a communiqué asking the government to stop the genocide. Two senior officers and a general were dismissed. After I was thrown out of the camp – with French soldiers escorting me away – I then went to Bukavu camp and back to Rwanda where the RPF authorities received me, and I ended up joining them.

The FAR officers were divided in their opinion over the genocide. Some from the north saw it as OK as they did not want to lose power but many officers from the south tried to stop the killing. For example one FAR officer from Cyangugu helped to save Tutsis by putting them in a camp under his protection. He is now dead. Many Tutsis survived because of this. Many of the [FAR] soldiers from the south were not happy fighting when their own side was killing innocent people.

For us in the FAR, we used French soldiers as both military and political advisers. Though Rwandan commanders gave the orders, there were many French advisers on hand. In terms of numbers, there were far more militia than the FAR, and many were trained by the presidential guard, who had themselves been trained by the French DAMI.[57]

According to Diogène's important testimony, there were French soldiers in the military camps in Zaire still acting on behalf of the interim government. French soldiers from Turquoise were responsible for ejecting him and fellow complainants from the FAR base, and were supporting Bagosora and his henchmen. It was another case of some members of Turquoise failing to see the bigger picture, and putting past and present loyalty to their FAR and interim government friends and allies before matters of justice and humanity.

In the localities, Hutu villagers in the Gikongoro region were reassured to see the French forces. 'We could hear the sounds of the gunfire near Gitarama on the other side of the river but when the French arrived they put a roadblock up to stop the RPF coming. We were happy to see the French soldiers as after they came we knew the war would not enter this area,' an old man commented while sucking on his pipe pushed into a bottle of banana wine. 'Apart from the genocide, there was no war in this area.'[58]

Aloys Mutabingwa testified that the French had singled him out for punishment for failing in his duties, but not because he was a genocidaire.

> One day I'd been denounced by the man in charge as my group hadn't done the night patrol. The French made me get into a helicopter, and they told me, 'You press-gang people and stop them working, we're going to throw you into the Nyungwe forest.' They took me as far as Dendezi, and there they released me telling me this had better be the very last time that I got in the way of other people's work. But they'd punished me; they'd completely stripped me; they didn't even leave me with any underwear. They told me, 'Now clear off, you can just scarper.' This was in broad daylight. It was 1994, in July. At that time I was a member of the *Interahamwe*, but I was also still a member of the army since I hadn't been dismissed.[59]

The French used such helicopter trips, it seemed, to discipline individuals they felt were stepping out of line. Rumours circulated widely in the villages about such action and helped foster a view that the French were in control of events. Several villagers testified that they had heard about such flights, though they were split over whether they were to punish the Hutu or surviving Tutsi population. Whatever the answer, the Geneva Convention would not have condoned them. At Murambi, just outside Gikongoro, thousands of Tutsis were slaughtered after having been transported to an unfinished technical school by the militia. At a memorial rally in April 1997, a survivor spoke of how French troops from Operation Turquoise had helped to bury the bodies when they arrived. The soldiers then made themselves a volley ball court on the ground above the mass grave.[60]

Operation Turquoise soldiers were increasingly having to deal with malnourished refugees and the devastating effects of cholera on those who had fled to the SHZ or to camps over the border in Zaire. They were ill-prepared for their role and unable to handle the pressure of organizing food for hundreds of thousands of displaced people, a situation, ironically, that Turquoise had helped to create. The actual humanitarian stage of the operation suffered from a lack of resources and poor relationships with aid organizations on the ground. Such bodies wanted to assess the needs and numbers of refugees properly before planning a response. They reacted angrily to French military personnel randomly telling them to hand out food as and when it became available; also, the food was often of questionable value, such as tonnes of sardines.

Moreover, the aid agencies were reluctant to be drawn into the complex political manoeuvres that were taking place. To help the French effort was to risk the ire of the RPF and, as a result, organizations like MSF, Oxfam and the International Red Cross refused to work alongside Operation Turquoise. Most of them were afraid that Paris would hijack their cooperation for propaganda purposes. In fact, one organization responded to pleas to help distribute sardines and high protein biscuits only to find France announcing its cooperation publicly; the agency immediately stopped assisting the military mission.[61]

Major Jean-Yves St-Denis, who flew in to help assess the situation in Goma for the UN, reported seeing 'a pile of bodies at least twenty feet high' and 'hundreds of bodies ... littering the roads. All of them ... had succumbed to cholera. For a while we followed a dumper truck filled with bodies that had been picked up by French soldiers. ... I remember the soldiers' eyes; they were lifeless and full of sadness.'[62] Turquoise had become overwhelmed by the tragedy it witnessed. Never equipped as a humanitarian mission, the soldiers ended up acting as morticians and death-cart drivers. Dallaire commented, 'Lafourcade had come into the country heavy with combat assets and light on the tools of humanitarian relief. Frozen in its tracks by the spread of cholera and by the knowledge of the health risks its troops would be exposed to due to the high infection rate of HIV/AIDS among Rwandans, Turquoise remained limited.'[63]

The important shift by the world media away from the genocide inside Rwanda to the refugees' plight was a godsend for Paris. News coverage of legionnaires working tirelessly with orphans and cholera victims in refugee camps was just what the politicians who had heralded Turquoise as a humanitarian mission wanted to see. The smokescreen behind which the killers lurked was to stay in place long enough for the world to forget from what it was that the refugees were fleeing. Members of the French public could again feel proud that their government had saved people who were dying in Goma while other Western powers looked on. The suffering, as Prunier noted, was 'mixed up', making it churlish to ask who was in most pain – the victims of genocide or of cholera. As the suffering and its causes became confused, so too did the whole political debate over how it came about, France's role and who was responsibile for the events in Rwanda.

On 21 July it was revealed that, despite the pictures being broadcast of malnourished desperate refugees begging for scraps on which to survive, the French military had given ten tons of food to the FAR soldiers near Goma. French diplomats seemed more concerned that the media would pick up on this appalling misuse of humanitarian aid than the fact that it showed again the complicity of some of Turquoise military with the FAR and genocidaire.[64] It certainly did not smack of the 'neutral' stance Mitterrand publicly insisted was being enacted by his forces.

Such impartiality was, according to one *Interahamwe* leader, far from the truth. He alleged that once the militiamen had reached Zaire, the French had allowed them to keep their weapons, and

> they had established a military base for us [at Mpanzi]. Once we'd put up our tents, the French arrived and went to find General Kabiligi; they immediately set up a group to attack Rwanda and destabilize the *inyenzis*. Once this base had been set up, it was divided into subgroups placed along the border. So they started attacking and a lot of damage was done as a result of

this criminal complicity between the French present in the camps and General Kabiligi. When we were in the camps, the weapons were brought in by the French, every sort of weapon, on lorries, even TVs arrived.[65]

Operation Turquoise finally began its planned retreat from Rwanda on 19 August. French legionnaires moved from their base near Gikongoro and were replaced by Ghanaian UNAMIR II soldiers. The result was panic for those who feared RPF reprisals. Tens of thousands of refugees continued to move into the SHZ and from there into Zaire. Official French statements on this sea of human misery tried to 'spin' the situation to their own benefit. Two days before Turquoise ended, Defence Minister François Léotard declared that:

> we did all that was possible to stabilize and reassure the popu-
> lation … it is now up to the RPF to make the necessary gestures.
> … I don't think it is fair to say that our intervention has only
> saved people temporarily. … Let us not forget that the safe
> humanitarian zone now contains more population than all the
> rest of Rwanda put together.[66]

In fact, while the SHZ had around 1.5 million people, the rest of Rwanda still contained about 3.2 million.

The number of people Operation Turquoise saved is variously put at between 10,000 and 17,000.[67] Dallaire's poorly-armed UNAMIR force of fewer than 500 men, by contrast, probably saved twice that many. With the distinction becoming hazier between the genocide on the one hand and refugees suffering in Bukavu and Goma on the other, images of French soldiers engaging in active humanitarian work had begun to obscure the political purpose of the intervention. It now became possible to consign to the bin of history pictures of militia killers waving French flags to greet their allies, survivors at Bisesero despairing after legionnaires had abandoned them and the RTLM welcoming the sons of Mitterrand to continue the fight against the RPF.

Fittingly, Operation Turquoise ended as it had begun. As the last of its troops left Cyangugu to cross to Bukavu in Zaire, Hutu crowds cheered them on their way.

***

Was Turquoise a success? While Prime Minister Balladur probably counted down the days until it finished, Mitterrand and Juppé justified the operation on the political stage, and military men like Lanxade and Hogard wrote glowingly about its strategic achievements. Writing six months after the operation, Admiral Lanxade declared that they had 'launched Turquoise as an urgent priority' and that it 'today presents a very positive balance sheet. Analysis of this operation should allow us to identify and strengthen, for the future, an operational concept adapted to actions with a humanitarian goal'.[68] The French chief of the armed forces had declared in July 1994 that the force had no mandate to arrest those responsible for the genocide, a position he felt was compatible with Turquoise being a 'fundamentally humanitarian' operation. Prunier, by contrast, described it as a 'public relations device with some political undertones. It was sold to the public as a humanitarian operation, which of course it was not.'

The timing of the intervention raises several issues. France knew that the genocide was killing thousands of people each day in early April, but its foreign minister only referred to the massacres as 'genocide' in mid-May, which was also when the vote went in favour of UNAMIR II intervention. Yet, while the UN was begging Western nations to donate troops and financial aid to this newly mandated force so that it could be sent as quickly as possible, Mitterrand chose to ignore its requests. One month and hundreds of thousands of deaths later the French president recommended sending an intervention force, this time UN mandated but effectively manned almost entirely by French troops. If France were so interested in stopping the genocide, why had it not backed the UN resolution to set up UNAMIR II in mid-May?

Having two separate UN missions acting under different mandates in the same country at the same time also presented a problem. It meant that Dallaire's under-resourced force ended up by having to mediate between the RPF and the other UN-mandated mission, Operation Turquoise, which, as an independent inquiry later noted, 'must be considered awkward to say the least'.[69]

In fact, the French intervention could well be referred to as Operations Turquoise, given that at any one time several different French missions seemed to be taking place with varying military and political aims according to who was in charge. While Barril and other operatives worked behind RPF lines on Operation Insecticide in an attempt to defeat Kagame, others, like Lafourcade, were negotiating with them. While Thierry Prungnaud was breaking rank to save Tutsis, high ranking officers like Rosier and Tauzin were happy to put a stop to any French intervention while their FAR and militia allies were busy completing their 'work'. Other French officers and troops, in sympathy with the FAR and militia, are alleged to have colluded in helping their allies continue the campaign against the RPF and even Tutsi refugees. On the political front some, like Prime Minister Balladur, had not wanted the operation to take place at all. In fact, Yannick Gérard at the foreign office had put forward a strong case for breaking all ties with the interim government and arresting the perpetrators of the genocide. Yet other politicians like Defence Minister François Léotard and of course Mitterrand, anxious to reap as much political capital as possible from their humanitarian expedition, would lace their speeches at home and abroad with references to how France alone had saved the Tutsis. The testimonies of former militia members and Tutsi survivors alleging that Operation Turquoise forces were complicit in rape, murder and looting need to be fully investigated.

On a wider canvas, the failure to disarm the FAR – in fact there is evidence of French complicity in feeding and rearming these forces even after the UN embargo was announced – plunged the region into a vicious, protracted war. For a whole decade *Interahamwe*, Hutu extremists and ex-FAR members continued to attack Rwanda from the safety of their bases in Zaire. The Red Cross estimates that at least four million people have died in this forgotten war since 1994. In 1999 Abdoulaye Yerodia, the foreign minister of the Democratic Republic of Congo (former Zaire), blamed Turquoise for 'bringing Rwandan Hutu militiamen into the Congo … it was France which carried out Operation Turquoise … an Operation which brought a lot of people into Congo, and one could clearly see armed men among them. Those who brought the armed men should assume their responsibility and organize another Operation Turquoise to take them away.'[70] The continuing presence of armed *Interahamwe* repeatedly derailed peace talks and prolonged Africa's most bloody conflict.

Thierry Prungnaud returned to France where, a few months after Turquoise had ended, a general in the ministry of defence called him in for a debriefing session. He asked him what he had seen and done during Operation Turquoise. Prungnaud told him, among other things, that he had recovered 'a list of 500 names of notables and others who had participated in or organized massacres'. The general's reply to this information shocked the Rwandan veteran who, in no uncertain terms was then told, 'listen, you forget everything, you recall nothing. ... He insisted I keep my mouth shut ... he was very precise that I must forget everything.'[71] In the eyes of such generals, anyone who fought against the RPF and Kagame could not be accused of any misdemeanour. It is a devastating indictment of the French military if their most senior officers are prepared to collude with mass killers merely because they are seen to be on the same military and political side.

By the end of August, politicians in Paris, especially Balladur, could settle back relieved to know that Turquoise was over and that the media were obsessed with the refugee camps. The medium and long-term tasks of rebuilding a shattered country, returning millions of its inhabitants, and dealing with the hundreds of thousands of geno-cidaires, ex-militia, FAR and those still eager to renew the civil war and genocide were all now problems that France could leave to the new Kigali government. Juppé tried to turn even this nightmare legacy and disastrous state of affairs in the region to France's benefit, claiming in a radio interview that, 'We have taken all the necessary precautions. We did not merely leave in the night, putting the key under the doormat.'[72] The French government's behaviour over the coming months proved that, as far as the new Kigali regime was concerned, it was quite happy to stand on the doormat and not give any clues on where to find the key to recovery.

Chapter 9

Burying Genocide

T he French 'humanitarian operation' left behind more than two million people crammed into refugee camps now blighting the Rwandan border. Piles of unburied bodies lay in heaps throughout Rwanda and the border refugee camps in Tanzania, Zaire and Burundi.[1] The genocide was over, the interim government had fled along with the genocidaires, leaving behind a tidal wave of human misery, disease, starvation, ethnic hatred and personal tragedy.

To brand Turquoise a success for posterity, politicians in Paris needed to justify the operation and parade it in the correct humanitarian robes. With the French role before July 1994 glossed over, interested journalists were encouraged to look instead at the human misery now lined up before the cameras in the camps at Goma and Bukavu. Foreign Minister Juppé told an interviewer five weeks after the end of the genocide that in Rwanda, 'one could not say that good was on the side of the RPF and evil on the other.'[2] If organizing the killing of a million people is not 'bad' or 'evil' what actually is?

The new RPF-based government in Kigali gained political recognition from the anglophone world early on. Within days of its creation in Kigali, the USA and Britain both officially recognized the broad-based regime and sent ambassadors to the Rwandan capital, while former colonial master Belgium also established immediate diplomatic ties. Mitterrand instead showed his antipathy. While anxious to take the credit for Turquoise he was not about to grant any political help to a new government he blamed for unseating one of his favourite francophone regimes. Paris pointedly sent Jacques Courbin to man a mere diplomatic cell in Kigali. No ambassador from France would grace Kigali and its anglophone government.

One month later, on 16 September, the new Rwandan president,

180

Hutu moderate Pasteur Bizimungu, travelled to The Hague for a two-day international conference on 'Rwanda in a regional context: human rights, reconciliation and rehabilitation'. It was the new regime's first chance to show its credentials to 150 delegates from around the world. When the new Rwandan leader got up to address the audience, the French ambassador to the Netherlands walked out of the event in a clear show of animosity.[3]

Diplomatic and political snubs aside, Mitterrand was more interested in hitting the new Rwandan government where it hurt – financially. Before fleeing from Kigali and Gisenyi, the interim administration made sure that everything that wasn't nailed down went with them or was destroyed. Rwanda's ministries and local government offices were plundered for typewriters, furniture, windows and even pens. Official vehicles were used to ferry the equipment away to Zaire. Any funds left from the Habyarimana and interim regimes were transferred to bank accounts set up in Belgium with the 17 billion Rwandan francs that former government members had taken into exile in Zaire.[4] Kagame's incoming broad-based government faced total devastation. Trying to run a country with a million dead, a third of the population displaced and the local and central administration in chaos was a nightmare. Many of the judges had been killed or had fled after taking part in the genocide. The story with the police, local mayors and prefects was the same. One former sub-prefect in the Gitarama region reported that when he took over in July 1995, one year after the genocide, things were still appalling. 'Everything had been looted. I got about on a beaten up ancient motorcycle. It took ages before, eventually, with German aid, we were able to buy some office furniture and even pens and paper to work with.'[5]

While aid agencies and the media concentrated on the refugee crisis, with cameramen vying with each other to bring the horror of the camps into the homes of Western viewers, the plight of the actual population in Rwanda went mostly unnoticed. New Rwandan vice-president Paul Kagame summed up the outcome of the 100 days of carnage in his country.

The genocidaires not only murdered a million people, they also destroyed our physical and social economic infrastructure, government, legal system, business and the whole economy. They

destroyed everything that supported human life. The survivors of
the genocide have suffered in silence. ... They lost their loved
ones, their property, and everything they called theirs; they were
tortured, raped and infected with HIV/AIDS and now live in
abject poverty. As if all this was not enough, we are over-
burdened with the need to forgive, to reconcile and to live with
former tormentors.[6]

A young Tutsi woman, Francine, saw her family being hacked to
death around her and spent the genocide hiding in the marshes to
escape the killers. But, unlike the French soldiers now returning to
their warm beds or the Western leaders in the USA, Britain and the
Élysée who had never even let the subject cause them to miss their pre-
dinner drink, the genocide survivors were condemned to a life of guilt,
regret and fear.

When you have lived through a waking nightmare for real, you
can no longer sort your day thoughts from your night ones as
before. Ever since the genocide I have felt pursued day and night.
In bed, I turn away from the shadows; on the road, I look back at
the figures that follow me. I am afraid for my child each time my
eyes meet those of a stranger's. ... I feel a sort of shame to have to
spend a lifetime feeling hunted, simply for what I am.[7]

In autumn 1994 Rwanda was about to collapse. Its new government
issued moving appeals to the West for aid to help rebuild its battered
and burnt infrastructure and for its Hutu population to return from
refugee camps now blotting the landscapes of neighbouring Burundi,
Zaire and Tanzania. The bankrupt new masters of a half-deserted
country were aware that rebuilding Rwanda would cost millions of
dollars, and this needed political will from the West and its banks.
The World Bank initially flourished a $35 million dollar cheque in
front of the Kagame regime, but then pulled back from handing the
amount over, claiming under its regulations that Rwanda had first to
repay a $6 million debt run up by the former interim regime since 6
April 1994. Its rules meant this debt could not be repaid from the
larger $35 million loan. By contrast, more than $200 million had
already been granted to aid the refugees, though the former Rwandan

army (FAR) and militia now controlling the camps funnelled off much of this.

The European Union also made noises about giving emergency aid to the Kigali government. Brussels voted for $200 million recovery aid to Rwanda only to see the French government veto the donation. The Paris agenda was simple – if they could not undermine the new Kigali regime by military means, then economic 'sanctions' were the next best weapon. The French demanded that no money be given until the refugee problem was resolved and that the new government in Kigali be broadened to include more Hutus and non-Kagame supporters.

Behind the demands was a clear French political agenda. One pro-French European Commission official told journalists:

> The French priority is the return of the refugees. The genocide comes second. You can't reconstruct a country if the people are out of the country. The RPF has strong links with the US. It has lots of arms and lots of money. It is necessary not to forget that the Americans helped the RPF and were the first to give aid. And the British followed on the American side.[8]

Put simply, France would not tolerate an anglophone regime in Kigali. Reconstruction of Rwanda, justice for those affected by the genocide, and help to those left starving in a country without food were less important to Paris than scoring political points and undermining the new government in Kigali.

British MEP Glenys Kinnock told the Strasbourg Parliament:

> The EU is refusing to release funds until the Rwandan government creates satisfactory conditions to enable the return of the refugees. But the government simply has no way of creating those conditions without receiving the aid. There seems to be a French hidden agenda here. Because of their association with the previous government, they are not wanting to do anything to ensure that the present government has a future. I am not saying France wants more bloodshed, but that will be the result.[9]

The new Rwandan interior minister Seth Sendashonga spoke of the Catch-22 position in which the French had put his country. 'We are refused both political confidence and material means, and at the same time are being asked to straighten out right away a situation of massive disaster.'[10]

Bernard Kouchner, who represented the Mitterrand government during the genocide, was equally critical of the French position. 'I don't want to malign my own country, only to help the victims. The government in Rwanda has opened up, but nobody has responded positively. I have had enough of people being mealy-mouthed, saying "this is politics". We need to help the Rwandan government create national reconciliation.'[11] The *Economist* magazine commented:

> The European grudgingness is not for lack of money. The EU has a pool of $166 million for long-term development and economic reform set aside for Rwanda, and this is largely unspent. The EU has released only $6.1 million to help restore electricity and water. The biggest finger in the EU dam is the French. ... The French argue that Rwanda's new government is illegitimate and tainted. It took power by force and, being Tutsi-dominated, does not represent the population at large.

As nearly a million Tutsis had been killed, it was not surprising that the Tutsis were now even more of a minority. Even so, the new broad-based government contained members from four other political parties, as well as more Hutus – including the president, prime minister and finance minister – than Tutsis.

> The price of isolating Rwanda could be high. A government without western friends may seek them in more dangerous places. A government that cannot pay its (more vengeful) soldiers puts its own political survival in peril. There is an urgent need to transfer power from soldiers to civilians. That means setting up a police force and a judiciary. At a recent count Rwanda only had three lawyers.[12]

Justin Forsyth, a senior Oxfam representative, spoke to the justice ministry in Kigali about problems in Rwanda, still without electricity and water, where revenge killings were commonplace because there was no machinery of law to punish atrocities. 'Genocide and civil war have shattered Rwanda's social fabric. Without substantial aid the country has no possibility of rebuilding its economy and its social structure.'[13]

However, French minister for cooperation Bernard Debré insisted the new anglophone government 'from Uganda', now in place in Kigali, allow refugees back, create a healthy judicial system and set a date for elections before any aid could be forthcoming. It was as if genocide, for Paris, were a purely political phenomenon, with no emotional or physical effects. No French minister had set foot in the country since the genocide to speak to survivors, examine the wrecked infrastructure, or step over the mounds of bodies left to rot in some massacre sites. Prunier commented on Debré's speech, remarking:

> Hey presto, the French magic wand had solved all the problems! It would have been funny if in the meantime half-starving orphans had not kept playing with leg bones for sticks and skulls for balls, if the refugee camps had not turned into social bombs whose fuses were likely to be lit by desperate men whom France kept helping, and if a new and very imperfect regime which was making a modest attempt at improvement had not been systematically starved, as if to see how soon it would break into another bout of homicidal madness. If this happened, one could after all feel justified – these people were all savages, and this new bunch were no better than the ones we had supported earlier.[14]

Foreign Affairs Minister Juppé went on national television on 26 November to announce, 'What is the Rwandan nation? It is made up of two ethnic groups, Hutu and Tutsi. Peace cannot return to Rwanda if these two ethnic groups refuse to work and govern together. ... This is the solution France, with a few others, is courageously trying to foster.' One commentator noted, 'One tends to pity the "few others" who have been welcomed on board this "Titanic" of a policy.'[15]

The last Franco–African summit of François Mitterrand's presidency took place in November 1994 with the spectre of Rwanda hanging over it. The place ally and friend President Habyarimana had occupied in the previous decade among other francophone leaders remained empty. Rwanda was pointedly not invited, a clear signal that, with Kagame at the helm, it was no longer considered a francophone country. Mitterrand left any discussion of the tiny African state off the agenda.

The 35 heads of state met at Biarritz on 7 November with the words of the new Rwandan prime minister ringing in their ears when he talked of the snub of not being invited. He had dismissed the francophone summits as 'picturesque meetings that never produce important decisions affecting our country'.[16] As the *Independent* pointed out, at the beginning of his Élysée tenure in 1981 Mitterrand's own Socialist Party had singled out three dictators at the summit, Mobutu of Zaire, Bongo of Gabon and Eyadéma of Togo, as men to be removed because of their appalling human rights record. Some 23 years on, Mobutu was rewarded for his recent support for France with a seat next to the French president.

Mitterrand decided that the best form of defence was attack when it came to the volley of criticism aimed at him and his government over their Rwandan record. In his opening address to the conference he told the delegates, 'One cannot ask the impossible from France, which is so alone, when local chiefs decide to … settle their quarrels with bayonets and machetes. After all, it is their country.'[17] If it were 'their country' why did France need to get so involved? As for local chiefs, it was politicians and the military that had carefully organized and planned the genocide, not a few savages deciding to settle old scores. With no sense of irony at the French military intervention in Rwanda, Mitterrand announced that now 'the time has come for Africans themselves to resolve their conflicts and organize their own security'.

Former cooperation minister Michel Roussin told the French newspaper *Le Figaro* on 10 November, 'there are still crimes committed whose responsibility has not been clearly established. In this context, to invite representatives of the new [Rwandan] government would not be proper.' If this were the criterion for exclusion from the francophone conference, no country would have come to Biarritz.[18] Bruno Delaye, Mitterrand's African special adviser, no doubt aware that the FAR were rearming and re-forming on Rwanda's border, added, 'We won't invite the new Rwandese authorities to the next Franco–African summit. They are too controversial and besides they are going to collapse any minute.'[19]

Added to this snub for the new Rwandan regime was the French government's attempt to further the 'double genocide' myth for its own political motives. At the UN, repeated statements from Hutu Power representatives during the summer of 1994 indicated that they saw the events in Rwanda as justified because the massacres were being carried out 'by both sides'. This theory of 'double genocide' was a vital component in reassuring the West that the slaughter was pure interethnic strife, thus implying that any intervention on one side only would be unjust. Hutu extremists alleged they were only defending themselves and that the massacres, while regrettable, were taking place because the population was afraid the RPF would kill them. The reality was that the genocide was a deliberately planned political event, not the result of sudden massive interethnic tension.[20]

Once the myth of 'double genocide' had been advanced, Mitterrand was quick to use it for his own political benefit. Turquoise, he argued, was put in place to 'stop a second genocide' – one in which the RPF would presumably kill a million Hutus. In the written version of his speech at Biarritz on 8 November, Mitterrand talked about the 'genocides' that had happened in Rwanda. When journalist Patrick de Saint-Exupéry quizzed him on this, the president replied, 'would you say that the genocide stopped after the Tutsi victory? I wonder.'[21] Prunier reported Mitterrand saying to another journalist, 'the genocide or the genocides? I don't know what one should say.'[22]

Historically, denial theories have always been used to raise doubt and confusion and to justify horrific crimes – witness German defences of the Holocaust that claimed that the Jews were engaged in a war against them or that Allied bombing was itself a 'holocaust'.[23] More recently, in July 2005, during the tenth anniversary of the Srebrenica genocide of 8000 Bosnian Muslim men and boys, the Serb government issued a statement deploring war crimes but equating the massacre of the unarmed civilians with the killing of Serbs during the Bosnian war. Ian Traynor, writing in the *Guardian*, felt 'the aim was ... to relativise and belittle a crime which judges in The Hague have classified as genocide.'[24]

France is still advancing this appalling 'double genocide' theory. In September 2003, Foreign Minister Dominique de Villepin, who made great play to the international community of the French 'non-interventionist' stance over Iraq, referred to 'the Rwandan genocides' in a broadcast on Radio France Internationale. Nearly a decade after the horror of 1994, Villepin, who at the time of the genocide had been working as a senior official at the Quai d'Orsay, was still rehearsing this appalling fabrication. Journalist Patrick de Exupéry, who covered Operation Turquoise and had witnessed the genocide, heard the broadcast while stuck in a Moscow traffic jam. He described Villepin's expression as 'terrible', with his disgust pushing him to write a book, *L'Inavouable* (*The Shame*) about French complicity in the genocide.[25]

• Visitors to churches in Rwanda that now stand as memorials to the thousands who were systematically murdered inside them can see the stark legacy of this lie. A bold, hand-written notice in blood red that hangs above the entrance to the church at Nyamata in which thousands were slaughtered declares '*non aux revisionnistes, non aux negativists*'. Anyone who would deny the genocide ever happened or 'revise' it to make it appear purely part of a civil war or ethnic clash is not welcome here. For the survivors, the claims that in some way they are to blame, that the killing was their fault, only adds to their suffering.

Paul Kagame has frequently complained to the UN about France allowing the ex-FAR and *Interahamwe* to set up new military camps in Goma, Bukavu and neighbouring areas of Zaire, without hindrance and in some cases with a great deal of help. According to UN ambassador Shaharyar Khan, Kagame reported to him on 15 August that his information showed that the militia and FAR had been systematically looting the former French SHZ and stealing vehicles in which to ferry the defeated troops over to Zaire. Reports surfaced in the media soon afterwards that French troops were continuing to arm and train some of the FAR, whose aim, according to Colonel Bagosora, was to return to Rwanda to 'wage a war that will be long and full of dead people until the minority Tutsi are finished and completely out of the country'.[26]

A confidential report from an international aid agency put together in Zaire in October pointed to the French continuing to support their former FAR allies. The source in Goma wrote in the report of 'rumours in existence about F[rance] supporting (training and rearming) former Rw[andan] troops ... official source of information (UNAMIR) confirmed later that retraining of former Rw[andan] troops by F[rance] was a fact.' The source alleged that such training was being carried out in the Zairian capital, Kinshasa.[27]

François Karera, former prefect of greater Kigali and alleged genocidaire, told US journalists, 'We do not have any fear regarding lack of arms, as we have countries ... prepared to support us financially and with weapons.'[28] By mid-November, aid agency MSF had pulled out of the Zairian refugee camps, citing lack of security and *Interahamwe* leaders being in control of the camps as the reason. The head of MSF-

France told a Japanese newspaper, 'The leaders of the refugees are those who carried out the massacres and they are trying to recapture power.'

It was estimated that the ex-FAR, Habyarimana's former army, now had up to 50,000 soldiers in a dozen refugee camps, from where it was already launching murderous raids into border villages in Rwanda. A United Nations report suggested that the Bukavu camps alone held around 10,000 ex-FAR and militia – around a third of the former Rwandan army.[29] British journalist Christian Jennings tracked down two architects of the genocide, MRND chief Joseph Nzirorera and Matthias Ngirumpatse,[30] ensconced in a large house outside Goma, in August 1994. Nzirorera insisted that even if he were tried and condemned to death, his party would return to Rwanda to kill more Tutsis. At the end of the interview he reached over and asked the British producer, who was with Jennings, if she would care to dine with him when next in Paris.[31] An investigation by Human Rights Watch detailed the way the FAR had been re-equipped for a renewal of war. According to the investigation, they

> continued to receive weapons inside the French-controlled zone via Goma airport ... it is unlikely that the French military authorities present in the zone, who conducted regular patrols at the border post between Goma and Gisenyi, and had a continuous presence at Goma airport, were not aware of weapons entering the safe zone. Yet the French authorities neither made an attempt to interdict these shipments nor report them to the Committee set up by the Security Council under Resolution 918.[32]

The report criticized the fact that weapons confiscated from the Rwandan troops fleeing into Zaire were later given to Mobutu's authorities. Since France knew that Zaire supported the interim government and its troops, it was 'hardly appropriate' to give the arms to these allies of the FAR. The French even left a weapons cache behind for the militia in the Rwandan town of Kamembe in the former SHZ. According to the Human Rights Watch researcher who saw the arms dump, it contained more than 50 assault rifles and several machine guns. *Africa Confidential* confirmed that Agathe Habyarimana, still residing in her luxury Paris house, accompanied Zairian leader

Mobutu on a trip to China, where it alleged she bought arms for Bagosora's reinvasion of Rwanda.

The Human Rights Watch reported the French military using their helicopters to move Bagosora, militia leader Jean-Baptiste Gatete and 'crack troops of the ex-FAR and militias out of Goma to unidentified destinations on a series of flights between July and September 1994'.[33] Allegations were made that Hutu militants continued to receive training at a French military facility in neighbouring Central African Republic. On at least one occasion members of Hutu militias from

> both Rwanda and Burundi travelled on an Air Cameroon flight from Nairobi to Bangui, capital of the Central African Republic, via Douala, Cameroon, between October 16 and 18 1994, to receive training from French forces there. The Burundian government, which learned of this independently, requested from the French government as to what kind of 'education' such Hutu militants were receiving.[34]

However involved the French were 'unofficially' with rearming and training the FAR, the failure to look to stabilizing a region rather than helping increase tension showed a lack of understanding and concern for the future of the civilians caught up in the strife – the very people its highly trumpeted 'humanitarian' operations had boasted they were there to help. There was, it seemed, little attempt to hide the brazen nature of the continued French support.

> Colonel Munyakasi [head of the ex-FAR in the Chimanga camp in south Kivu on the Rwandan border] has bragged of French military offers to help train his men. There is no firm evidence of direct French involvement, or of illicit French weapons shipments of the kind that breached the UN arms embargo towards the end of the [civil] war. But contacts are maintained, and French military attachés have flown to Goma and Bukavu from France and Kinshasa in recent weeks.[35]

The instability that such an organized and well-armed group caused in an already volatile region became apparent in the coming decade. With the Mobutu regime in free fall and the ageing, infirm dictator confined to his grandiose mansion in the jungle around Gbadolite, his poorly paid and ill-disciplined Zairian army took what rich pickings it could from exploiting the Rwandan situation. Kivu, the area where most refugee camps were embedded, became a launch pad for violent cross-border raids into Rwanda by the ex-FAR and *Interahamwe*, who also took the opportunity to attack Tutsis who had settled in the Zairian border region.

In its 2000 report, the OAU, clearly held French policy responsible for destabilizing the region.

> The consequences of French policy can hardly be overestimated. The escape of genocidaire leaders into Zaire led, almost inevitably, to a new, more complex stage in the Rwandan tragedy, expanding it into a conflict that soon engulfed all of central Africa. That the entire Great Lakes Region would suffer destabilization was both tragic and, to a significant extent, foreseeable. Like the genocide itself, the 'convergent catastrophes' that followed suffered from no lack of early warnings. What makes these developments doubly depressing is that each led logically, almost inexorably, to the next. What was lacking, once again, was the international will to take any of the steps needed to interrupt the sequence. Almost every major disaster after the genocide was a result of the failure to deal appropriately with the events that preceded it, and what was appropriate was evident enough each step of the way.[36]

For survivors of the genocide, any attempt to come to terms with the emotional and physical trauma of the events of 1994 and with the loss of their families, homes and livestock rested in seeing the perpetrators brought to justice. Within a year of the genocide more than 100,000 alleged killers were being held in prisons across Rwanda, though the justice system was too overwhelmed to cope with investigating the crimes and putting the accused on trial.

To placate its conscience as much as to bring justice, the West set up a court in Arusha, Tanzania to try leaders of the genocide – those it held responsible for planning, financing and organizing the killing. The ICTR (International Criminal Tribunal Rwanda) was established in November 1994 and the first trial began in January 1997. For the survivors, the hope was that the world community, having turned its back on the actual genocide, would now at least do its duty by financing and helping to organize a court to bring those responsible to justice. It is ironic that the court should be located in the same town as the peace talks and agreement meant to end the ethnic and political tension and bring unity to Rwanda had been held.

According to the ICTR's own public relations statement, 'The purpose ... was to contribute to the process of national reconciliation in Rwanda and to the maintenance of peace in the region, replacing an existing culture of impunity with one of accountability.' The court's remit was to 'prosecute persons responsible for genocide and other serious violations of international humanitarian law committed in the territory of Rwanda between 1 January 1994 and 31 December 1994'. The dates are important because, after pressure from France, all actions before 1994 were deemed outside the court's mandate. No account of Operation Noroît, French complicity with the Habyarimana regime or other embarrassing findings would be forthcoming. The genocidal massacres at Kibilira in October 1990, Bagogwe in 1990/1 and Bugesera in 1992 would be ignored. France did not want its military put on the witness stand to explain what had taken place while it was in Rwanda on a non-UN mandated mission supporting a government killing its own people. As it began its proceedings in 1997, the president of Human Rights Watch, Ken Roth, attacked 'the total lack of enthusiasm by France for the work of the ICTR'.

For the small insignificant town of Arusha, the ICTR has become a milch cow – for taxi drivers, bar and restaurant owners, food sellers and even the shabby prostitutes who sidle up to wealthy white UN workers money is abundant. In 2002/3 the UN General Assembly gave the ICTR a budget of $177,739,400, much of which went in wages to its 887 staff. It is authorized to recruit up to 949 people.

Many of the accused have French or French Canadian lawyers. Though French-speaking African lawyers were available, most opted for highly-paid barristers based in Paris and Montreal; 16 of the 49 suspects the ICTR held in May 2003 had French lawyers and 17 had French Canadian ones. The snail's pace of the proceedings makes for dire viewing. Emotionally traumatized witnesses are flown in from Rwanda to give evidence. Women survivors who were raped and now suffer from HIV and AIDS are then distraught to find that some of the accused, also HIV positive, are on expensive anti-retroviral drugs courtesy of the UN. The women were told that the UN could not afford to provide anti-retrovirals to the victims but nor could the impoverished Kigali regime afford the cost. For the survivors it amounted to a second failure of the UN – first it had ignored their pleas to save them during the genocide in 1994; now they were refused drugs to keep them alive while the rapists and those who ordered the crime are given the life-saving treatments.

Individuals suffering from hangovers are holding their heads at the well-staffed ICTR media centre. It has been another heavy night of partying following the departure of one of their number back to Europe. Today is Friday and by 12 noon what little 'action' there has been that morning to seek justice for the genocide survivors has been abandoned for the weekend. No cases are currently being heard – all have, yet again, been suspended to hear legal arguments.

I sit patiently waiting for an answer from the highly-paid ICTR spokesman, Roland Amoussouga. It is rather like waiting for a trial verdict because it seems to take years and when it finally comes it is often less than satisfactory. After four days of waiting, I finally cornered Amoussouga outside his office, but my questions about French involvement with the Habyarimana or interim governments and the genocide are none too subtly rebuffed. 'I refuse to give any information about French complicity with the accused. I have no comment to make to you, no comment at all. I say it again, no comment – and I advise everyone else in this building to give you the same answer.'[37] I had clearly hit a sensitive nerve. However, Amoussouga's reaction made perfect political sense, leaving aside the fact that his highly paid job was allegedly to give information to waiting journalists and researchers rather than to dismiss them from his esteemed presence with a flea in their ear. Other independent journalists, and one trial prosecution lawyer, asserted that international politics had direct links to the court and its actions. France, like other Security Council members, was a key financial backer of the court and anything that might implicate a donor nation was taboo. Incredible as it seemed, France received no mention during the trials that had taken place. Documents sent to the ITCR from France, gathered during Operation Turquoise, had entire paragraphs blanked out with black ink.[38] A US prosecutor commented on the strain such international courts are

193

under given the diplomatic and financial pressures they feel from outside donor nations. In September 2005 the ICTR launched an internal inquiry into Amoussouga who was alleged to have influenced the appointment of Frenchman Pascal Besnier to the high profile (and paid) job as head of the court's defence management section. Needless to say, the ICTR will now waste countless more dollars and much time investigating this alleged nepotism, yet another distraction from its supposed role of bringing justice to the victims of the genocide.

The court also seems to have adopted the unfortunate habit of making some of its key staff 'unwell'. In May 2004 Judge Andresia Vaz from Senegal became the second judge to withdraw from a trial since the start of that year. Judge Asoka de Zoysa Gunawardana from Sri Lanka had resigned due to 'ill health', while judge George Lloyd Williams from St Kitts had pulled out citing personal reasons. The leakage of such top tribunal lawyers alarmed Rwanda, which pointed the finger at pressure on them from non-African countries – one of which was alleged to be France. Rwanda's representative at the ICTR, Aloys Mutabingwa, said: 'We are aware that the Tribunal is caught in a web of political crisis, but that should not be the issue.' After hinting that France was one of the sources of the said pressure, he added that such action was 'undermining the due process of the court'.[39]

On 22 October 2004 Bagosora's defence lawyers asked the ICTR for the French authorities' permission to meet former ambassador Marlaud and Colonel Jean-Jacques Maurin. Bagosora, accused of masterminding the genocide, obviously believed that these two Frenchmen could assist his defence. Maurin had been appointed as adviser to Habyarimana and the Rwandan military during Operation Noroît in April 1992, helping to advise and liaise at daily meetings with his Rwandan military counterparts. Both Maurin and Marlaud had been present at the French embassy in Kigali on 7 April, the day after Habyarimana's death, where, according to Maurin, they tried to persuade Bagosora to 'take control of the situation'. This was despite the fact he was 'already in control of the violence'.[40] Bagosora's French defence lawyer, Raphael Constant, told the press in January 2005 that he was delighted with the Paris government's cooperation towards his client and that he hoped to arrange a meeting between Maurin, Marlaud and Bagosora in the near future.

The ICTR had become more like the 'IGTR' – 'International Gravy Train Rwanda'. By June 2006 it had handed down 22 judgements involving 28 accused. Twenty-five of them were convicted and three acquitted. A further 27 of the accused had trials on-going. These trials had cost hundreds of millions of dollars, but while making many individual lawyers and court staff rich they did little to change the view that this was an expensive Western conscience-salving exercise in which truth was secondary to political and financial interests.

In March 2003 France became the first Western country to sign an agreement with the ICTR to provide prison accommodation for those found guilty. Several countries have elected to allow the prisoners to serve time in their prisons, including Benin, Swaziland, Mali and Rwanda. ICTR registrar Adama Dieng praised the French, commenting that France, which had 'previously supported the Tribunal in judicial and technical fields, was again setting an example to other member states by being the first European country to sign such an agreement'. Not surprisingly, a comfortable home in a French prison was the convicted genocidaires' most popular choice of destination.

For all its obvious flaws, the ICTR has achieved some important results in its decade of existence. It has, for the first time, defined the crime of genocide, as used in the 1948 Genocide Convention, and that of rape as a method of genocide. The trial of Jean Kambanda, the Interim government Prime Minister of Rwanda, marked the first time a head of state has pleaded guilty to genocide, and has been punished for it. The ICTR has faced mounting difficulties in the complexity of bringing witnesses, many suffering from acute trauma and illness, from Rwanda to testify, and to provide witness protection and security given the sensitivity many have in facing their former attackers. Other difficulties that have been overcome successfully include translation of the proceedings into many languages and investigation of crimes that took place several years previously. Not least of the ICTR's achievements has been making publicly available to researchers and legal experts the immense paper archive and important evidence that has come out of the trials.

The ICTR's mandate is set to end at the end of 2008, though it is highly unlikely that the remaining trials will have been finished by then Agathe Habyarimana remains free despite being mentioned at trials in relation to the *Akazu* network, held responsible for masterminding and planning the slaughter. Investigators seeking to find evidence against her meet a wall of silence and fear. The Hutu extremist network is still powerful and political considerations dictate that finding out the truth is a low priority. Juvénal Uwilingiyimana, an alleged genocidaire and former minister for parks who had expressed his willingness to cooperate with the ICTR and 'spill the beans' on his former colleagues, was found dead in a Brussels canal in December 2005. It would seem that the still powerful *Akazu* network in France, Belgium, Canada and other Western countries had ensured that such a traitor never broke ranks.

In early April 1994 many of those who had carefully planned the genocide during the preceding months took the opportunity to flee the scene of their crime. It was one thing to decide on the logistics for the 'final solution' to the Tutsi problem; it was quite another to be caught with blood on their hands. With chaos descending on Kigali from 7 April, many ringleaders used their political connections to get airlifted to safety and to a comfortable life in France. Some chose to remain in Paris after 1994; others took off to equally compliant or uninterested Western and francophone African countries to enjoy a contented retirement there.

On 9 April 1994 Agathe Habyarimana, *Madame de l'Akazu*, was airlifted with her family to Paris where she has kept a luxury house for the past decade, occasionally tottering to the local church to say mass. The Mitterrand government welcomed Agathe with a 200,000-franc golden-handshake and since then she has enjoyed an equally positive reception under Jacques Chirac's presidency. She has kept up her links with her French backers and in 2003 attended *Le Sommet de la Franco-phonie*, a meeting of French-speaking heads of state and others interested in promoting French language and culture. She has remained impassive on the genocide, and has 'gone to ground' insofar as publicity is concerned. No French politicians or media have questioned either her role in the genocide or why she is allowed to continue residing in France.

In 2004 the Rwandan government issued a statement calling for Agathe's arrest. Kigali maintained that she, along with her brothers Selaphe Rwabugumba and Protais Zigiranyirazo, were 'key masterminds' of the genocide and must be brought to justice either in Rwanda or at the ICTR. 'We have sent out a formal request to Interpol to have these people arrested and brought to justice for crimes of genocide,' Emmanuel Rukangira, a state attorney said. 'Each were key members of the *Akazu* clan.' Belgium handed Zigiranyirazo, or 'Mr Z' as he was known, over to the ICTR in 2001 and he is now on trial for his involvement in the genocide. 'It is high time that these people who have been trotting around the world were brought to justice,' Rukangira added.[41] Agathe has been mentioned in several cases at the war crimes tribunal and investigators have actively been attempting to find witnesses prepared to testify against her. Given that many of the *Akazu* are now in prison, dead, on trial or enjoying their liberty in Europe or North America, the difficulty the investigators face is immense. Rather like trying to crack the secret organizations that protected former SS and *Einsatzgruppen* members after the end of the Second World War, the *Akazu* has remained a properly closed book.

Agathe Habyarimana briefly broke her silence in an interview with the French paper *Libération* in December 1998. She called accusations against her 'outrageous' and alleged that those who had killed her husband wanted to 'tarnish me or drive me mad'. She also denied that she had controlled Rwanda before the genocide and expressed willingness to go to the ICTR to answer charges against her.

Despite such bravado, she has now gone to ground again and remains untouched by the justice system. France has made no move to deport her despite the grave charges that hang about the former Rwandan first lady. To deport a woman the Paris government has showered with gifts for 30 years, who has paraded with the president at the Élysée and been a guest at the tables of the elite in French political and social circles, could not be stomached.

Catholic priest Father Wenceslas Munyeshyaka, former head of the Sainte Famille church in Kigali, is another alleged genocidaire now residing in France. During the genocide thousands of Tutsi and Hutu civilians fleeing the fighting and genocide happening around them sought refuge in his church. However, witnesses and survivors told African Rights investigators that Munyeshyaka collaborated openly with the militiamen who entered the church on numerous occasions to massacre Tutsis. He was said to have given the killers lists, pointed out Tutsi refugees to be murdered and forced a large number of Tutsi girls and women to sleep with him as a condition for being evacuated to the nearly Hotel des Mille Collines.

One witness, Brother Damescène, spoke of how Munyeshyaka, the militia chaplain, 'was always with them [the militia] wearing a bullet-proof vest and [carrying] a gun.'[42] On 17 June the priest had entered the church, pistol in hand, accompanied by the *Interahamwe*. More than 100 Tutsis were massacred while Munyeshyaka looked on with grim satisfaction. Another massacre followed on 19 June. Munyeshyaka told survivor Anastase Karayiga that he should now help him cover up what had happened.

> Very early in the morning on 20th June, Fr Wenceslas, together with some gendarmes, forced the men who were staying at St Famille, including me, to take the bodies in St Famille courtyard, people killed the day before, and dispose of them in the garage of St Famille's office of procurement. He didn't want the foreign journalists who had come with UNAMIR for the evacuation to find the bodies scattered over the courtyard.[43]

Numerous witnesses also testified to the priest's sexual abuse of young girls. One woman, Rose Rwanga, told investigators how her 16-year-old daughter Hyacinthe, who refused to sleep with the priest, was later singled out and killed. Rose later told the BBC that she strongly condemned Munyeshyaka. 'I'm ready to go to any court anywhere to hear him say why he let my daughter be killed.'[44]

Munyeshyaka fled from Kigali for the French 'safe zone' before slipping across the border into Goma, from where he and 28 other Catholic clergy sent a letter to the Pope that spelled out their hatred of all things Tutsi.

> Everyone knows, except those who do not wish to know or understand it, that the massacres which took place in Rwanda are the result of provocation and the harassment of the Rwandese people by the RPF. To speak of genocide and to insinuate that only Hutus killed Tutsis is to be ignorant [of the fact] that Hutus and Tutsis have been each other's executioners. We dare even to confirm that the number of Hutu civilians killed by the army of the RPF exceeds by far the Tutsi victims of the ethnic troubles.[45]

It was the 'double genocide' myth rolled out again as justification. Mitterrand, Juppé and Villepin are in good company on that matter.

From Goma, Munyeshyaka was flown to France where he was given a visa and, under the protection of the White Fathers, a religious order with close links to the Habyarimana regime, was installed in the parish of Bourg-St-Andéol in the Ardèche department. The Catholic hierarchy closed ranks around him with Monsignor Jean Bonfils, the bishop of Viviers, saying he would tolerate 'no attacks on the priest'. Munyeshyaka's defence to a journalist who interviewed him was that he had acted to help the refugees at St Famille. When asked then why he was hiding in France, he replied, 'that is none of your business.'

On another occasion a genocide survivor cornered Munyeshyaka in his new parish church after mass, but the priest lost his temper, shouting, 'What do you want, how far are you going to pursue me ... go fuck yourself!'[46] However, with powerful church allies, including the White Fathers, and clerical legal funding to fight his accusers in court, Munyeshyaka has so far continued to evade the courts and justice. On 10 June 2004 the European Court for Human Rights condemned the slowness of the French judicial system in bringing the Munyeshyaka case to a conclusion. Nine years after complaints were first made the priest had still to face his accusers. The court in Strasbourg judged that that the length of the procedure violated its articles 6 and 13. Clearly, politics was holding up the legal process. The priest and his supporters were in no rush to get to court to prove his innocence, which they declared on occasions when the media and survivors came looking. The Catholic Church sent 46-year-old Munyeshyaka to a new parish in Les Andelys in the diocese d'Evreux, though he moved to a White Father safe house when the press became interested again in his case during the tenth anniversary of the genocide in 2004.

Yves Dupeux, the lawyer who represented the priest, also defended another fugitive from justice who had fled to France. Dr Sosthène Munyemana, the so-called 'butcher of Tumba', had a string of allegations from genocide survivors hanging over him. He fled to France just before the RPF took Butare, and settled in Talence. Witnesses claimed he killed with his own hands, stockpiled ammunition for the militia and compiled lists of Tutsis in Tumba to be killed while he was working with the *Interahamwe* to encourage and organize the genocide. One survivor said he saw Sosthène take a bayonet from the 'trouser of a soldier next to him' before driving it into the stomach of a Tutsi. When Operation Turquoise came, 'he wore banana leaves [a symbol of belonging to the *Interahamwe*] ... while parading with the militia' to welcome the Gallic troops. 'Sosthène waved a large French flag.'[47]

In France it was not just lawyers who hastened to defend the alleged killer. Journalist Claire Gabillat, writing in a medical journal, presented both Munyeshyaka and Munyemana, despite not having talked to any witnesses in Kigali or Tumba, as 'martyrs' who had tried to bring 'peace'. The accusations against them were, she alleged, due to the RPF. As African Rights has pointed out, Ms Gabillat provided no evidence to support her allegations, and it is not the RPF but civilian survivors who are accusing them of their killing. 'To dismiss their grief and their evidence as an RPF plot is inhuman and smacks of cheap politics.'[48]

Laurent Bucyibaruta, former prefect of Gikongoro, scene of some of the most devastating Tutsi killings, fled to France after the genocide to become a resident of the tranquil and scenic town of Bar-sur-Aube. An MRND loyalist, Bucyibaruta had, along with Deputy Damien Biniga, seen the Tutsi population in their region almost totally wiped out during the second quarter of 1994. While the latter wholeheartedly threw his energy into organizing the massacres, Bucyibaruta made no attempt to stop the killers in their 'work'. In late April 1994 he issued a message to the local population, after a meeting with interim government officials. His fear was that the killings were beginning to take on another dimension over and above the slaughter of Tutsis, and people were being killed 'for their property or are betrayed and killed out of hatred'.[49] He was, however, less concerned about the Tutsis' fate than about the international community cutting off the interim government's aid. Bucyibaruta's comfortable retirement to the Champagne region in the east of France has not gone unnoticed by those affected by the genocide, even if the French interior ministry and judiciary has continued to look the other way.

Genocide suspect Colonel Tharcisse Renzaho, prefect of Kigali, who carried out a census of the city's Tutsi population before the killings began, is now on trial at Arusha. His family meanwhile enjoy residency in Verpillière, in the Isère alpine region of France. Genocidaires who have enjoyed hospitality away from justice in France also include Fabien Neretse, while francophone countries including Cameroon and Gabon continue to give sanctuary to other wanted killers.

On 9 February 1995, the UN Security Council passed Resolution 978 urging 'states to arrest and detain, in accordance with their national law and relevant standards of international law, pending prosecution by the International Tribunal for Rwanda or by the appropriate national authorities, persons found within their territory against whom there is sufficient evidence that they were responsible for acts within the jurisdiction of the International Tribunal for Rwanda'.[50] France protested that this resolution was not obligatory and, in effect, it had no need to enforce it. Belgium, by contrast, has not only sent several suspected genocidaires to the ICTR who were arrested on its national territory, but has also tried and imprisoned those found guilty of atrocities during 1994.

According to the Geneva conventions, to which France is a signatory, 'each High Contracting Party shall be under the obligation to search for persons alleged to have committed, or to have ordered to be committed, such grave breaches, and shall bring such persons, regardless of their nationality, before its own courts.' A decade after the genocide, with its chief architect, among others, still living in Parisian luxury, such high-minded words and articles seem redundant when faced with a political and judicial will to do nothing. In his book on the search for global justice, Geoffrey Robertson wrote:

'Crimes against humanity will only be deterred when their would-be perpetrators – be they political leaders, field commanders or soldiers and policemen – are given pause by the prospect that they will henceforth have no hiding place: that legal nemesis may some day, somewhere, overtake them.'[51] Just as thousands of Nazis fled to comfortable South American exile in the years after the Second World War, so genocidaires have relied on France to continue to support their comfortable post-1994 retirement.

Nyamata survivor Innocent Rwililiza, speaking five years after the genocide, had harsh words to say about Western justice and his constant fear that the lack of it could again trigger yet another mass killing.

One thing that surprises me today is that many of the genocide's promoters have become everyday people again, whether they dispersed undisturbed, whether they stroll down streets in France, in Europe, in Kenya. They teach at university, preach in churches or give treatment in hospitals and, in the evening, they listen to music and supervise the children's schooling. ... If you ran into one in Paris, with his fashionable suit and his round glasses, you would say, 'well, there's a very civilized African'. You would not think: There is a sadist who stockpiled, then distributed two thousand machetes to peasants from his native hill. So because of this negligence, the killings can begin again, here or elsewhere.[52]

Four years after the genocide, France followed Belgium's example by holding an inquiry into its role in Rwanda. From 3 March to 15 December 1998, the French parliament, the National Assembly, presided over by Paul Quilès, looked into the interventions of its army and politicians in the central African country between 1990 and 1994. Quilès had been Mitterrand's minister of defence in 1985–86, which raised doubts about his ultimate objectivity in judging the actions of his former boss.

Pressure for such an inquiry had been building, especially from aid organizations with first-hand knowledge of what had happened in Rwanda. In early 1998 MSF, with human rights groups *Action contre la faim* and *Ligue des droits de l'Homme*, issued a statement calling for an inquiry into the French government's role in the organization and implementation of the genocide between 1990 and 1994. MSF president Dr Philippe Biberson stated:

> France's African policy has been conducted without any form of democratic accountability for too long. The French government supported the Habyarimana regime to the bitter end, and failed to exert the necessary pressure when the genocide was launched, and has even continued to provide support after that time. It is high time the French government broke its traditional silence on its shameful role in the genocide.[53]

The Quilès inquiry heard evidence from 88 people – 20 politicians, 21 diplomats, 34 army personnel and 13 African experts. French newspapers and journals added to the highly-charged atmosphere by publishing documents testifying to French military involvement in training the Rwandan army, selling arms after the UN embargo and taking part in identity searches at roadblocks.

The inquiry aimed to resolve key questions about France's involvement in Rwanda – its motivation, the extent of its military support, and its reaction to human rights abuses and information about both pre-1994 massacres and the genocide. Questions were also asked about

202

how the closest ally of the Habyarimana and interim governments had failed to exert pressure to stop the appalling actions they carried out.

However, there were vital flaws in the inquiry. It interviewed only 88 witnesses despite four years of complicit involvement by all areas of the French government and military, while some officers from the special operations command refused to have their testimonies published and around 40 per cent of their statements were not included in the report.[54] The inquiry spent much time on the plane crash that killed Habyarimana without reaching a verdict, while skimming over controversial areas like breaking the UN arms embargo, evacuating 'secret employees' from St Agathe's orphanage and the role of Barril and the secret service in Rwanda from 1990 to 1994. Quilès explained that Barril, who did not testify, was not needed because the inquiry was made up of 'parliamentarians, not judges and police', a statement suggesting that the truth was not a mandatory objective for those tasked with finding it. The government also failed to declassify important documents relating to Rwanda, thus leaving important gaps in understanding the political motivation of Mitterrand's government. Some witnesses gave their testimony in private session, and none were required to give their evidence on oath; needless to say, many used their witness box appearance more to justify their actions than hint at the truth.

The politicians who gave evidence to the inquiry were in no mood to give their doubters any leverage. Former Prime Minister Édouard Balladur gave a particularly barnstorming performance, telling his questioners that 'France was the only one to have intervened to limit the horror. The others [countries] did nothing.' The minister attacked the 'violent, biased and often hateful campaign' directed against the French government. Foreign Secretary Alain Juppé was equally forthright before the world's media, which suddenly found an interest in the subject once a politician was seen to be in trouble.

Our diplomacy ended up giving a bad conscience to an international community capable only of expressing noble sentiments while doing nothing. So how can one explain that we are today investigating an action our country should be proud of? I can neither understand nor accept that the good intentions of our humanitarian intervention of that era, which saved tens of thousands of lives, are now being questioned.

Balladur again denied that Paris had 'participated in military operations on the side of the Rwandan armed forces between 1993 and 1994', though admitted that as far as arms deliveries made after the UN embargo were concerned, 'despite my stated wishes, I was not disposed to have the necessary information'. In other words, such deliveries could well have happened, but he denied any knowledge of them.[55]

The eventual inquiry report concluded that the Rwandan president, anxious to maintain power at all costs, had sucked Mitterrand into a military conflict in Rwanda. The Rwandan dictator 'took advantage of the invasion of October 1st [1990] to stop many Hutu and Tutsi opponents and to mobilize the "Hutu people" against the Hima–Tutsi threat'.[56] Quilès decided that Mitterrand's government did know about the massacres taking place in the country from 1990 to 1994, many of them carried out by the same presidential guard and FAR units its soldiers were training. It also uncovered the close involvement of Operation Noroît with the military command of the Rwandan army and in some field operations.

Yet, there was no analysis of the 'unofficial' war France launched and that included illicit gunrunning, frontline action, training Rwandan government forces and surveillance of the RPF; there had either been a catastrophic failure to gather information by the secret services, or the information was not shared or ignored. Instead, Quilès found that

France did not encourage the Rwandan genocide from April to July 1994 that saw close to 800,000 [2001 Rwandan government census estimated 937,000] Tutsis and moderate Hutus decimated. This genocide was committed against Rwandans by Rwandans even if the United Nations was unable to prevent the violence from escalating because, following the failure of the operations in Somalia, the United States did not want to consider an immediate increase in UN forces.

The blame, such as there was, was directed at Rwandans and the international community.

Quilès made some progress in attempting to establish the truth, even if it is blurred in the report's final conclusion. It is stated that 'France considered the Habyarimana regime a lesser evil' – a curious statement that is not clarified. Given that the Rwandan government was known to be anti-democratic, to have harboured a network of known extremists and Hutu radicals and to have supported the massacres of thousands of its population and opposition politicians, it begs the question if this were the lesser evil what was the greater threat? Was the RPF really capable of being worse – or was its anglophone stance the real problem?

The error, then, was naivety and being too supportive of a friend, rather than a cynical disregard for human rights and the reality of massacres and genocide. The inquiry chose to believe each and every word from the politicians and military officers called, coming to the conclusion that there were 'errors of judgement' and a failure at times to adapt the actions to the situation. However, while France committed errors, it was 'not at all implicated in the unleashing of the violence.'

When the report was published in mid-December 1998 critics attacked its conclusions as a 'whitewash'. For one such critic, the real question to be asked was 'how a democracy at peace like France, a rich country without any serious adversaries, became so deeply involved in a criminal policy that fills any conscience with revulsion. ... The parliamentary fact-finding mission was hurriedly put together so as to wipe away the main aspects of France's responsibility. Thus it is really a mission of disinformation.'[57] Survie, a French pressure group seeking reform of Franco-African relations, was forthright in its criticisms of the National Assembly inquiry.[58] Other questions it pointed out were not answered was why, after Foreign Secretary Juppé called the atrocity in Rwanda a 'genocide' in mid-May 1994, did the French government continue into June and even July to recognize the interim government carrying out the mass killing? It noted that the inquiry heard the evidence of only four Rwandans, three of whom were ex-Habyarimana ministers or ambassadors.

Less surprisingly, Rwandan President Paul Kagame alleged that Operation Turquoise was aimed at reorganizing the ex-Rwandan armed forces and *Interahamwe* militia. 'When this could not be achieved in Rwanda, France proceeded to re-arm and re-train these forces in Bukavu and Goma in the then Zaire.' Kagame accused the French government of complicity with the Habyarimana regime, citing a letter of support Mitterrand sent to the militia. He concluded that it was no surprise that the National Assembly inquiry had found no responsibility attached to France for its actions; it was, after all, the same key people who were investigating themselves.[59]

Conclusion

'The only way France can renew and reinforce its relationship with Rwanda is by first accepting its past mistakes and asking for forgiveness. Failure to do this will be like building a house on sand, with no concrete foundation.'

(David Glucksmann)

The Rwandan genocide ended the twentieth century on a note of unimaginable evil. A century that had begun with the extermination of up to 10 million Congolese people in a violent grasp for colonizing riches by Leopold II of Belgian, ended with Hutus taking up axes and machetes to annihilate their fellow countrymen, whose only crime was to come from a different ethnicity. The suffering, unlike the bodies of the dead, cannot be counted.

For France, the genocide marked the nadir of its francophone policy. It exploded the myth of *La Gloire* and exposed the arrogance and prejudice that bedevilled the Élysée's African policy. That the subject is still such a sensitive one to politicians and military figures in Paris a decade after the genocide is testimony to the continued undercurrent of guilt, anger and frustration. With each new revelation from survivors, journalists and ex-soldiers who break rank with the official version of events, there is a move towards an acceptance, unofficially at least, of French responsibility for what occurred.

Prunier has likened France's role to that of a person giving a bottle of brandy to an alcoholic. The drink does not cause the man's death but it contributes.[1] Why did France choose this path? Why did it give a country so much political and military support when it was already, according to information its own sources were sending back to Paris, on the verge of an implosion of catastrophic proportions? In 1990, the defence attaché at the French embassy in Kigali had sent a note to the foreign office in Paris detailing his view that the Tutsis in Rwanda were already fearful of genocide. According to this diplomat, any total

206

victory by the Habyarimana regime could result in even more repression and persecution of the minority ethnic group, leading to 'the total elimination of the Tutsi'.[2] His warning went unheeded.

Other commentators have likened the French response to the Rwandan crisis, after the invasion of the RPF in October 1990, to 'sleepwalking' into a disaster 'on the assumption that established policy would continue to work'.[3] This was the well-established neocolonial strategy that had been in place for the previous nine years. The Mitterrand government had decided, after just a few months of experimentation in 1981, that a foreign policy based on human rights, fair trade and democracy was inappropriate for modern-day France. Personal and financial dealing with francophone dictators and military intervention were once more the order of the day.

In this atmosphere, in 1990 it was hardly news if another African head of state wanted French paratroopers to crush an invasion. For Mitterrand, it would have been controversial to have resisted a call to send Gazelle helicopters, heavily armed paratroopers and special services to repel the RPF, especially since much was made of these invaders being not Rwandans, but Maoist, Ugandan, anglophone 'Khmer Noir' revolutionaries hell-bent on carving out a whole Tutsi empire in the Central Lakes region that would expel France and all its interests. In October 1990 Mitterrand could have backed a negotiated peace and refused Habyarimana military support. That the option was never discussed or considered shows how much Paris had stigmatized the RPF 'enemy' and reinforces the view that the Élysée saw all such African questions as best solved by military might rather than discussion and conciliation.

In supporting Habyarimana, the French president was supporting a personal and political friend and ally, and sending a signal to other African leaders of his intent to protect *la Francophonie*. On another level, it allowed Mitterrand to bask in the glow of *la Gloire* in action, the tricolour again rescuing troublesome natives from their constant wars and interethnic violence. Mitterrand, on his luxury tour of the Middle East in October 1990, failed to take any proper briefing before deciding to intervene militarily in Rwanda. Questions that needed to be answered went without even being asked. Would the French intervention help promote democratization and bring peace to the country? And what was the real nature of the regime he was supporting?[4]

For three years, 1990–93, the civil war was characterized by rising violence towards Tutsis. The same forces France was training and arming were carrying out horrific massacres all over the country and Habyarimana created two new bodies, the *Interahamwe* and *Impuza-mugambi* militias comprised not of drunken ill-disciplined men but of highly politicized, well-trained, armed youth responsive to government demands. And, as seen, witnesses have testified to the French actually helping to train some of these militias. Equally, the French military knew full well that the *Interahamwe* were terrifying and killing inno-cent civilians. Indeed, in early 1994, two weeks before he was assas-sinated on 21 February, opposition politician Félicien Gatabazi referred to the militia's training camps around the country in a well-publicized speech. For France to deny it knew this was taking place defies reality.

Discounting the massacres as 'rumours', France gave Habyarimana all the military backing he needed. The French effectively took over running the campaign against the RPF, using their frontline troops to do everything bar fire the impressive armaments and field batteries flown in to assist their Rwandan allies. While Mitterrand, Huchon and the Africa Cell backed this policy, it was left to a single under-secretary from the French embassy in Tanzania to consider a 'soft' diplomatic approach by supporting negotiations at Arusha.

Operation Noroît quietly went about shoring up a regime that was murdering political opponents and civilians alike. The *Akazu*, which planned the genocide, and its detailed plans for eliminating the Tutsi race were out in the open, with Radio Rwanda and RTLM broadcasting daily inflammatory messages aimed at dehumanizing the Tutsi population. For the literate, the extremist newspaper *Kangura*, among others, was as fulsome in its denigration of its ethnic enemies as it was in praising Mitterrand as 'a very real friend'. Human rights agencies had been warning of impending ethnic meltdown for three years, while diplomats in Kigali knew months before the genocide that something horrific was about to happen.

According to French Rwanda expert René Lemarchand:

It is difficult to believe that the French were not aware of the potential for genocide created by the systematic manipulation of ethnic identities, by the mob killings of Tutsi over a period of years, and by the incitements to violence broadcast by Radio

Mille Collines. If so, it defies Cartesian logic to comprehend how the self-styled 'patrie des droits de l'homme' could shove under the rug such massive human rights violations in the name of threats posed to its higher geopolitical interests by the Trojan horse of Anglo-Saxon imperialism. It only took a logic of calculated risks for the authors of the genocide to grasp this paradox.[5]

Events from 1990 to March 1994 are easily brushed over as analysts concentrate on the genocide, yet this period is critical for judging French responsibility for the eventual carnage. Without Paris's military support for Habyarimana's regime the RPF would have seized power sometime in 1993, if not earlier. Mitterrand's involvement unwittingly gave the *Akazu* network time to plan the genocide down to producing detailed death lists, getting local officials primed and in place, and building up arms caches around the country. The *Interahamwe* were brought into being, armed and trained, while radio RTLM was also established to give 'direction' to the Hutu population and the genocidaires during the summer of 1994.

Mitterrand and his political and military advisers chose to ignore the impending doomsday scenario. One reason for this is the Hutu extremist sympathizers who held sway in vital policy-making areas in Paris. A French official is quoted as saying shortly after the genocide began, 'We got rid of the most extremist [officials] of our past policy, in fact, [they were] totally pro-Hutu.'[6] The question then is why did it take so long for such men to be moved aside if their views were so well known? Agnès Callamard, in her analysis of the situation reckoned:

the political responsibility for inaction in this respect was enormous. Second, the political establishment could not have chosen a worse time to wake up from four years of collective amnesia. If some French actors were totally pro-Hutu, they were the only ones who could have some influence upon the Rwandese extremists during the first phase of the genocide and could perhaps have limited the killing.[7]

When the surface-to-air missiles struck Habyarimana's plane on 6 April 1994 to usher in 100 days of carnage, France's reaction was to reverse totally the policy it had followed for the past three years. Troops were sent in not to fight the RPF but to get everyone out. The French plainly knew within hours of the crash that genocide, or at least killing on an unprecedented scale, was under way. Through their secret intelligence, radio intercepts and surveillance, as well as their close relationships with Bagosora, Agathe and members of *Akazu*, the French military and government had a clear idea of what was taking place. The new interim government, incredibly put together in the French embassy after the genocide began, can have left few doubts in the minds of Ambassador Marlaud and the French foreign office which way policy would go in Rwanda. Bagosora was a recognized extremist, as were the cabinet chosen to rule the country. All were well known to the French, and yet little attempt seems to have been made to put pressure on them to halt the carnage. Paris became the first government to recognize the 'bunch of killers' as the new government – and continued to do so throughout the genocide.

Members of the interim government were welcomed at the Élysée three weeks into the genocide. The French supported the Rwandan ambassador's condemnation of the RPF at the UN and call for a 'ceasefire' that again confused the genocide with the war. The 1998 National Assembly inquiry noted that French politicians and diplomats had become so caught up in Rwanda's affairs that they ended up 'holding conversations, discussions ... with a criminal government' and, even after Operation Turquoise had been launched, were still recognizing the interim regime. This meant that Paris was 'either not taking into account the reality of the genocide or not analysing the responsibilities of the Interim government in this event'.[8] A more cynical view would be that Mitterrand and Huchon knew exactly what was happening and that Bagosora and his coterie were responsible for it, but for wider political and geostrategic objectives were still prepared to support them. While Clinton used every trick in the diplomatic book to avoid getting involved in a country in which (with or without genocide) the USA clearly had no interest, Mitterrand and his military advisers were determined to get the best outcome for France out of the carnage. It begs the question if, at the end of the genocide the interim government instead of the RPF had emerged victorious, would Mitterrand have continued to support a regime that had murdered a million of its people? The conclusion, based on the French reaction to the genocidaires before and during the summer of 1994 is affirmative. No doubt some mottled words of caution would have been issued for public consumption, but just as many champagne corks would have been flying at the Élysée and in military ranks at the defeat of the 'anglophone' forces. The genocide was irrelevant. Another francophone state would have been 'saved'. It is a picture of terrifying Machiavellian cynicism.

As it was, France did everything possible to keep its Rwandan extremist allies in power for as long as possible – and in holding up the RPF advance it again allowed the genocide to continue. Rwandan military chiefs flew to Paris to meet Huchon and the MAM in a successful bid to gain more weaponry for their cause. Encrypted telephone systems were sent to allow the French military a direct means of communication with their Rwandan FAR and presidential guard allies. Arms shipments were flown in, via Goma, with assistance from Paris. Barril operated not just as Madame Habyarimana's 'investigative' bodyguard, but also to train Rwandan special forces in 'Operation Insecticide' against the RPF.

Operation Turquoise became one of the most controversial interventions undertaken by France in Africa. To attempt to save thousands of people from a genocidal regime was a humanitarian task *par excellence*. However, the motivation for the operation and its eventual realization in the field have left a distinct feeling in the minds of those who witnessed it that yet again France was playing a 'double game'.

Operation Turquoise, with its arsenal of weapons and special forces personnel, arrived with a plan based more on stopping the RPF advance than on rescuing those at risk; when such unfortunates were found, as at Bisesero, there was either no will or no transport to rescue them. The interim government, Rwandan army commanders and troops, and the *Interahamwe* retreated into the French 'safe zone' where they were not only allowed to keep their weapons, but in some cases were also escorted or given transport into Zaire. No arrests were made, no information on the killers handed over to the UN, no attempt to put radio RTLM off the airwaves. It hardly smacked of an operation doing everything in its power to bring justice and stability to the country, or smash the genocidaires. Other witnesses, as seen, have testified that some of the more 'extremist' French troops participated in helping the *Interahamwe* in the genocide and were involved in gross human rights violations, including the rape of Tutsi refugees. While many of its troops and officers acted with courage and dedication to their humanitarian task, Turquoise remained an operation presided over by many politicians and military top brass still 'fighting' the 'Anglo-Saxon' RPF threat.

France's actions in the months after the genocide betray the mindset that many a media appearance had testily denied. For example, French representatives stormed out of conferences when the president of the new regime in Kigali stood up; France denied aid to Rwanda, blocked EU help to the country and perpetuated the 'double genocide' myth to conceal the responsibility of its FAR allies. It also continued to give military support to the re-forming militia and FAR in the refugee camps outside Rwanda, and put pressure on the new ICTR in Arusha to restrict its mandate to 1994 while deterring it from investigating any French involvement in the genocide. These facts make French protestations that it was in no way responsible for the genocide look ridiculous. It beggars belief that *Akazu* head Agathe Habyarimana can continue to live in Paris and openly go to conferences and church. For the survivors of the horror it is living proof that France seems no more prepared under Chirac to face up to its history in Rwanda than it was under Mitterrand.

In a rare BBC interview, Jean-Christophe Mitterrand, former head of the Africa Cell, vehemently denied an allegation that 'this killing machine would never have been created if you and your father hadn't given this government so much encouragement.' He replied, 'Bullshit – and I answer in English!' When asked if he had sleepless nights because of the events in Rwanda, he responded:

> No, not at all. That's to say if you're talking about the question of responsibility, not at all. If you're talking about the horror of the photos or the films of the massacres, then obviously yes. But you can discover the same ... in Mauritania or Senegal. You could ask me the same question about them. You can find the same thing in certain images you can see from Bosnia-Herzegovina. Obviously that can give you sleepless nights. But I reject the question in the sense you have put it to me, in suggesting that I have some kind of responsibility.[9]

The argument is effectively that in countries like those, namely lawless, black and full of savages, genocide happens. So what can you expect? Rwanda was just another over-populated African country.

Like Jean-Christophe, French politicians and generals at the heart of French Rwandan policy react with indignation at any attempt to tarnish their reputations, but other scandals have forced many leading players besides Jean-Christophe into the political wilderness. Alain Juppé, foreign minister in 1994, was found guilty in February 2004 of misappropriating public funds to benefit Chirac's RPR party while acting as deputy mayor of Paris and given an 18-month suspended sentence; Michel Roussin, cooperation minister from 1993 to 1995, was caught up in the same scandal and forced to resign during the November 1994 Biarritz francophone conference. He was gaoled briefly on corruption charges in 2000 and was among 47 former Chirac allies put on trial in March 2005. The 66 year-old former minister was found guilty, given a four-year suspended prison sentence and fined $60,000. In all, 43 of the accused politicians, aides and party officials were found guilty of corruption. In August 1998 former defence minister François Léotard pulled out of frontline politics after being placed under formal investigation on charges of alleged money laundering. Roland Dumas, foreign secretary from 1988 to 1993 and later president of the constitutional council, the highest court in France, was sentenced in May 2001 to 30 months in prison for his part in the Elf corruption scandal. Chirac was exempted from standing trial for corruption only because Dumas's council had passed a law granting total immunity to the president while in office. According to former president Giscard d'Estaing, 'Chirac can have his mouth full of jam, his lips can be dripping with the stuff, his fingers covered with it, the pot can be standing open in front of him. And when you ask him if he's a jam eater, he'll say: "Me, eat jam? Never, Monsieur le Président".'[10] It was an accusation that could well have been levelled at many of the Mitterrand protégés and allies who refused to take any blame for their behaviour and policy decisions towards Rwanda. Except the jam here is the blood of a million innocent Rwandans with which such Paris politicians and military are covered.

French policy was not unified. The defence and foreign offices disagreed over the amount of support proffered to Habyarimana and the interim government, and some soldiers were traumatized by the role they were expected to play alongside their killer hosts. But over and above the policy debates stood a president wholly committed to an interventionist solution, regardless of the suffering this could and did cause. The man who had been caught up in the atrocities of the Vichy regime and Algerian war, and was a keen Milosevic supporter, could go to his grave knowing he had been the personal hero of thousands of genocidaires in Rwanda where his nickname 'Mitterahamwe' had been well earned.[11]

Mitterrand's close relationship with the Habyarimanas was reminiscent of his affection and loyalty for René Bousquet, the Vichy chief of police personally responsible for sending French Jews to the gas chambers in Poland. Mitterrand, who described Bousquet as 'a man of action, passionately interested in politics and very sympathetic', could well have similarly described Bagosora, Agathe and his other genocidal Rwandan friends.

As the Rwandan legal system creaks under the weight of the thousands of accused still to stand trial a decade after the events, there is the first sign that France may at some point admit its responsibility for the genocide. In November 2004 French ambassador to Rwanda Dominique Decherf told the IRIN news agency that 'France is willing to cooperate in good spirit and goodwill with the [Rwandan] commission', which Kagame's government had set up to investigate officially the role of France. In April 2005 French film makers David Glucksmann, Raphaël Hazan and Pierre Mezerette previewed their film *Tuez-les tous* (Kill them all) to a Kigali audience that included high-ranking government officials and Mr Decherf. Glucksmann told the crowd that, 'This film is an alarm to our government that it should not continue with the silence. We hope it will make our President come to Kigali one day and apologize … our film depicts the role that French soldiers played in training the militia, prior to the Genocide.' He added that his idea to produce such a film was to 'inspire fellow Frenchmen to accept their role in the Genocide and ask for pardon'. Ambassador Decherf commented, 'The work is being done to clarify the exact responsibility [of France]. There is no denial of the responsibility in principle, we have to see through the historical truth and what exactly is the extent of the responsibility … this is a political move.'[12] In April 2006 the Rwandan government nominated six members of a commission of inquiry charged with finding evidence of the French role in the genocide. The president of the commission is the head prosecutor Jean de Dieu Mueyo.[13] The timing of the start of the commission's work – during the twelfth anniversary of the genocide – is no coincidence, and reflects the view of the Kagame government that France is heavily implicated in the horror of 1994.

Outside the Nyamata church a few kilometres from Kigali, a small boy sits on a wall in silence after school surrounded by the few goats he tends. It is his favourite spot and he comes to be alone with his thoughts and feelings. Cassius witnessed what Dante would not have imagined when the *Interahamwe* surrounded this church in April 1994 and butchered the 5000 people inside – including his beloved Papa and Maman.

> Every day I go there. ... Every day I look at the holes in the walls, I go to the shelves, I look at the skulls, the bones which were once all those people who were killed around me. In the beginning I felt a tendency to cry on seeing these skulls without names and without eyes looking at me. But little by little you get used to them. I stay sitting for a long moment, and my thoughts go off in the company of all those before me. I force myself not to think of particular faces when I look at the skulls, because if I venture to think of someone I know, fear catches up with me. ... The sight and smell of these bones causes me pain and, at the same time, soothes my thoughts though they trouble my head.[14]

A sign in Kinyarwandan hangs above the doorway of the church. It reads simply, 'If you had understood yourself and you had understood me you would not have killed me.' The West failed to understand that a Rwandan life mattered as much as one in London, New York or Paris. It failed to see beyond the politics of genocide to the human tragedy of the crime. The cynicism displayed by Mitterrand and his government in supporting a regime of killers for four bloody years has left it with a great responsibility for the genocide. Meanwhile, *Madame de l'Akazu* sits safely in her comfortable Parisian house cloaked in a secure French political cocoon that mocks the Rwandan dead. Given that it has taken France half a century even to begin to come to terms with its role in the deportation of 100,000 Jews to the death camps under its Vichy regime and in the Algerian war of independence, it is not surprising to find its politicians and military shying away from admitting their failures and responsibilities in the Rwandan genocide. It remains a stain on the tricolour and a nation that rightly still makes proud reference to its values of *liberté, fraternité* and *equalité*.

On 16 July 1995, the then newly inaugurated president Jacques Chirac spoke at the first annual Memorial Day for the Jews deported and murdered under the Vichy regime.

> On this day [in 1942] France, the country of light, and the rights of man, land of welcome and refuge, carried out an irreparable act. Abandoning its word, it delivered its protected people to their torturers. These dark hours have sullied our history forever and are an insult to our past and our traditions ... we must recognize the faults of the past and the faults committed by the state.[15]

It remains to be seen when a president of the French republic will ever have the courage to make the same speech about Rwanda.

Notes

Chapter 1: A Policy of Bad Habits

1. Interview, Gikongoro, 15 June 2003.
2. Hatzfeld 2005: 5.
3. Prunier 1997: 63.
4. *Guardian*, 8 November 1994.
5. Jennings 2001: 12.
6. Legum 1962: 254.
7. French 1996.
8. Martin 1989: 111.
9. 'France and Africa: dangerous liaisons', *The Economist*, n.d., p. 21.
10. Assemblée nationale 1998: I, 30.
11. Assemblée nationale 1998: I, 30.
12. Prunier 1997: 103.
13. Kalfèche 1988: 54.

Chapter 2: Invasion and Intervention

1. Prunier 1997: 82n.
2. Peterson 2000: 280.
3. BBC Panorama 1995.
4. Cole 1997: 140.
5. McCallum (online publication).
6. Cole 1997: 143.
7. Smyth 1994: I: 6.
8. Jennings 2001: 83.
9. Mitterrand 2001. See also Palosuo 2001; Sancton 2000.
10. *Africa Confidential*, vol. 32, no. 17, 30 August 1991, p. 5.
11. Interview, Frederic Charillon, Centre in Social Studies of the Ministry of Defence, Paris, 14 April 2003.
12. Coret and Verschave 2005: 480–4.
13. Jennings 2001: 75.
14. Lanxade 2001: 164.
15. Interview, Gérard Prunier, Paris, 15 April 2003.
16. Lanxade 2001: 164.
17. Quoted in *Libération*, 18 May 1994.
18. Prunier 1997: 104.
19. BBC Panorama 1995.
20. BBC Panorama 1995.
21. Assemblée nationale 1998: I, 32.
22. de Brie 1991.
23. Ferney 1993: 173.
24. Prunier 1997: 110.
25. Reported in *Le Monde*, 1 February 1993.

26. Lemarchand 1995: 8.
27. BBC Panorama 1995.
28. McNulty 2000: 111; Barril 1995: 15–16.
29. McNulty 2000: 111.
30. Assemblée nationale 1998: I, 131.
31. Prunier 1997: 148.
32. Assemblée nationale 1998: I, 172.
33. McNulty 2000: 122.
34. Assemblée nationale 1998: I, 174.
35. Martres's testimony to Assemblée nationale 1998.
36. Coret and Verschave 2005: 107.
37. Austin 1999: 34.
38. Braeckman and Human Rights Watch 1994: 60–3.
39. Braeckman and Human Rights Watch 1994: 60–3.
40. Prunier 1997: 184.
41. Sibomana 1997: 38.
42. Smyth 1994.
43. Human Rights Watch 1999: 654.
44. Favier and Martin-Roland 1999: 478.
45. Human Rights Watch 1999: 119. Quoted testimony of Éric Gillet, reported by *L'événement du Jeudi*, 25 June–2 July 1992; Assemblée nationale 1998: I, 158–68.
46. Assemblée nationale 1998: I, 139.
47. Jennings 2001: 85–6.
48. Interviewed by Georges Kapler, Rwanda, 2004.
49. Interview, Kigali, 20 June 2003.
50. Prunier 1997: 148.

Chapter 3: Civil War and Peace Talks

1. This may have been one of the common pits the human rights federation (FIDH) discovered in January/February 1993 in the Kigombe–Ruhengeri commune.
2. Coret and Verschave 2005: 20–8.
3. Human Rights Watch Arms Project 1994: 23.
4. Indangamuntu 1994 (online publication).
5. Gouteux 2002: 31–3.
6. Interview, Clement, Butare, 23 June 2003.
7. Prunier 1997: 149n.
8. *Africa Confidential*, 6 March 1991, vol. 32, no. 5, pointers.
9. Assemblée nationale 1998: I, 188.
10. Prunier 1997: 159.
11. Prunier 1997: 127.
12. Péan 2005.
13. Callamard 1999: 164.
14. Callamard 1999: 164.
15. Verschave 1994.
16. Human Rights Watch 1999: 118.
17. Prunier 1997: 163.
18. Human Rights Watch 1999: 96.
19. Human Rights Watch 1999: 64.
20. Prunier 1997: 165n.
21. Prunier 1997: 174.
22. Human Rights Watch 1999: 119.
23. Assemblée nationale 1998: I, 47.

24. Callamard 1999: 160.
25. Interview, Kigali, 20 June 2000.
26. BBC Panorama 1995.
27. Assemblée nationale 1998: I, 160.
28. Human Rights Watch Arms Project 1994: 23.
29. Melvern 2000: 48.
30. Jennings 2001: 87.
31. Prunier 1997: 164n.
32. BBC Panorama 1995.
33. BBC Panorama 1995.
34. Interviewed by Georges Kapler, Rwanda, 2004.
35. Dupaquier 1992.
36. Interview, Vénuste Kayimahe, Kigali, 23 June 2003.

Chapter 4: Militia, Massacres and Arusha

1. Prunier 1997: 86.
2. Jennings 2001: 75.
3. *Africa Confidential*, vol. 33, no. 20, 9 October 1992, p. 7.
4. BBC Panorama 1995.
5. BBC Panorama 1995.
6. BBC Panorama 1995.
7. Kakwenzire and Kamukama 1999: 79.
8. Sibomana 1997: 50.
9. Interviewed by Georges Kapler, Rwanda, 2004.
10. Huband 1994a: 14.
11. BBC Panorama 1995.
12. Assemblée nationale 1998: I, 144–6.
13. Jennings 2001: 90.
14. Prunier 1997: 110.
15. Sibomana 1997: 43.
16. Prunier 1997: 137.
17. Human Rights Watch Arms Project 1994: 11.
18. Report by Mr. B. W. Ndiaye, special rapporteur on his mission to Rwanda from 8 to 17 April 1993, United Nations, E/CN.4/1994/7/Add.1, 11 August 1993.
19. AFP (Paris) 22 April 2005.
20. Callamard 1999: 170.
21. Human Rights Watch 1999: 121–2.
22. On 26 January 1991 *Le Monde* reported a racist hate campaign in Rwanda following the Bagogwe massacre three days earlier.
23. Prunier 1997: 154n.
24. Sibomana 1997: 53.
25. Adelman n.d.: 9.
26. Prunier 1997: 177.
27. *Le Canard enchâiné*, 17 February 1993, p. 3.
28. Prunier 1997: 179.
29. Des Forges 1995: 5.
30. RPF press release, Washington, 8 February 1994.
31. McGreal 1993: 20.
32. Prunier 1997: 190.
33. Human Rights Watch 1999: 124.
34. Callamard 1999: 174, quoting Bayart 1994.
35. Dallaire 2003: 42.

36. Dallaire 2003: 71.
37. Dallaire 2003: 76.
38. BBC Panorama 1995.
39. Human Rights Watch 1999: 655.
40. Gouteux 2002: 169.
41. Gouteux 2002: 283.
42. Gattegno 2005.
43. Deacon 1990: 315.
44. Madsen 1999: 113.
45. Madsen 1999: 113.
46. Jennings 2001: 27.
47. Human Rights Watch 1999: 666.
48. *Le Figaro*, 31 March 1998; Gouteux 2002: 176.
49. Human Rights Watch 1999: 665.
50. Prunier 1997: 176.
51. Human Rights Watch 1999: 143.
52. Human Rights Watch 1999: 127.
53. Human Rights Watch 1999: 121.
54. Jouan 1996: 144.
55. Human Rights Watch 1999: 146.
56. Human Rights Watch 1999: 154.
57. Human Rights Watch 1999: 157.
58. *Africa Confidential*, vol. 35, no. 4, 18 February 1994.
59. BBC Storyville 2005.
60. Hatzfeld 2005: 79.
61. Hatzfeld 2005: 209–10.
62. Adelman and Suhrke 1996: 34. This information came from interviews in Geneva in March 1995 and in Kigali and Dar es Salaam in August 1995.
63. Prunier 1997: 205.
64. Prunier 1997: 211.

Chapter 5: Retreat

1. From 1998 until 2004 Judge Jean-Louis Bruguière headed the inquiry into the fatal plane crash.
2. Prunier 1997: 219.
3. Human Rights Watch 1999: 655.
4. See Lanxade 2001.
5. Statement by International Panel of Eminent Personalities (online publication).
6. Ambrosetti 2001: 65.
7. Interview, Kigali, 16 January 2004.
8. Dallaire 2003: 276.
9. Dallaire 2003: 282.
10. Dallaire 2003: 286.
11. Callamard 1999: 175.
12. Callamard 1999: 286.
13. Callamard 1999: 289.
14. On 13 May 2005 a notorious bandit called Firmin Mahé was involved in a fire-fight with French troops in the Ivory Coast in which he was slightly injured. He was captured but died on the way to hospital. At an internal inquiry Poncet was alleged to have given an order to his troops to transport Mahé to hospital but to 'take your time. You understand me.' Poncet, who had been decorated by President Chirac in July 2005, was suspended from duty on the order of Minister of Defence Madame Michele Alliot-Marie in October,

and later transferred to a desk job while military and civil enquiries took place into the incident. Three other soldiers who carried out the actual suffocation of the prisoner were also accused of murder.

15. Coret and Verschave 2005: 213. Froduald Karamira was a top Hutu Power figure who played a lead role in planning and implementing the 1994 genocide; he used Hutu hate radio to support the *Interahamwe* carrying out widespread massacres in 1994. He was sentenced to death and executed in Kigali on 24 April 1997. Justin Mugenzi, minister of trade and industry in the interim government, was captured after fleeing to Cameroon after the genocide and put on trial at the ICTR. Jean-Bosco Barayagwiza, policy director in the ministry of foreign affairs during the genocide and founding member of Hutu hate radio RTLM, was found guilty at the ICTR along with Ferdinand Nahimana, former director of RTLM, and Hassan Ngeze, former owner and editor-in-chief of the extremist *Kangura* newspaper, of genocide, conspiracy to commit genocide, direct and public incitement to commit genocide and crimes against humanity, including extermination and persecution. Jerome Bicamumpaka, minister for foreign affairs in the interim government, later fled to Cameroon where he was arrested and is currently on trial at the ICTR for genocide. Pauline Nyiramasuhuko, minister for family and women's affairs, is presently on trial at the ICTR on charges of genocide.

16. Coret and Verschave 2005: 216.

17. Human Rights Watch 1999: 655. Jean Kambanda was later arrested in 1997 after fleeing to Nairobi. At his trial before the ICTR he pleaded guilty to genocide and was sentenced to life imprisonment. While in office as interim government prime minister he had made radio broadcasts declaring 'genocide is justified in the fight against the enemy.'

18. Jennings 2001: 108–9.

19. Casimir Bizimungu was arrested in Kenya in 1999 and transferred to the ICTR. His trial, on charges of genocide and conspiracy to commit genocide, began in 2003 and is still going on.

20. Bijard 1994b: 36.

21. Interview, Kigali, 22 June 2003.

22. Jennings 2001: 106–7.

23. Assemblée nationale 1998: I, 269.

24. Assemblée nationale 1998: I, 269.

25. *Inkotanyi*, literally 'tough fighters', was used to refer to the RPF. It had monarchical overtones and hence was used by Hutu militants as a derogatory term, a way of referring to the past colonial period when the Tutsi had been in control.

26. Assemblée nationale 1998: I, 263.

27. L'orphelinat Sainte-Agathe (1994) (online publication).

28. See Survie 1994. Survie was founded in 1984, and has campaigned hard for an end 'Françafrique' and for the establishment of fair, transparent and democratic Franco-African relations. It has been especially active in its research into, and condemnation of the French role in the Rwandan genocide, and actively monitors the continued close cooperation between African dictators and the Élysée, for example with the state visits of two such men to President Chirac in September 2006, Faure Gnassingbé of Togo and Idriss Déby of Chad.

29. African Rights 2001: 35.

30. African Rights 2001: 29.

31. African Rights 2001: 30.

32. African Rights 2001: 30.

33. African Rights 2001: 35.

34. African Rights 2001: 85.

35. Human Rights Watch 1999: 612–13.

36. Human Rights Watch 1999: 660.

37. Gourevitch 1999: 132.

38. Gourevitch 1999: 143.
39. Alain Frilet 1994: 2–3.
40. Human Rights Watch 1999: 660.
41. Gourevitch 1999: 143.
42. Human Rights Watch 1999: 659.
43. Human Rights Watch 1999: 659.
44. Gouteux 2002: 63.

Chapter 6: Arming the Genocide

1. *Umuganda* in Kinyarwanda referred to the unpaid weekly work each person was expected to undertake in the local community.
2. Jones 1999: 148.
3. Quoted by Hirondelle News Agency, Arusha, 10 March 1998.
4. Melvern 2000: 75.
5. Coret and Verschave 2005: 241.
6. Prunier 1997: 337–8.
7. UN Blue Book, S/1994/531, Document 58, p. 274.
8. Human Rights Watch 1999: 658.
9. Reported by Patrick de Saint-Exupéry in *Le Figaro*, 12 January 1998.
10. Human Rights Watch 1999: 638.
11. 'Poursuivant sa visite en Asie centrale, François Mitterrand a rendu hommage à la politique régionale du Turkménistan,' Sophie Shihab, *Le Monde*, 20 April 1994: 9.
12. Quoted in *Golias magazine*, no. 106, January/February 2006: 63.
13. Hatzfeld 2005: 145–6.
14. Human Rights Watch 1999: 658.
15. Human Rights Watch 1999: 279n.
16. Prunier 1997: 278–9.
17. BBC Panorama 1995.
18. Assemblée nationale 1998: I, 299.
19. McNulty 2000: 117.
20. Interview with Romeo Dallaire (online publication)
21. Dallaire 2003: 395.
22. Mari 1994.
23. Interview with Mehdi Ba, Paris, April 2006.
24. Callamard 1999: 182.
25. Human Rights Watch 1999: 664.
26. Human Rights Watch 1999: 664.
27. Human Rights Watch 1999: 664.
28. Human Rights Watch 1999: 664.
29. Human Rights Watch 1999: 664–5.
30. Human Rights Watch 1999: 665n.
31. McNulty 2000: 116.
32. Gouteux 2002: 151.
33. UN Blue Book, S/PRST/1994/21, Document 55, p. 272.
34. Security Council resolution S/RES/918 (1994), 17 May 1994, UN Blue Book, Document 62, pp. 282–4.
35. BBC Panorama 1995.
36. Human Rights Watch 1999: 661.
37. *Le Figaro*, 3 April 1998.
38. Jennings 2001: 112.
39. Human Rights Watch 1999: 662.
40. Jennings 2001: 113.

41. Human Rights Watch 1999: 663.
42. Jennings 2001: 113.
43. Smith 1994, quoted in McNulty 2000: 118.
44. Binet 2003: 48–9.
45. Smith 1994: 118.
46. Prunier 1997: 278n.
47. Quoted in *Golias magazine*, no. 106, January/February 2006: 65.
48. *L'Humanité*, 29 June 1994.
49. Barril 1995: 12–19, 86–7, 100.
50. Human Rights Watch 1999: 666–7.
51. *La Libre Belgigue*, 11 September 1995.
52. Human Rights Watch 1999: 667.
53. Human Rights Watch 1999: 667.
54. Human Rights Watch 1999: 668.
55. *Africa Confidential*, vol. 36, no. 14, 15 July 1994.
56. Hatzfeld 2005: 74.
57. Sehene (online publication)

Chapter 7: Operation Turquoise

1. Nundy 1994a: 11.
2. Prunier 1999: 285.
3. Prunier 1999: 285.
4. Prunier 1999: 285.
5. Human Rights Watch 1999: 669.
6. Assemblée nationale 1998: II, 375.
7. Prunier 1999: 304n.
8. McNulty 1997: 16.
9. Human Rights Watch 1999: 674.
10. African Rights 1995a: 1142.
11. African Rights 1995a: 1146.
12. *Le Monde*, 23 June 1994.
13. Dallaire 2003: 369.
14. Dallaire 2003: 371
15. Dallaire 2003: 418.
16. Dallaire 2003: 422.
17. Dallaire 2003: 426.
18. Prunier 1999: 287.
19. UN Security Council 1999.
20. S/1994/728, Document 68, United Nations Blue Book Series, pp. 304–6.
21. S/1994/734, Document 70, United Nations Blue Book Series, p. 307.
22. Adelman and Suhrke 1996: 57.
23. Prunier 1999: 291.
24. Dallaire 2003: 437.
25. Dallaire 2003: 438.
26. Interviewed by Georges Kapler, Rwanda, 2004.
27. Assemblée nationale 1998: I, 306.
28. Prunier 1999: 291.
29. Peterson 2000: 284.
30. McGreal 1994a: 24.
31. Saint-Exupéry 2004: 25.
32. Bijard 1994a: 36.
33. Interview by Georges Kapler, Rwanda, 2004.

34. RTLM, ICTR tape 011, K0143673, broadcast 28 April 1994.
35. RTLM, ICTR tape 046, K0159033, broadcast 19 June 1994
36. RTLM, ICTR tape 035, K0113819, broadcast 20 June 1994.
37. McGreal 1994b: 26.
38. Interviewed by Georges Kapler, Rwanda, 2004.
39. Kim Willsher, 'Court to look at French role in 1994 genocide', *Guardian*, 27 December 1994, p. 23.
40. Interview by Kapler, Rwanda, 2004.
41. Ibid.
42. Ibid.
43. Dallaire 2003: 449.
44. Dallaire 2003: 451.
45. Human Rights Watch 1999: 676.
46. Brendan Boyle, Reuters, 5 July 1994
47. John Bierman, *Financial Post* (weekly edition), 8 July 1994, p. 7.

Chapter 8: Bisesero and Withdrawal

1. Many of the testimonies in this chapter came from interviews given by survivors to the author at Bisesero in January 2004. Alfred Musema was director of Gisovu tea factory and the ICTR later charged him with genocide and crimes against humanity. He was found guilty and sentenced to life imprisonment.
2. African Rights 1998: 9.
3. Dr Clement Kayishema, prefect of the Kibuye prefecture, and Obed Ruzindana were accused and convicted of genocide when they were brought before the ICTR in Arusha. Dr Gérard Ntakirutimana was also convicted of genocide at the ICTR after helping to lead attacks against the Tutsis at Bisesero. Kayishema was sentenced to life imprisonment, while Ruzindana and Ntakirutimana received sentences of 25 years each.
4. Interview with Anastase in Bisesero.
5. Interviewed by Georges Kapler, Rwanda 2004.
6. Saint-Exupéry 2004: 72.
7. African Rights 1998: 62.
8. See Marin Gillier's testimony in Assemblée nationale 1998: 402–6. Patrick de Saint-Exupéry account is in Saint-Exupéry 2004: 45–88.
9. Saint-Exupéry 2004: 84.
10. Human Rights Watch 1999: 680.
11. Ibid.
12. Thierry Prugnaud interviewed by Laure de Vulpian on French Culture radio, 22 April 2005, reprinted in *Billets d'Afrique*, no. 136, May 2005.
13. Ibid.
14. Human Rights Watch 1999: 681.
15. Bonner 1994; Human Rights Watch 1999: 681.
16. Interview, Arusha, 9 June 2003.
17. Interview, Mehdi Ba, April 2006.
18. Human Rights Watch 1999: 681.
19. 'The French in Rwanda', *The Economist*, vol. 332, no. 7870, 2 July 1994, p. 39.
20. S/1994/798, document 73, *United Nations Blue Book Book Series*, p. 310.
21. Prunier 1997: 297.
22. Human Rights Watch 1999: 683.
23. Human Rights Watch 1999: 683.
24. Dallaire 2003: 459.
25. Ibid.
26. Prunier 1997: 337n.

27. Interviewed by Georges Kapler, Rwanda, 2004.
28. Interview, Butare, 23 June 2003.
29. Georges Rutaganda was committed for trial at the ICTR at Arusha on charges of genocide and crimes against humanity. He was found guilty of the charges on 6 January 1999 and sentenced to life imprisonment.
30. Interview, Butare, 23 June 2003.
31. *Le Canard Enchâiné*, 8 April 1998.
32. Interviewed by Georges Kapler, Rwanda, 2004.
33. Prunier 1999: 295.
34. Dallaire 2003: 455.
35. Human Rights Watch 1999: 686.
36. Human Rights Watch 1999: 684.
37. Human Rights Watch 1999: 685.
38. Prunier 1999: 295.
39. Ibid.
40. Dallaire 2003: 457.
41. Human Rights Watch 1999: 685.
42. Bizimungu was arrested in Angola in April 2002 and transferred to the ICTR in Arusha to face charges of conspiracy to commit genocide, genocide, five counts of crimes against humanity for murder, extermination, rape, persecution and other inhumane acts, and serious violations of the Geneva conventions. His trial is ongoing.
43. Dallaire 2003: 474.
44 Human Rights Watch 1999: 686.
45. Prunier 1999: 299.
46. Human Rights Watch 1999: 686.
47. Human Rights Watch Arms Project 1995: 5.
48. Kiley 1998; Human Rights Watch 1999: 688.
49. Richter 1994.
50. Gourevitch 1999: 157.
51. Interviewed by Georges Kapler, 2004.
52. Assemblée nationale 1998: I, 328.
53. Interviewed by Georges Kapler, Rwanda, 2004.
54. 'Radio Mille Collines', *Le Monde*, 31 July 1994.
55. Interview, Stephen Rapp, Arusha 2003.
56. Human Rights Watch 1999: 688.
57. Interview, Kigali, 19 June 2003.
58. Interview, Gikongoro region, June 2003.
59. Interviewed by Georges Kapler, 2004.
60. Kagabo 2004.
61. McGreal 1994c: 10.
62. Dallaire 2003: 482.
63. Dallaire 2003: 483.
64. Assemblée nationale 1998: I, 329.
65. Janvier, interviewed by Kapler, 2004.
66. Prunier 1999: 301.
67. Prunier 1999: 303.
68. McNulty 1997: 19; Lanxade 1995: 7–16.
69. UN Security Council 1999.
70. IRIN–CEA update 708, 6 July 1999.
71. Thierry Prungnaud interviewed by Laure de Vulpian on France Culture radio, 22 April 2005, reprinted in *Billets d'Afrique*, no. 136, May 2005.
72. Prunier 1997: 311.

Chapter 9: Burying Genocide

1. Adelman and Suhrke 1996: 43.
2. African Rights 1995a: 1154.
3. *Billets d'Afrique*, no. 15, October 1994.
4. Prunier 1997: 321.
5. Interview with Albert in Gitarama, 22 June 2003.
6. 'Rwanda: week of genocide commemoration begins, Kagame in plea to international community', IRIN news, 5 April 2004.
7. Hatzfeld 2005: 28.
8. Huband 1994b: 21.
9. Carvel 1994: 13.
10. Prunier 1997: 337.
11. Carvel 1994.
12. 'Abandoned Rwanda', *Economist*, 26 November 1994, vol. 1333, no. 7891, p. 19.
13. For detail of funding failure to the new Kigali regime see: Waller, David (1996) Which Way Now? (revised edition), Oxford, Oxfam publications; Rwanda: Kigali under Europressure, *Africa Confidential* 4 November 1994, vol. 35, no. 22: 4-6; Austin, Kathi, 'Rwanda's next nightmare', *Washington Post,* 20 November 1994, p.c.02; *Rapport de l'observatoire permanent de la coopération française* (1995) Paris: Desclée de Brouwer: 170-172; Chossudovsky, Michel, 'IMF-World Bank policies and the Rwandan holocaust', *Third World Network Features*, 26 January 1995 (online publication); Chossudovsky, Michel and Garland, Pierre, *The Use of Rwanda's External Debt (1990-1994)*, *The Responsibility of Donors and Creditors*, 30 March 2004 (online publication).
14. Prunier 1997: 340–1.
15. Prunier 1997: 339.
16. Nundy 1994b.
17. Prunier 1997: 339.
18. *Rapport de l'observatoire permanent de la coopération française* 1995: 164–5.
19. Prunier 1997: 317.
20. See the work of Jean-Pierre Chrétien, especially 1992 and 1993.
21. Chrétien 1993: 164.
22. Prunier 1997: 339.
23. Prunier 1997: 339.
24. Traynor 2005: 15.
25. Saint-Exupéry 2004: 14.
26. Human Rights Watch Arms Project 1995: 1.
27. Block 1994.
28. Block 1994. François Karera was prefect of Kigali-Rural province in central Rwanda during the 1994 genocide. He was arrested in Nairobi and charged with four counts of genocide and crimes against humanity before the ICTR. He is still awaiting the start of trial proceedings.
29. UNHCR/FRS/A/04:para.5, quoted in Adelman and Suhrke 1996: II, 56.
30. Joseph Nzirorera, former national-secretary of MRND and minister of public works, and Mathieu Ngirumpatse, former MRND president and justice minister, helped create the *Interahamwe*. Their trial is currently ongoing at the ICTR in Arusha where they are charged with genocide, crimes against humanity and extermination.
31. Jennings 2001: 62.
32. Human Rights Watch Arms Project 1995.
33. Human Rights Watch Arms Project 1995: 5.
34. Ibid.
35. McGreal 1994d.
36. Organization of African Unity 2000.
37. Interview, Arusha, 8 June 2003.

38. Gouteux 2002: 386.
39. Hirondelle News Agency, 18 May 2004.
40. Human Rights Watch 1999: 656.
41. 'Census finds 937,000 died in genocide', IRINnews.org, Kigali, 2 April 2004. An expert witness Nikko Nsengimana testified to the ICTR at the trial of Jean de Dieu Kamuhanda, former higher education minister, that the *Akazu* was the core of power, and centered around Agathe Habyarimana. 'The brains behind the Tutsi genocide are *Akazu* with their armed wing the Interahamwe,' he told the court. Kamuhanda was sentenced to life imprisonment for genocide in January 2004. see '*Akazu* was the Mastermind of the genocide.' Hirondelle News Agency, Lausanne, 8 May 2003.
42. African Rights 1995b: 7.
43. African Rights 1995b: 15.
44. BBC Panorama 1995.
45. African Rights 1995b: 25.
46. Gouteux 2002: 110.
47. African Rights 1996: 23.
48. African Rights 1996: 35.
49. Human Rights Watch 1999: 346.
50. S/RES/978 (1995), Document 120, UN Blue Book, p.471.
51. Robertson 2002.
52. Hatzfeld 2005: 80.
53. MSF 1998 (online publication).
54. Atienga 1998 (online publication).
55. CNN (1998) (online publication).
56. Assemblée nationale 1998: I, 341. 'Hima' people are a subgroup of Tutsis who traditionally come from southern Burundi and Uganda.
57. Atienga 1998 (online publication)
58. Special report on Rwanda, *Billets d'Afrique*, 21 December 1998, no. 66A, January 1999.
59. Panafrican News Agency, quoted by Nabakwe 1998.

Conclusion

1. Prunier 1997: 352.
2. Assemblée nationale 1998: II, Annexes, 133, quoted in Coret and Verschave 2005: 106.
3. Gregory 2000: 440.
4. Chrétien 1992: 18.
5. Lemarchand 1995: 11.
6. Callamard 1999: 175.
7. Callamard 1999: 175.
8. Assemblée nationale 1998: I, 344.
9. BBC Panorama 1995.
10. Henley 2002.
11. Prunier 1997: 165.
12. Munyaneza 2005.
13. AFP (Kigali) 10 April 2006.
14. Hatzfeld 2005: 8.
15. Webster 2001: 297.

References

Adelman, Howard (n.d.) 'The role of the non-African states in the Rwandan genocide', Centre for Refugee Studies, York University, Online Content Enhancement Project (OCEP) Documents, 34 pp. paper.

Adelman, H. and A. Suhrke (1996) *The international response to conflict and genocide: lessons from the Rwanda experience*, Steering Committee of the Joint Evaluation of Emergency Assistance to Rwanda, four volumes, Copenhagen, March

African Rights (1995a) *Rwanda: death, despair and defiance*, London: African Rights (revised edition)

(1995b) *Backwards and forwards: the struggle for justice, Father Wenceslas Munyeshyaka arrested and released in France*, Rwanda series, Witness to Genocide, issue 1, London: African Rights

(1996) *Dr Sosthène Munyemana, the butcher of Tumba: at liberty in France*, Witness to Genocide, issue 2, London: African Rights

(1998) *Bisesero: resisting genocide*, London: African Rights

(2001) 'Left to die at ETO and Nyanza: the stories of Rwandese civilians abandoned by UN troops on 11 April 1994', *Witness to Genocide*, issue 13, London, African Rights.

Ambrosetti, David (2001) *La France au Rwanda: un discours de légitimation morale*, Paris: Karthala

Assemblée nationale (1998) *Enquête sur la Tragédie rwandaise (1990–1994)*, Mission d'Information commune, Report No 1271, Paris: Edition

Atienga, Thomas (1998) 'Politics-right: France denies responsibility for Rwanda genocide', Inter Press Service at www.oneworld.org/ips2/Dec98/ 18_21_071.htlm

Austin, Kathy (1999) 'Light weapons and conflict in the Great Lakes Region of Africa', in Jeffrey Boutwell and Michael T. Klarke, *Light weapons in civil conflicts*, Lanham, Rowman & Littlefield Publishers Inc., pp. 29–48.

Barril, Paul (1995) Interview in *Playboy*, French edition, by Christian Chatillon, March, pp. 12–19, 86–7, 100.

Bayart, Jean-Francois (1994) 'Fin de partie au sud du Sahara? La politique africaine de la France', in S. Michailof (ed.) *La France et Afrique: vade-mecum pour un nouveau voyage*, Paris: Karthala

BBC Panorama (1995) *The bloody tricolour*, directed by Stephen Bradshaw, broadcast 20 August

BBC Storyville (2005) *Shake hands with the devil*, directed by Peter Raymont and produced by White Pine Pictures, broadcast September

REFERENCES

Bijard, Laurent (1994a) 'Turquoise, l'opération sans boussole', *Le Nouvel Observateur*, 30 June–6 July

(1994b) 'Le Pouvoir hutu à l'heure de la débâcle', *Le Nouvel Observateur*, no. 1549, 14–20 July

Binet, Laurence (ed.) (2003) *Génocide des Rwandais Tutsis 1994*, Paris: Médecins Sans Frontières

Block, Robert (1994) 'Aid agency says France is rearming the Hutus: UN "aware" of troops training', *Independent on Sunday*, 6 November.

Bonner, Raymond (1994) 'As French aid the Tutsi, backlash grows', *New York Times*, 2 July

Braeckman, Colette and Human Rights Watch (1994) *Qui a armé le Rwanda? Chronique d'une tragédie annoncée*, les dossiers du GRIP, Institut européen de recherche et d'information sur la paix et la sécurité, Brussels: GRIP, no. 188

Callamard, Agnes (1999) 'French policy in Rwanda', in Howard Adelman and Astri Suhrke, *The path of a genocide: the Rwanda crisis from Uganda to Zaire*, New Brunswick, NJ: Transaction Publishers.

Carvel, John (1994) 'France blamed for Rwanda violence', *Guardian*, 16 November.

Chossudovsky, Michel, (1995) 'IMF-World Bank policies and the Rwandan holocaust', *Third World Network Features*, 26 January at http://www.hartford-hwp.com/archives/35/033.html.

Chossudovsky, Michel and Garland, Pierre, (2004) *The Use of Rwanda's External Debt (1990-1994), The Responsibility of Donors and Creditors*, 30 March at http://www.globalresearch.ca/index.php?context=viewArticle&code=CHO200 40330&articleId=364

Chrétien, Jean-Pierre (1992) 'Le regime de Kigali et l'intervention française au Rwanda: sortir du silence', *Bulletin CRIDEV*, no. 105, February–March.

(1993) 'Le Rwanda et la France: la démocratie et les ethnies', *Esprit*, March.

CNN (1998) 'Ex-French officials deny France aided Rwandan genocide', CNN world news at http://www.CNN.com/world/Africa/9804/21/ Rwanda.inquiry/index.htm

Cole, Alistair (1997) *François Mitterrand: a study in political leadership*, London, Routledge

Coret, Laure and Francois-Xavier Verschave (2005) *L'horreur qui nous prend au visage – l'état français et le génocide au Rwanda: rapport de la Commission d'enquete citoyenne*, Paris: Karthala

Dallaire, Romeo (2003) *Shake hands with the devil*, Toronto: Random House

Deacon, Richard (1990) *The French secret service*, London: Grafton Books

de Brie, Christian (1991) 'Faibles lueurs dans le cotonneux brouillard du consensus', *Le Monde Diplomatique*, June

Dupaquier, Jean-François (1992) 'La France au chevet d'un fascisme africain', *l'Evènement du Jeudi*, 25 June

Favier, Pierre and Michel Martin-Roland (1999) *The Mitterrand decade*, Paris: Le Seuil, vol. 4

Ferney, Jean-Christophe (1993) 'La France au Rwanda: raison du prince de raison d'état?' *Politique Africaine*, vol. 51, October

Forges, Alison Des (1995) 'Chronology', in Gilles Peress, *The silence*, Zurich: Scalo Publishers

French, Howard W. (1996) 'France's army keeps grip in African ex-colonies', *New York Times*, 22 May

Frilet, Alain (1994) 'La France prise au piège de ses accords,' *Libération*, 18 May

Gattegno, Hervé (2005) 'Greenpeace, vingt ans après: le rapport secret de l'Amiral Lacoste', *Le Monde*, 10 July

Gourevitch, Philip (1999) *We wish to inform you that tomorrow we will be killed with our families*, London: Picador

Gouteux, Jean-Paul (2002) *La nuit rwandaise*, Paris: Dagorno

Gregory, Shaun (2000) 'The French military in Africa: past and present', *African Affairs*, July, vol. 99, no. 396, pp. 435–49

Hatzfeld, Jean (2005) *Into the quick of life*, London: Serpents Tale

Henley, Jon (2002) 'How to succeed in politics without really lying', *Guardian*, 19 April

Huband, Mark (1994a) 'Militiaman claims France trained Rwanda's killers', *Guardian*, 22 June.

(1994b) 'France blocks Rwanda aid in cynical power game', *Observer*, 9 October

Human Rights Watch (1999) *Leave none to tell the story: genocide in Rwanda*, New York: Human Rights Watch

Human Rights Watch Arms Project (1994) 'Arming Rwanda: the arms trade and human rights abuses in the Rwandan war', *Human Rights Watch/Africa*, vol. 6, no. 1, January

Human Rights Watch Arms Project (1995) 'Rearming with impunity: interational support for the perpetrators of the Rwandan genocide', *Human Rights Watch*, vol. 7, no. 4, May

'Indangamuntu 1994: ten years ago in Rwanda this identity card cost a woman her life', Prevent Genocide International, at http://www.preventgenocide.org/edu/pastgenocides/ rwanda/indangamuntu.htm

Interview with Romeo Dallaire, Holocaust Memorial Museum, Washington, 12 June 2002, transcript at http://www.ushmm.org/conscience/events/dallaire/dallaire.php

Jennings, Christian (2001) *Across the Red River*, London: Phoenix

Jones, Bruce (1999) 'The Arusha peace process', in Howard Adelman and Astri Suhrke (eds) *The path of a genocide: the Rwanda crisis from Uganda to Zaire*, New Brunswick, NJ: Transaction Publishers

Jouan, Antoine (1996) 'Rwanda, Octobre 1990–Avril 1994: les errances de la gestion d'un conflit', *Relations Internationales et Strategiques*, no. 23, autumn

Kagabo, José (2004) 'Le sens d'une commémoration', *Le Monde diplomatique*, March

Kakwenzire, Joan and Dixon Kamukama (1999) 'The development and consolidation of extremist forces in Rwanda 1990–1994', in Howard Adelman and Astri Suhrke, *The path of a genocide: the Rwanda crisis from Uganda to Zaire*, New Brunswick, NJ: Transaction Publishers

Kalfèche, J.-M. (1988) 'De l'abus du domaine reserve', *L'Express*, 4 November

Kiley, Sam (1998) 'A French hand in genocide', *The Times*, 9 April 1998

Lanxade, Jacques (1995) 'L'Opération turquoise', *Défense Nationale*, February

Lanxade, Jacques (2001) *Quand le monde a bascule*, Paris: Nil Editions

Legum, Colin (1962) *Pan-Africanism: a short political guide*, London: Pall Mall Press

Lemarchand, René (1995) 'Rwanda: the rationality of a genocide', *A Journal of Opinion*, vol. 23, no. 2

'L'orphelinat Sainte-Agathe, "sauvé" par la France', *Réseau Voltaire*, 1 December 1994 at http:// www.reseauvoltaire.net/article5872.html

McCallum, Wayne Stuart (n.d.) *Defence policy and the French left's accession to power 1981–1986*, at http://venetic com/frenchdefencepolicy.html

McGreal, Chris (1993) 'Eyewitness: guerrillas in the mist sense victory', *Guardian*, 22 February
(1994a) 'Slim pickings at Rwanda's deadly checkpoints', *Guardian*, 28 June
(1994b) 'French compromised by collaboration in Rwanda', *Guardian*, 1 July
(1994c) 'Balladur pleads with UN to speed up plan for Rwanda', *Guardian*, 12 July (1994d) 'Routed Rwandan army plans intifada-style comeback', *Guardian*, 19 December

McNulty, Mel (1997) 'France's Rwandan débâcle', *War Studies*, vol. 2, no. 2, Spring (2000) 'French arms, war and genocide in Rwanda', *Crime Law and Social Change* (Kluwer Academic Publishers, Netherlands) vol. 33

Madsen, Wayne (1999) *Genocide and covert operations in Africa 1993–1999*, New York: Edwin Mellen Press

Mari, Jean-Paul (1994) 'Rwanda, voyage au bout de l'horreur', *Le Nouvel Observatoire*, 19 May 1994

Martin, Guy (1989) 'France and Africa', in Robert Aldrich and John Connell (eds) *France in world politics*, London: Routledge

Melvern, Linda (2000) *A people betrayed*, London: Zed Books

Mitterrand, Jean-Christophe (2001) *Mémoire meurtrie*, Paris: Plon

MSF (1998) 'Médecins Sans Frontières calls for a commission of inquiry into the role of the French government in the Rwandan genocide', press release, MSF, 2 March 1998 at http://www.globalpolicy.org/security/issues/ rwanda1.htm

Munyaneza, James (2005) 'Apologize for genocide, French film directors tell Paris', *New Times*, Kigali, 29 April

Nabakwe, Ruth (1998) 'Rwanda insists France is to blame for genocide', Africa News Online, 18 December

Nundy, Julian (1994a) 'French agonize on Rwanda strategy', *Independent*, 6 July (1994b) 'Paris shuns new Kigali leadership', *Independent*, 7 November

Organization of African Unity (2000) *Rwanda: the preventable genocide*, Report of the OAU

Palosuo, Eija (2001) 'Son of a socialist king', *Time Pacific*, no 46, 19 November

Péan, Pierre (2005) *Noirs fureurs, blanc menteurs: Rwanda, 1990–1994*, Paris: Editions Mille et une Nuits

Peterson, Scott (2000) *Me against my brother: at war in Somalia, Sudan and Rwanda*, London: Routledge

Prunier, Gérard (1997) *The Rwandan crisis: history of a genocide*, London: Hurst & Co, revised edn (1999) 'Operation Turquoise: a humanitarian escape from a political dead end', in Adelman and Suhrke, *The Path of a genocide*, New Brunswick: Transaction Publishers

Rapport de l'observatoire permanent de la coopération française (1995) Paris: Desclée de Brouwer

Richter, Rosemary (1994) 'France's killing fields', *The Times*, 6 July

Robertson, Geoffrey (2002) *Crimes against humanity: the struggle for global justice*, Harmondsworth: Penguin

Saint-Exupéry, Patrick de (1998) 'France–Rwanda: le temps de l'hypocrisie', *Le Figaro*, 15 January (2004) *L'inavouable: La France au Rwanda*, Saint-Amand-Montrond: Éditions les Arenès

Sancton, Thomas (2000) 'His father's son: don't blame Jean-Christophe Mitterrand: corruption was in the air', *Time Europe*, vol. 157, no 3, 22 January

Sehene, Benjamin (n.d.) Rwanda, the ethnic trap, at http://victorian.fortunecity.com/cloisters/870/theethnictrap.html

Sibomana, André (1997) *Hope for Rwanda: conversations with Laure Guilbert and Hervé Deguine*, London: Pluto Press

Smith, Stephen (1994) 'Les Mystères de Goma: refuge zairois des tueurs rwandais', *Libération*, 4 June

Smyth, Frank (1994) 'Rwanda's French connection', *New York Times*, 3 July

Statement by International Panel of Eminent Personalities to the media on the release of its report (see Organization of African Unity 2000) on 7 July 2000 at http://www.theperpective.org/rwanda.html

Survie (1994) *Dossier noir de la Politique africaine de la France*

Traynor, Ian (2005) 'Serbs turn their backs on their past', *Guardian*, 11 July

UN Department of Public Information (1996) *The United Nations and Rwanda, 1993–1994*, The Blue Book Series, vol. 10, New York: United Nations

UN Security Council (1999) *Report of the independent inquiry into the actions of the United Nations during the 1994 genocide in Rwanda*, 15 December

Verschave, François-Xavier (1994) *Complicité du génocide? La politique de la France au Rwanda*, Paris: La Découverte

Waller, David (1996) *Which way now?* (revised edition) Oxford, Oxfam publications.

Webster, Paul (2001) *Petain's crime: the full story of French collaboration in the holocaust*, London: Pan (updated edition)

Willsher, Kim (1994) 'Court to look at French role in 1994 genocide', *Guardian*, 27 December 1994

Index

Abu Dhabi, 24
Action contre la faim, 202
Africa Cell, 11–12, 19, 21, 24, 39,
    45–6, 53, 62–3, 109, 208, 212
Africa Watch, 58
African Rights, 98, 197, 200
Afrika, Janvier, 35, 56–7, 130, 140,
    168
Agence France-Presse, 21
Air Zaire, 115
Akagera River, 121
Akazu, 44, 51–2, 54, 64, 66–7, 73,
    78–9, 81, 83, 87, 90–1, 101–2,
    167, 195–7, 208–10, 212
Albania, 115
Albright, Madeleine, 6
Amahoro stadium, 96, 99
Amasasu, 60
Ambrosetti, David, 7
Amin, Idi, 15–16, 18
Amnesty International, 50, 124
Amoussouga, Roland, 193, 214
Angola, 31
Annan, Kofi, 74
Ardèche, 199
Arusha, 40, 42–6, 64, 66–7, 69, 75,
    77, 79, 82, 84–5, 88, 103, 106,
    112, 124, 133, 191–2, 200, 208,
    212
Auckland, 70

Ba, Mehdi, 7, 112
Bagambiki, Emanuel, 133, 136,
    140–1
Bagogwe, 29, 57, 59, 62, 192

Bagosora, Théoneste, 52, 81–2, 88,
    99, 103–4, 109, 116, 119, 126,
    168, 173, 188, 190, 194, 210, 214
Balch, Jean, 94
Balkans, 45
Balladur, Édouard, 63, 65, 104,
    122–4, 159, 177–9, 203–204
Bandetse, Édouard, 133
Bangui, 47, 190
Barayagwiza, Jean-Bosco, 45, 88,
    107, 133
Barigira, Félicien, 130
Barril, Paul, 26, 28, 70–2, 80, 82–3,
    119–21, 144, 178, 203, 211
Bar-sur-Aube, 200
Bayart, Jean-François, 68
Bayonne, 131
Belgium, 9–10, 17, 33, 38, 50, 75,
    82–83, 85, 88, 96, 115, 125, 132,
    180–1, 197, 201–2
Benin, 193
Bérégovoy, Pierre, 46
Bernard, Daniel, 27, 40
Besnier, Pascal, 194
Biarritz, 186, 187, 213
Biberson, Philippe, 118, 202
Bicamumpaka, Jérôme, 88, 107, 110,
    166
Bigogwe, 34, 55–7, 59, 72, 119–120,
    144
Biniga, Damien, 200
Birindwa, Faustin, 67
Bisesero, 146–7, 149, 152–8, 176,
    211
Biya, Paul, 71

Bizimana, Jean-Damascène, 105–6, 120
Bizimungu, Augustin, 100–1, 113, 120, 167
Bizimungu, Casimir, 90–1
Bizimungu, Pasteur, 171, 181
Blair, Tony, 19
Bonfils, Jean, 199
Bongo, Albert-Bernard, 22, 186
Bonner, Raymond, 151, 153
Bosnia, 78, 212
Bourg-St-Andéol, 199
Bousquet, René, 20, 214
Boutros-Ghali, Boutros, 31, 103–4, 114, 126, 128, 159
Bradol, Jean-Hervé, 109
Braeckman, Colette, 7, 112, 114
Brazil, 128
Brazzaville, 12
Britain, 13, 19, 104, 182
Bruguière, Jean-Louis, 79–80
Brussels, 16, 85, 121, 183, 196
Bucyibaruta, Laurent, 200
Bugarama, 54, 140–1
Bugesera, 54, 57, 59, 61, 62, 74, 192
Bujumbura, 48, 78, 90
Bukavu, 3, 130, 167, 172, 176, 180, 188–90, 205
Bulgaria, 115
Bunel, William, 48
Burkina Faso, 22
Burundi, 10, 16, 48, 77–8, 90, 121, 180, 182, 190
Bushiru, 52
Butare, 9, 18, 28, 121, 124, 163, 168, 171, 199
Byumba, 29, 38, 40, 66

Cairo, 31, 112
Callamard, Agnes, 209
Cambodia, 26
Cameroon, 35, 71, 190, 200
Canada, 16, 17, 196
Canisuius, Pierre, 136
Canovas, Gilbert, 29

Cape Town, 102
Carbonare, Jean, 56–7
Cattier, Immaculée, 37
Central African Republic, 25, 71, 190
Chad, 27, 70, 80, 129
Chaillot, 41
Charillon, Frédéric, 22
Chevènement, Jean-Pierre, 24
Chimanga camp, 190
China, 128, 190
Chirac, Jacques, 123, 196, 212–13, 216
Chollet, Colonel, 33–4, 52, 171
CIEEMG, 31
Clinton, Bill, 6, 100, 103, 107, 210
Coalition pour la Défense de la République (CDR), 41, 45–6, 54, 66–7, 73, 78, 103
Cobain, Kurt, 5
Commandos de Recherche et d'Action en Profondeur (CRAP), 34, 131
Comoros, 25
Congo, 130, 161, 169, 206; see also Democratic Republic of Congo; Zaire
Constant, Raphael, 194
Cot, Jean-Pierre, 20
Courbin, Jacques, 180
Cresson, Edith, 46
Cros, Anne, 91
Cruvellier, Thierry, 157
Cuingnet, Michel, 92–3
Cussac, Bernard, 32, 47, 50, 75
Cyangugu, 3, 113, 124, 128, 136, 144, 156, 158, 160–1, 166–7, 172, 176

Dallaire, Romeo, 7, 68–9, 74, 76–7, 81, 83, 86–7, 99, 104, 111, 125–9, 143, 152, 160, 164, 166–7, 169–70, 174, 176–7
Damascène (survivor), 148, 151, 153, 154, 155
Damescène, Brother, 197

Dar es Salaam, 66, 77–8
de Gaulle, Charles, 10–11
de Grossouvre, François, 71
Debarge, Marcel, 46, 63–4
Debré, Bernard, 80, 82, 101, 117, 185
Decherf, Dominique, 214
Decraene, Philippe, 62
Delaye, Bruno, 12, 39, 45–6, 63, 73, 101, 106–8, 111, 167, 169, 186
Delort, Dominique, 47–8
Democratic Republic of Congo, 8, 9, 178; *see also* Congo; Zaire
Democratic Socialist Party (PSD), 89, 91
Dendezi, 173
d'Estaing, Giscard, 91
Détachement d'assistance militaire et d'instruction (DAMI), 33, 47, 49, 58, 60, 76, 172
d'Evreux, 199
Diagne, Mbaye, 96
Didot, Alain, 81
Dieng, Adama, 195
Dieu Mueyo, Jean de, 215
Dijoud, Paul, 33, 40, 42
Direction générale de la Sécurité extérieure (DGSE), 11, 28, 47, 49, 70, 72–73, 121
Djibouti, 25, 106
Douala, 190
Dumas, Roland, 22, 24, 213
Dupaquier, Jean-François, 7
Dupeux, Yves, 199
Duval, Jean-René (Diego), 150–2, 156–7

École technique officielle (ETO), 96–9
Egypt, 30–2, 56, 115
Ehlers, Willem, 116
Elf, 213
El Salvador, 20
Escadron d'Intervention des Commandos de l'Air (EICA), 131

Ethiopia, 12
European Union (EU), 30, 183–4, 212
Eyadéma, Gnassingbé, 22, 186

Fashoda, 12, 25, 74
First World War, 9, 25
Fontbonn, Paul, 70
Fontenay-aux-Roses, 31
Forces armées rwandaises (FAR), 28, 30, 32, 39–40, 47, 49, 54, 58–61, 72, 75, 77, 81, 83, 87, 89, 94–5, 100, 105–6, 108, 112–15, 117–18, 120, 126, 130, 136, 143, 152, 157, 160, 163–6, 169–73, 175, 178–9, 183, 186, 188–91, 204, 211–12
Foreign Legion, 157
Forsyth, Justin, 184
Fossey, Dian, 8
France, 4, 6–7, 10–13, 17, 19, 21–5, 27–8, 30–2, 35–6, 40, 42, 46–7, 57, 62–9, 71–2, 74–6, 79, 81–5, 90, 95, 97, 100, 103–4, 106–11, 114, 116–18, 122–5, 127–9, 131–2, 134–5, 139, 143, 145, 156, 158–9, 165–8, 170–2, 174, 177–80, 183, 185–90, 192–193, 194–214, 216
French Cultural Centre, 10, 36, 50, 91
Frilet, Alain, 101

G-7, 145
Gabillat, Claire, 200
Gabiro, 34
Gabon, 21, 25, 186, 200
Gahinga, 49
Gako, 34
Gasana, James, 47
Gashwati forest, 54
Gasiza, 14
Gatabazi, Félicien, 208
Gatete, Jean-Baptiste, 190
Gatuna, 40
Gbadolite, 191

Geneva, 111, 168, 174, 201
Genocide Convention, 60, 168–9, 195
Gérard, Yannick, 165–7, 178
Germany, 9, 16–17, 20
Giciyi, 14
Gikongoro, 1, 128, 132, 156, 160–3, 169, 171–4, 176, 200
Gilleron, Pierre-Yves, 70–1
Gillet, Éric, 50
Gillier, Marin, 151, 153, 156–8
Giscard d'Estaing, Valéry, 11, 125, 168, 213
Gisenyi, 9, 15, 17, 23, 28–9, 34, 55–6, 58, 115, 118, 121, 124, 127, 132, 144, 160, 164, 166, 170–1, 181, 189
Gisovu, 146
Gitarama, 17, 102, 124, 173, 181
Glucksmann, David, 206, 214
Goma, 57, 115–18, 128–9, 143–4, 156, 167, 170, 174–6, 180, 188–90, 198, 205, 211
Gouteux, Jean-Paul, 114
Greenpeace, 70
Groupe d'Intervention de la Gendarmerie nationale (GIGN), 61, 71, 131
Guell, Germaine, 116
Guichaoua, André, 91, 96
Gunawardana, Asoka de Zoysa, 194

Habyarimana, Agathe, 15, 23, 44, 51–2, 56, 67, 80–1, 84, 87, 101, 103, 120–1, 189, 195–7, 210–12, 214
Habyarimana, Jean-Baptiste, 18
Habyarimana, Jean-Pierre, 21
Habyarimana, Juvénal, 1, 2, 12, 14–19, 22–6, 28–38, 40–6, 48–9, 52–4, 56–8, 60–71, 73–85, 87–91, 94, 100, 102, 109, 111, 114, 118–19, 136, 144, 146, 159, 168, 181, 185, 189, 192–4, 197–8,

202–5, 207–9, 213
Hague, The, 181, 187
Harare, 43
Hassan II, King, 22
Hazan, Raphaël, 214
Héraud, Jacky, 80
Hicks, Irvin, 43
Hitler, Adolf, 16, 76, 109
Hogard, Jacques, 177
Hotel Ibis, 163
Hotel Meridien, 121
Hotel Mille Collines, 96, 100
Huchon, Jean-Pierre, 29–30, 33, 42, 46, 63, 112–14, 121, 124, 157, 208, 210, 211
Hugeux, Journalist, 151
Human Rights Watch, 7, 38, 47–8, 59, 75, 99, 106, 113, 116–117, 144, 170, 189–90, 192
Hutu Power, 63, 100, 186

Ignatia, Sister, 1, 3, 13
Impuzamugambi, 54, 208
Indo-China, 13
Interahamwe, 2, 4–5, 35, 54–7, 73–4, 76, 88, 92, 97–100, 102, 107, 109, 111, 117, 119, 121, 125, 130–1, 133, 137–42, 147, 149–50, 153, 155–6, 160, 163, 168, 173, 175, 178, 188, 191, 198–199, 205, 208–9, 211, 215
International Commission on Human Rights, 83
International Criminal Tribunal for Rwanda (ICTR), 43, 191, 192–7, 201
International Federation for Human Rights, 50
International Monetary Fund, 22
International Organization of the Francophonie, 104
Iran, 32, 45
Iraq, 45, 103, 187
Isère, 200
Israel, 115–16

Ivory Coast, 11, 25, 88

Jehanne, Philippe, 118
Jennings, Christian, 23, 57, 116–17, 189
Johannes, Franck, 117
Johannesburg, 102
Jouan, Antoine, 7
Juppé, Alain, 73, 85, 106–7, 111, 118, 122–3, 165, 177, 179–80, 185, 198, 203, 205, 213

Kabiligi, General, 175
Kagame, Paul, 19, 24, 26, 41–2, 44, 67, 79–80, 84–5, 109, 124, 135, 152, 158, 160, 164, 170–1, 178–9, 181–3, 185, 188, 205, 214
Kalisa, Anastase, 146, 148–9, 151, 154–6
Kamarampaka stadium, 141
Kambanda, Jean, 89, 102, 195
Kamembe, 113, 141, 189
Kamilindi, Thomas, 100
Kampala, 19
Kanombe, 52, 115
Kantano, Habimana, 134–5
Karamira, Froduald, 88
Karayiga, Anastase, 198
Karera, François, 52, 188
Kayibanda, Grégoire, 10, 15–17
Kayigema, Vincent, 151
Kayimahe, Vénuste, 36, 50, 91
Kayishema, Clement, 147
Kayitesi, Claudine, 107
Kayumba, Cyprien, 112, 116
Keating, Colin, 128
Kennedy, John, 102
Kenya, 77, 201
Khan, Shaharyar, 160, 166, 188
Khmer Rouge, 26
Kibilira, 58, 192
Kibungo, 54, 60
Kibuye, 128, 132, 146–8, 156, 160, 170
Kicukiro, 97

Kigali, 4, 7, 9–10, 15, 17, 21, 23–5, 28–30, 32, 34–6, 38, 40–3, 46–8, 50, 52–3, 56–8, 62–4, 66–9, 71, 73–8, 80–2, 84–8, 90, 93, 96–7, 100–2, 111, 114–15, 118–21, 125, 129, 139, 143, 147, 152, 160, 164, 171, 179–81, 183–5, 188, 193, 195–8, 200, 206, 208, 212, 214–15
Kigoma, 121
Kiley, Journalist, 151
Kiley, Sam, 168
Kinnock, Glenys, 183
Kinshasa, 108, 112, 160, 188, 190
Kitchener, Lord, 13
Kivu, 190, 191
Kivu, Lake, 8, 142, 146, 160
Kouchner, Bernard, 125–7, 184
Kovanda, Karel, 106, 109, 128

La Baule, 22, 41, 159
Lacaze, Jeannou, 70
Lacoste, Pierre, 70
Ladsous, Hervé, 170
Lafourcade, Jean-Claude, 143, 158, 160, 166–7, 170, 174, 178
Lanxade, Jacques, 24–5, 29–30, 73, 83–4, 119, 129, 167, 177
Lemaire, Captain Luc, 96
Lemarchand, René, 208
Léotard, François, 122–3, 153, 169, 176, 178, 213
Les Andelys, 199
Lewis, Stephen, 75
Libreville, 47
Ligue des droits de l'Homme, 202
Lizinde, Théoneste, 18
Lloyd Williams, George, 194
Logiest, Guy, 18
London, 32, 106, 215
Lorgeoux, Jeanny, 44
Lorient, 116
Lovanium University, 15

McGreal, Chris, 66, 132

McNulty, Mel, 110
Mafart, Alain, 70
Maïer, René, 81
Major, John, 6, 103
Mali, 35, 195
Mandela, Nelson, 4–5, 18, 102, 144
Manichimwe, Prefect, 162
Manishimwe, Samuel, 133, 141
Mantion, Jean-Claude, 70
Marchal, Luc, 86, 88, 114
Marchand, Commander, 13
Marlaud, Jean-Michel, 48, 69, 75, 88–9, 91, 93–4, 194, 210
Martres, Georges, 16, 25, 34–6, 40, 46, 53, 61, 73, 80, 170
Maurin, Jean-Jacques, 34, 52, 81, 194
Mauritania, 212
Mayuya, Stanislas, 18, 52
Médecins Sans Frontières (MSF), 174, 188, 202
Médecins Sans Frontièrs (MSF), 118
Mérimée, Jean-Bernard, 110, 128, 159
Mezerette, Pierre, 214
Mfizi, Christopher, 52, 53
Mibilizi, 139, 141
Michaux-Chevry, Lucette, 111
Middle East, 8
Military Assistance Mission (MAM), 33, 112, 121, 211
Military Cooperation Mission, 112
Milosevic, Slobodan, 214
Minaberry, Jean-Pierre, 80
Minaberry, Sylvie, 80
Mitterrand, Danielle, 23
Mitterrand, François, 8, 11–13, 16, 19–25, 27, 29–30, 36, 41–3, 45, 52–3, 61–3, 65, 67, 70–3, 75, 79–80, 83–4, 88, 91, 100–1, 104–9, 112, 118–119, 122–3, 125–6, 131–2, 135–6, 144–5, 153, 159, 167, 175–8, 180–1, 184–7, 196, 198, 202–5, 207–10, 212–15
Mitterrand, Jean-Christophe, 12, 19,
21–2, 24, 33, 41, 44–6, 53, 62–3, 212–13
Mobutu Sese Seko, 15–16, 22, 67, 108–9, 117, 125, 128, 159, 167, 186, 189–90
Mombasa, 73
Mont St Louis, 54
Montoya, Robert, 70
Montreal, 192
Morocco, 22
Moscow, 188
Mouvement républicain national pour la démocratie et le développement (MRND), 16–17, 41, 44, 54, 57, 59, 90, 189, 200
Mpanzi, 175
Mugenzi, Justin, 88
Muhabura, 49
Muhoza, 49
Mukakalisa, Auréa, 140
Mukamira, 57, 144
Munyakasi, Colonel, 190
Munyakazi, Yusufu, 130, 168
Munyemana, Dr Sosthène, 199–200
Munyeshyaka, Wenceslas, 197–200
Murambi, 174
Murambi camp, 140
Musema, Alfred, 146, 148, 154, 155
Museveni, Yoweri, 18, 24, 26, 67, 77, 108
Musinga, King, 52
Mutabingwa, Aloys, 55, 72, 133, 141, 160, 173, 194
Mutara, 59
Mwami, King, 9
Mwanyumba, Duncan, 193
Mwinyi, Ali Hassan, 67, 77
Mwogo, 169

Nahimana, Ferdinand, 88, 90, 133, 170
Nairobi, 93, 112, 120, 126, 190
Naples, 145
National Resistance Army, 18
Ndadaye, Melchior, 71

Ndengejeho, Pascal, 91
Ndiaye, Bacre Waly, 59, 60
Neretse, Fabien, 200
Netherlands, 181
Network Zero, 52, 53, 56, 60
New York, 24, 74, 76–7, 85, 103, 110, 215
New Zealand, 71, 128
Ngarambe, Joseph, 89, 91
Ngeze, Hassan, 88, 133
Ngirabatware, Augustin, 90
Ngirumpatse, Matthias, 189
Ngulinzira, Boniface, 44, 97
Nicaragua, 20
Niger, 35
Nigeria, 31, 128
Nimes, 131
Nkubito, Alphonse, 91
Noroît, 61
North Africa, 13
Nsabimana, Deogratias, 49
Nsanzimane, Sylvestre, 90
Nsanzuwera, François-Xavier, 100
Nsekalije, Alois, 52
Nshimiyimana, Philimon, 155
Ntahobari, Sébastien, 120
Ntakirutimana, Gérard, 147, 151
Ntarama, 4, 6, 117
Ntaryamira, Cyprien, 77, 78
Nyamata, 4, 188, 201, 215
Nyambuye, 13
Nyanza, 6
Nyarushishi, 141
Nyarushishi camp, 128, 136–7, 140–2, 162
Nyiramasuhuko, Pauline, 88
Nyirigira, Jean-Bosco, 50
Nyungwe forest, 54, 173
Nzabahimana, Eric, 149, 154
Nzirorera, Joseph, 189

Obote, Milton, 16, 18
Office rwandais d'information (ORINFOR), 52

Oman, 107
Operation Amaryllis, 82–4, 86, 94–6, 102, 105, 109, 115, 117, 131, 163, 167, 170
Operation Chimera, 47
Operation Insecticide, 178, 211
Operation Noroît, 25, 27–9, 32–3, 38–9, 48, 61, 68–70, 72, 81, 104–5, 124, 136, 152, 157, 167, 192, 194, 204, 208
Operation Turquoise, 84, 104, 120, 122–5, 127–31, 133, 136, 141, 143–4, 147–8, 152–3, 156–61, 164–77, 179–80, 187, 193, 199, 205, 210–11
Operation Volcano, 47
Organization of African Unity (OAU), 44, 125, 145, 167, 170, 191
Ostende, 113
Ottawa, 77
Oueddei, Goukouni, 70
Oxfam, 174, 184

Pakistan, 128
Paris, 7, 10–13, 16, 19–24, 26–7, 30–1, 33–4, 36, 39–43, 45, 47, 49, 52–3, 58, 61, 62, 63, 64, 65, 66–7, 71, 73, 75, 79–81, 83–4, 87, 92, 94, 100–1, 103–4, 106–8, 112, 114–16, 118–20, 122, 126, 129, 152, 165–7, 170, 174–5, 179–80, 183, 185, 189, 192, 195–7, 201, 203, 206–7, 209–13, 215
Pasqua, Charles, 71
Patassé, Ange-Félix, 71
Peeters, Louis, 99
Penne, Guy, 65
Perrine, Jean-Michel, 80
Pétain, Marshal, 20
Peterson, Scott, 131
Pol Pot, 26
Poland, 214
Polisi, Dennis, 85
Pompidou, Georges, 11

Poncet, Henri, 86, 88, 95
Prieur, Dominique, 70
Prouteau, Christian, 71
Prungnaud, Thierry, 61, 153–4, 156–8, 178
Prunier, Gérard, 7, 24, 39, 45, 64, 91, 123–4, 159–60, 175, 177, 185, 187, 206

Quai d'Orsay, 13, 101, 107, 187
Quesnot, Christian, 33, 45, 63, 73, 107, 109, 112, 124, 157
Quilès, Paul, 202–4

Rainbow Warrior, 70, 72
Rassemblement Pour la République (RPR), 213
Rawson, David, 62
Rebero camp, 72
Red Cross, 149, 150, 174, 178
Régiment des dragons parachutistes (RDP), 153
Régiment parachutiste d'Infanterie de Marine d'Assault (RPIMA), 47, 61, 131, 157
Renzaho, Tharcisse, 52, 200
Réseau Zero, 52
Robertson, Geoffrey, 201
Rocard, Michel, 27
Rosier, Jacques, 152, 157, 178
Roth, Ken, 192
Roussin, Michel, 63, 70, 83–4, 105, 118, 186, 213
RPF, 152, 212
Rubirizi, 98
Ruhengeri, 9, 29, 34, 37–9, 46, 49–50, 56–7, 59, 124, 144, 164
Rukangira, Emmanuel, 196
Rurangangabo, Beatrice, 137, 140
Rurangangabo, Gilles, 137, 138
Rusegama, Frank, 47
Rusesabagina, Paul, 100, 101
Rusizi River, 141
Russia, 104, 129
Russizi, 133

Ruta, Shaban, 66
Rutaganda, Georges, 163
Ruzindana, Obed, 147
Rwabalinda, Ephrem, 112, 113
Rwabugumba, Selaphe, 196
Rwabukumba, Séraphin, 52
Rwagafilita, Pierre-Celestin, 52, 73
Rwaganyasor, Innocent, 52
Rwandan Government Forces (RGF), 69, 77, 86, 143, 166
Rwandan Patriotic Front (RPF), 14, 19, 24–6, 28–31, 33–6, 39–51, 54–6, 58–9, 61–7, 69, 71–3, 76–7, 79–80, 82–7, 91, 94, 101–2, 104–6, 109–10, 112–13, 119–20, 124–9, 132, 134–6, 143–4, 154–7, 159–64, 166, 168–74, 176–80, 183, 187, 198–200, 204–5, 207–11
Rwanga, Hyacinthe, 198
Rwanga, Rose, 198
Rwema, Epimaque, 4
Rwigyema, Fred, 19, 28
Rwililiza, Innocent, 76, 121, 201

safe humanitarian zone (SHZ), 155, 159–60, 163–6, 168–70, 174, 176, 188
St-Denis, Jean-Yves, 174
Saint-Exupéry, Patrick de, 7, 72, 120–1, 132, 150–2, 187
St Kitts, 194
St Paul's College, 14
Saint-Quentin, Grégoire de, 81
Saitoti, George, 77
Salim, Salim, 44
Sandinista National Liberation Army, 20
Sankara, Thomas, 22
Satagwa, Elie, 52
Second World War, 19, 20, 201
Segatwa, Elie, 78
Sendashonga, Seth, 183
Senegal, 25, 35, 128–9, 194, 212
Seromba, Charles, 93, 148, 154, 156

Serubuga, Laurent, 33, 52
Seychelles, 115
Sibomana, André, 32, 54, 58, 62
Simbikangwa, Pascal, 52
Simpson, O. J., 5
Sindikubwabo, Théodore, 102, 107, 118
Sofremas, 116–17
Somalia, 45, 107, 204
Sorbonne, 103
South Africa, 5, 12, 18, 30, 102, 115–16, 123, 144
South America, 20
Srebrenica, 187
Sri Lanka, 194
Strasbourg, 183, 199
Survie, 7, 95, 205, 221n
Swaziland, 195
Switzerland, 17, 76

Talence, 199
Tanzania, 8, 10, 40, 42–3, 67, 77–8, 108, 112, 180, 182, 191, 208
Tauzin, Didier, 136, 144, 157, 160, 169, 178
Temmerman, Els de, 87
Temmerman, Luc de, 120
Thibault, Didier, *see under* Tauzin, Didier
Togo, 25, 186
Toulon, 116
Tracqui, Philippe, 32
Traynor, Ian, 187
Trepel de Lorient, 131
Tripoli, 112
Tumba, 199, 200
Tunis, 112
Turkmenistan, 107
Twagiramungu, Faustin, 74, 89
Twagirayezu, Jean Baptiste, 149

Uganda, 8, 10, 15–16, 18, 26, 28, 42, 64, 67, 72, 74, 77, 82, 108, 121, 132, 185

Ukraine, 129
UNICEF, 24
United Kingdom, 6, 115
United Nations, 6, 43, 66, 145, 159, 177–8, 189, 204
United Nations Assistance Mission to Rwanda (UNAMIR), 68–9, 74–6, 81–2, 86–8, 96–101, 104–6, 110–11, 120–1, 124–5, 127–9, 131–2, 143, 164, 167, 176–7, 198
United Nations Development Programme (UNDP), 97
United Nations International Commission of Inquiry (UNICOI), 115
United States, 6, 13, 16–17, 19–20, 24, 26, 32, 74–5, 103–4, 107–8, 180, 182, 204
Urbano, Jean-Claude, 117
Usabyimbabazi, Anathalie, 153
Uwilingiyimana, Agathe, 74, 82, 95
Uwilingiyimana, Juvénal, 196

Vasset, Brigitte, 118
Vaz, Andresia, 194
Védrine, Hubert, 24
Verpillière, 200
Verschave, François-Xavier, 7, 11, 42
Vichy, 20, 65, 214, 215, 216
Victoria, Lake, 121
Vietnam, 32
Villepin, Dominique de, 187, 198
Viviers, 199
Volcano, 171
Volcano National Park, 8

White Fathers, 15, 198, 199
World Bank, 16, 22, 46, 64, 66, 182

Yerodia, Abdoulaye, 178

Zaire, 8, 14, 16, 27, 67, 108,

115–17, 121, 125, 128–0, 159,
162, 166–76, 178, 180–2, 186,
188–9, 191, 205, 211

Zigiranyirazo, Protais, 52,
197